# CASTE, CLASS AND POLITICS
## Emerging Horizons of Political Sociology

# Caste, Class and Politics

## Emerging, Horizons of Political Sociology

S. AKINCHAN

GYAN

GYAN PUBLISHING HOUSE

New Delhi 110 002

Caste, Class and Politics
Emerging Horizons of Political Sociology
*(Sociology, Political Science)*

ISBN : 81-212-0486-0
Library of Congress Card No. 900334



Published 1995 in India by
Gyan Publishing House
5, Ansari Road
New Delhi -110 002



Laser typesetting at DTP Allied Services, Wazirpur, Delhi
Printed at Mehra Offset Press, New Delhi.

# Contents

# Preface

During the past couple of years a growing tendency is perceptible to encourage interdisciplinary approach to understand the complex social phenomenon. A new combination of sociology, political science and psychology has given birth to political sociology. It makes an attempt to relate general sociological theories to the available body of knowledge of political science and psychology especially to understand political behaviour in social settings.

Political sociology is a well established discipline in the western world but it is in its infant stage in the third world. Neither the western social scientists showed interest not the scientists from third world had time to study the political behaviour of the members of newly developing societies—socially, economically as well as politically. There must be some unique problems in third world because of different socio-economic, cultural and political background of the national concern.

To keep pace with the West, by overcoming and modifying the ethnocentric bias of the Western writers and for a perceptive understanding of our own culture, society and politics, we should develop our own thinking and writing. Original work of endogenous hand and mind are scattered in the form of countable articles, monographs and dissertations. There is an acute demand of the writings in the form of text books in the field of political sociology.

The University Grants Commission also seems to be encouraging the development of interdisciplinary approach in general and political sociology in particular by granting various projects in this field and allowing a number of Universities to start teaching in political sociology.

After careful examination of number of books on political sociology and syllabi of a number of Universities it was observed that there was no relationship between the two. Even the subject matters were not similar in most of the books. After rigorous scrutiny of books and syllabi the course content of the present book is framed to meet the demands of the students of political sociology of a number of Universities.

Not only we hope but believe that this book brings political sociology closer to students and other serious readers in related disciplines.

**S. Akinchan**

# Chapter - 1

# The Perspective of Political Sociology

The emergence of political sociology, in recent years symbolizes an intellectual concern to relate general sociological theories to the body of available theories about political behaviour. If sociology can be defined as the systematic study of collective human behaviour then politics like other separate disciplines such as economics, demography, anthropology, psychology, etc. would appear as a coordinate, but distinctive branch of general sociology. The contrast, therefore, between sociology and politics, in so far as their relevance to the study of human behaviour is concerned will also appear to be false. Political behaviour, like economic behaviour, is a particular kind of social behaviour for the reason that political or economic institutions are also one kind of social institution. In view of this, if there is anything as general sociological theory, it indispensably includes theories about economic and political behaviour of man. This is because a general sociological theory, as a set of general, testable, explanatory propositions applicable to the total area of collective human behaviour, must be capable of explaining different though interrelated aspects of human behaviour, so as to become intellectually feasible as well as operationally valid for the specialized branches of social science. Short of these attributes a general social theory, incapable of the crucial distinction between classification and analysis of social phenomena, would not go beyond a general discussion within the realm of philosophy of history. Obviously one cannot deny that there is a great deal of similarity both in vocabulary and in method which is shared between various areas of social sciences and that the various areas at many points depend upon one another for their substantive conclusions. But to put them together under a single explanatory heading is to adopt what Runciman calls a kind of pre-Socratic approach, such as everything is water and wet, every social act, institution or relationship is basically economic. Thus in recent years it has been realized that there is a strong case for abundoning the pre-Socratic view of sociology as an unqualified term and for referring to its specialized branches, such as industrial sociology, legal sociology, economic sociology and sociology of values. In the same manner, we may refer to political sociology for the purpose of systematically studying all political phenomena within the framework of general sociology.

Though politics has been studied ever since a systematic study of Aristotle but political behaviour in itself is rather a new trend in modern times. This makes the modern political science a relatively new distinction between the political and the social, which constitutes the background of the emergence of sociology of politics. This does not mean that politics has been studied in isolation from the society rather the two have been supposed to be co-terminous with each other. It is in the context of the study of modern societies, conceived of as a complex system with growing interdependences among its various constituent elements, that the need to study political phenomena in the total societal perspective has been stressed.[1] Thus political structure has come to be characterized as a distinct sub-system of societal system which represents the adaptative dimension of society.[2]

The emergence of sociology of politics as an analytical imperative in the study of the modern social systems, has been coupled with the birth and development of various political institutions, such as universal suffrage, large-scale bureaucracy, mass parties, federation, centre and periphery, and para-political structures. Universal suffrage dates in England only from 1929, in France from 1945, in Belgium from 1949. Marx was dead before even the Third Reform Bill of 1885, Bentham, the foremost of the early champion of universal suffrage, died the day before the Reform Bill of 1832 received the royal assent. Bagehot's classic study *The English*

*Constitution* was written under the imminence of the extended franchise of 1867. France did have manhood suffrage till the second half of the nineteenth century, but nobody systematically studied how it operated; Proudhon who remained the strongest doctrinal influence on French radical politics until after the experiment of commune, merely dismissed it in a typical mixture of silliness and insight as 'a device to make the people lie'. Only in the United States can political democracy be regarded as an institution of reputably long standing: Toqueville's famous study, Democracy in America, which he conceived after the fall of Charles Xth in 1830 and completed a decade later, remains the lonely forerunner of all our twentieth century preoccupations with 'mass society'.

A similar position can be observed in the context of the political parties. The two classics—Ostrogorski's Democracy and the organization of political parties and Michel's Political Parties—appeared only at or the turn of the century. The first study of the single party as a political institution did not appear until 1936. Even the topic of bureaucracy, like popular despotism, a worry to be found in Mill on liberty, became a subject of generalized political inquiry only shortly before Weber.

That an aura of novelty and even of naivete still surrounds many of the topics with which contemporary sociologists of politics deal, is not surprising. It is even less surprising when we look also at the oneness of many of their methods. Application of Sociological methods to political phenomena could be traced back to the 'Political Arithmetic' of the Seventeenth century followed by William Petty's remarkable work on the Political Anatomy of Ireland. However, modern statistical methods, developed only in the late nineteenth century, and many are still more recent than this. The first International Political Congress did not meet until 1853, chairman of which was the Belgian astronomer Quitelet, who was not a sociologist by origin, but only later in his career took from Lallace the idea of applying probability theory of statistics to human populations. Sampling theory and techniques of statistical correlations emerged only thereafter. We find significant contribution in the Journal of Royal Statistical Society which could now-a-days be called as quantitative politics or sociology. The notion that political or other attitudes might be in some sense measurable, dates from the late 1920's in the United States, and sample survey data on costing is largely a quarter of century old. For these reasons alone, it is not surprising that the scientific study of politics should still be more productive of new questions than providing answers to the old ones.

In order to understand the institutions and ideas which brought modern political sociology into being, we can go back to the period between Gerson and Grotius whose importance was first fully recognized by J.N. Figgis in a classic series of lectures at Cambridge in 1900. The notion of territorial sovereignty had superseded the traditional belief in the theocratic unity of Christendom and such development brought into focus a clear distinction between the society and the state. However, this could be regarded as no more than a revision to the Aristotle's Politics which exercised a considerable influence from the mid-thirteenth century onwards and many of his generalizations (such as that a large middle class is the best guarantee against revolution) are precisely the sort of assertions that a modern political sociologist would dignify by the title of hypothesis. In Aristotle, however, one finds no distinction between social and political relations. Such distinction could become meaningful only after the emergence of the modern idea of the state as such. This could be credited to what Figgis saw as unconscious alliance between Machiavelli and Luther. Once this distinction began to be realized, it was possible to ask the question: Which determines which? To Machiavelli, it is the state by which the society is moulded; and to Marx it is the society which determines the form and nature of the state. The proper answer is a reciprocal relationship between the two. It was Montesquieu who was the first important author to show an awareness of this, though there are hints of it even in Bodin. Montesquieu clearly saw both that social determinants affect the nature of government and also that society can be changed by precisely those rulers who understand the social determinants. The vision about this reciprocal relationship overshadowed by the problem of sovereignty which identified a prescriptive position than a concern to distangle the causes and effects at work within the fabric of civil society. Even Hobbes, inspite of his hard-headed nominalism, is not a political sociologist because his social contract is not a sociological hypothesis but a hypothetical model enlisted to booster up a psychological model and the ethical theory implied by it. Thus we could see explicit difference between thinking about politics in philosophical and sociological terms, especially in the context of such concept as authority, legitimacy, and the structure of rights and duties in the state. As a matter of fact, we need to understand also the whole transition from the exposition of natural law to the claim for natural rights which took place between Grotius and Rousseau. In Rousseau, the famous contrast between men and citizen was a contrast between man in a state of nature and man in civil society, rather than between political man and social man. Sociology is the case of Adam Ferguson whose History of civil society treated the state as the all embracing association rather than family. To him although the family was a generic term including both family and nation, yet it was not as comprehensive a term as the state. Hence his inability to distinguish social from political relations. Let us remember that though Rousseau is rightly credi-ted with emphasizing the common humanity of men over and above their membership of a delimited citizen body but this is not exactly what we understand by a distinction between society and the state. From this view point, Saint Simon can be treated as an early precursor of modern political sociology. One time associate of Auguste Comte, the father of sociology, St. Simon's writings foreshadowed all the intellectual preoccupation of his time, such as positivism, historicism, internationalism, industrialism and technocracy. It was he who first saw that the economic structure of society is in some sense the basis for the form of the State although (unlike Marx) he saw that all institutions were the product of ideas and that political economy was the veritable and unique foundation of politics. But the contrast throughout St. Simon's writings between the 'political' and the 'social' was actually a contrast between the government and the administration—a contrast which was to occur a little more drastically in Engels and Lenin, what St. Simon tried to do was taking politics out of administration rather than describing how the governmental and the political is related to the administrative and the social. Thus his contrast stopped short of a real enquiry into the inter-relation of society and the state. The society predicted by St. Simon is a sort of hierarchy of available expertise; he pictures subordination without coercion rather than coexistence of the political and the social.

Even the position of anarchists about the contrast between society and the government does not reflect what we exactly mean by a contrast between social and political. The radicalism of Paine and the anarchism of Godwin rest on assumptions which tend to confuse this distinction. None of the writers of this school realized that some form of political association was necessary to make societies possible at all and that political relations must coexist with social relations, although they did not necessarily overlap with one another. To say that the government was the brute engine which has been the only perennial cause of the bias of mankind or that one could do away with the state and yet have constitutional guarantees for the rights that society ought to recognise, was, as Rancimam has observed, an unargued optimism about human nature. Thus although anarchists properly distinguished between cooperation from coercion and administration from government they failed to realize an inherent contradiction in their arguments about a sort of non-political government. Social organization presupposes that some people must have some power over some other people which is recognized by others as legitimate, and this competition for power must somehow be regulated or institutionalized. As a matter of fact, an understanding of how social institutions coexist with political has been more clearly realized by Toqueville in his discussion on the importance of voluntary association in American democracy. Toqueville however did not realize, at any stage of his exposition, the implication of his arguments in the context of a distinction between the social and the political.

The first explicit discussion on the state as distinct from society can be found in the writings of Hegel who happened to be the most distinguished contemporaries of Saint Simon. By emphasizing that particular interests which are common to everyone fall within civil society and lie outside the absolutely universal interest of the state proper, he simply warned against confusing the state with 'civil society'. Hegel's position, however, is not clear in regard to position of civil society itself. Although he appears to conceive of civil society as something separate, he actually subsumed it under the state where interest was absolutely universal by definition. Hegel, in fact, meant too much by the state, he seems to understand sometimes by it what Malinowski meant by 'culture' or Durkheim meant by 'collective consciousness'. He could never see that the social and the political could coexist in juxtaposition or even in opposition, and that the problem to be considered is relation between the political and the separate, non-political element is 'civil society'. This obviously required an explicit separation of society and the state. The terms which could not be formulated until Marx, who for the first time gave a full analysis of the distinction between society and the state during the course of his early criticism of Hegel.

Marx held the view that political hierarchy is in fact separate from though interrelated with the non-political organization of society, so that for Hegel, to assert their fusion is a necessary (and indeed desirable) fact is to force a metaphysical harmony upon an empirically real contradiction. This shift of emphasis proved to be crucial. Marx agreed with the anarchists that the state is a wicked imposition, but, unlike them, he offers a full scale analysis of how and why it is related to society under different economic conditions. Thus Marx was aware not only of the differences between the society and the state but also of the separate difference between a sociological and a metaphysical discussion of politics.

Losenz Von Stein, one of the important contemporaries of Marx, was the first author to discuss society as an independent concept. For him, 'the principles of the state stands in direct opposition to the principles of society and, thus, the character of the life of a people is the continuous struggle between the state and the society. This is almost exactly the sort of argument we find in Marx's writings of the same period. The state is founded 'he wrote in 1844,' upon the contradiction between the public and the private life'; and in 1845, 'only political superstition believes now-a-days that civil life must be held together by the state when in fact the state is upheld by civil life'. Thus the writings of Von Stein, when read together with those of Marx, will signify the 'emergence of a distinction which had been only latent or metaphysical before, and which now and only now makes possible a sociology of politics'.[3]

It would be worthwhile to discuss the writings of Weber in this regard. For him, the state cannot be defined in terms of what it does. There is scarcely any task that some political association has not taken in hand, and there is no task that one could say has always been exclusive and peculiar to those institutions which are designated as political. A sociological definition of state will imply specific means peculiar to it, as to every political association, namely physical force. A state short of this peculiarity will emerge as 'anarchy'. As a human community a state successfully claims within a given territory the monopoly of the legitimate use of force. Hence, politics will mean to us striving to share power or to influence the distribution of power, either among states or among groups within a state. Thus the term 'political' will mean the distribution, maintenance or transfer of power.

Weber's distinction between the society and the state is not quite what we need in the context of the sociology of politics. This is mainly because of political anthropologists account of societies which are not anarchic, but where there is no centralized monopoly of the use of force. Prof. Schapera, for example, stressed the fact that the public life of the Bergdama or the Bushman though not fulfilling definition of the state, is still 'subject to a definite system of control and is neither chaotic nor causal in operation'. In fact, we can talk about 'stateless societies' when force may be used but where there is no recognized central monopoly of it. However, we can retain the undoubted value of Weber's definition without going against the ordinary use of 'State', which does imply the notion of centralization.

Valuable clues of our needed distinction can be found in Durkheim. He wrote extensively on this subject in his long essays entitled 'Professional Ethics and Civic Morals'. For Durkheim tendency to attach cardinal importance to national territory was of relatively recent date. He felt that it was rather arbitrary to deny any political character to the great nomad societies whose structure was sometimes very elaborate. Thus we could retain Weber's emphasis on territorial unity without denying the title of the state even to centralized and organized nomadic societies. It seems better, however, to keep centralization alone as a criterion and to drop territory, so that we can, if we have to, talk not only about stateless societies but about 'non-territorial states'. Durkheim's failings in this regards, as his critics claim to have detected is that he surreptitiously reimposes a capital on society instead of talking about societies as such and thus, like Comte, smothers the state in society itself. Durkheim has, however, made two essential points. First, he has stressed that a patriarchal family, though it may be a social unit containing both governess and governed is not a state; secondly, he emphasizes that the idea of the state presupposes the existence of other social grouping under it. The useful aspect of Durkheim views about the difference between the social and the political will emerge clear when we add to it the Aristotelian basic contrast between the public and the private which among the recent authors has been most emphatically revised by Hannah Arendt. To talk about political relations, even in stateless societies, is to talk about relation on the public side of the private public line. If political organization is synonymous with familial organization then it is not political. The family is not political unit whether it rests on legitimate force or not, and a society where every family was politically autonomous would not be a society, but only a clan ridden territory in a state of anarchy. Weber, in fact, has arrived at the same point in his emphasis on the role of an administration staff in the exercise of political power. If we add to this definition of 'political' an explicit emphasis on public/private distinction, then we have perhaps the best definition of what 'political sociology' is about.

Since the 'social' embraces the political, economic, religious, and all other collective areas of behaviour, an attempt to distinguish it from the political may seem either a tautology or a paradox. For the purpose of distinction between the social and the political, the social as a separate category should include the sort of residual category of social relations that cannot be covered by some more specific term: Such forms of relation as friendship or the sort most naturally describable only as social relations. And if we follow Webers emphasis on the capacity for physical coercion, then the 'politics' of informal group or voluntary associations, are, strictly speaking, outside the scope of political science. Beyond this, we do not require further venture of technological refinement. The only point we have to keep in mind is Weber's warning of properly defining the political, against trying to define the state by what it does rather than what it possesses. This is precisely because there is scarcely anything that the state does not do? We may generally agree with Weber's view that if a state ceases to retain its recognized monopoly of force, then we wish to say it is no longer a state. Thus, possession of the monopoly of physical force and legitimacy of its organs will appear to be its chief characteristics.

The mistake of identifying the state in term of what it does can be found in Hobhouse who defined the state as the community organized for certain governmental purposes. Such definition amounted to relapsing back into Hegel's confusion between the society and the state. The same mistake can be found in the functionalist school of modern political thinkers. For example, Gabriel A. Almond writes;" ....a political system is that system of interactions to be found in all independent societies, which perform the functions of integration and adaptation (both internally and vis-a-vis other societies) by means of the employment, or threat of employment of more or less legitimate physical compulsion". There is no denying that such approach to political phenomena is useful and interesting. But does it mean specifically to define the political system by its functions, i.e., by what it does? Supposing that the answer is in negative, will then the state, if it chooses to use its legitimate coercive means for functions that are not integrative or adaptive, cease to be a state? If we accept this position, it will amount to our turning into many tantologies that have proved a perennial weakness of functionalism itself.

The subject matter of political sociology, therefore, covers all those institutions and forces of behaviour which as we have described earlier, fall under the category of what we term as 'political'. This will include the reciprocal relations between the political and the social in the sense of all other 'social ' institutions and behaviour not subsumed also under the political. The political is thus not entailed by the social, but it does entail, both the coercive and the public. This sort of distinction did not clearly emerge until Hegel, and it is only since a few decades that political sociology in the true sense of the term, has acquired the status of a definite and distinguishable discipline.

In fact, the first attempt to comprehend causative and social phenomena of political behaviour can be found in the study of Merriam and Crosnell that was conducted in the Chicago area for investigating the socio-economic characteristics of non-voters in a delimited universe. Later, around 1930 Lasswell published his work on psychopathology of politics that was based on the Freudian psycho-analytical model to understand the political decisions made by important leaders. For this, he utilized the psycho-analytical concepts of Vicissitudes of 'instinct', 'repression', 'submission', 'the dreams', 'repetition-compulsion' and others. He was mainly concerned with the type whether the political decisions involving further direction and orientation of a nation made by political leaders were rational. He also tried to see whether alternative choices of action were clearly perceived and decisions arrived at on the sole criterion of maximum advantage with minimum costs and risks. From a detailed analysis of biographics of important leaders, he concluded that the frustrations associated with their own childhood sublimated into the adult personality. To this extent, the "unconscious" and the "irrational" element does enter into major political decisions. This was the first attempt to apply certain psychological concepts for the study of political phenomena. Since then the discipline of psychology has been used by many for an analysis of political phenomena. Such attempts broadly fall into three main categories. They are : (i) The elite had been studied through the examination of case histories as revealed in historical material through primary psycho-dynamic research biographical notes or statistical records of decision behaviour; (ii) with the help of the empirical data on public opinion on attitudes, mass behaviour was investigated; (iii) the deviant groups and social movements were studied to specify the psychological consequences of exposure to different types of political situations and institutions.

However, the application of sociology for the study of political behaviour preceeded at a tremendous speed in the U.S., whereas the application of psychology considerably lagged behind, with the exception of the psychological studies of political socialization which clearly developed into a specialized offshoot of the discipline. It is not necessary, at this stage, to go into the details for such a lag. However, a few specific reasons may be cited (1) the psychoanalytical concepts are not easily amenable to empirical investigation, and (2) all the new-Freudians like Addler, Sullivan, Young and Eric Fromm refuted the psychological pre-determinism. Instead, having accepted the basic Freudian mosel, they stressed the influence of "socialization" and "reference groups" on the adult personality.

The psychological roots of the early development of political sociology can be traced back into the 'behavioural movement' in social sciences which emphasizes the necessity of looking at and explaining the 'observed' political behaviour underlying particular institutional legal arrangements. For instance, knowledge about all the details of the American constitution does not tell us very much about the political process in contemporary Indian society. It does not tell us that non-political decisions are made in practice, or about the particular nature of social bond between a member of Parliament and his constituents, and so on. None of this means abandoning attention to law, constitutional arrangements and the like, but rather seeing there as one kind of variable among a host of others which could be used to explain those aspects of the political process in which we might be interested.

This trend can be seen in as early as the 1900's studies to investigate voting behaviour, party identification, and attitudes and opinions. Development in the techniques of survey design, sampling, interviewing, questionnaire—design and personality measurement during the 1930's and 1940's further accelerated the trend. The current extent of this change was pointedly demo-nstrated by a survey of American political scientists. Asked to specify the area within which the most significant work in political science was taking place, they gave more weight to 'comparative government' and 'political behaviour' than to the study of traditional 'Public Law' and political theory.[4] The political scientists most frequently mentioned as making the more important contribution to the subject since the Second World war were the behaviouralists like Robert A. Dahl, Harold D. Lasswell, Herbert Simon, David Truman, V.O. Key Jr., David Caston, S.P. Huntington, Lucien W. Pie and Herbert Hyman.[5]

The origin of the behavioural movement in the field of politics owes its origin to the two, though not unrelated, intellectual developments—one in philosophy and the other in psychology. References in this direction should be made to the contributions of Pavolov of Russia and John Walson and B.F. Skinner of the United States who wrote extensively in the subject of 'behavioural psychology' by emphasizing that the development and employment of the stimuli—response model should be used for explaining human behaviour. Thus behavioural psychology turned away from the clinical problems and practices of Freudian psychology and stressed the observable stimuli, which human being experiences as the root cause of behaviour. Another development took place in the realism of philosophy. Drawing inspiration from David Hume, the logical postivists insisted on the separation of facts from values. They argued that it was necessary to distinguish factual propositions (which are observable and objectively verifiable) from value propositions that indicate subjective preferences and as such are not objectively verifiable. The basic message of both behavioural psychology and logical positivism was a brute and hard-nosed empi-ricism[6] in the realm of social sciences.

The new trend witnessed its manifestation in the writings and expressions of certain enlightened political scientists who could grasp the essential nature of the movement and thus sought to swim across the current of traditionalism. References in this regard may be made to the *Human Nature in Politics* by Graham Wallas that was published in 1908 and the *Process of Government* written by Arthur Beilley of America that appeared in the same year. It had its strong reiteration in the presidential address of James Bryce (delivered at the American Political Science convention in 1909) when he insisted: "We must have facts, facts, facts". It well demonstrated that the powerful currents of behavioural psychology and logical positivism that had made a high watermark in their respective fields contributed their share to the culmination of the behavioural movement that was abroad in the Anglo-American universe.

As a matter of fact, the "first sightings in the roily waters of political science of the phenomenon variously called political behaviour approach, a behaviouralist research, evidently occurred in 1920s.[7] After the ground breaking work done by Graham Wallas and Arthur Bentley a host of American authors emerged on the scene. Mention in this direction may be made of the New Aspects of Politics (1925) by Merriam, The Science and Method in Politics (1927) by George E. Caltin, Quantitative Methods in Politics (1928) by Stuart Rice, Political Behaviour: The heretofore unwritten laws, customs and principles of politics as practised in the United States (1928) by Frank Kent, and Psycho-pathology of politics by Harold

Lasswell. These notable works, among others, showed that as the behavioural movement emerged, it carried with it the signs of its intellectual paternity— a thorough going commitment to empirical data as the only verifiable source of objective knowledge and an even more thorough going commitment to a reconstruction of the categories of explanation describing political phenomena[8] has been replaced by a growing urge to derive analytical models from the behavioural disciplines like sociology, psychology and economics. Prominent among the pioneers of this approach are David Easton, Harold Lasswell, and Gabriel A. Almond. More recently, this approach has attained full expression in the works of Myron Weiner, Joseph La Paloobara, Sidney Verba, Karl Dentch, G.B. Powell, R.A. Dahl, David Apter, Edward Shils, Paul Brass and Ethiel de sola Pool and host of others who have sought to study political issues in the context of 'non-political' phenomena in a number of ways.

Thus contradistinguished from the classical or traditional theory, contemporary trend in the methodology of political science is to focus research on actualities, that is on the disclosure of facts and their inter-relationship, basing its findings on painstaking observation and measurement, especially on a rapidly growing stock of pertinent statistics. As such, it has tended to focus the development of new language and new concepts in establishing intellectual links among its several sub-fields, and its exponents are largely responsible for the development and use of such concepts as power, political system, political communication, political socialization and the like. The concepts gross traditional sub-field lines and their persuit is essential to the attainment of what they believe should be the correct major goal of political theory: the building of a body of an empirical and enduring theory about political life! Thus the emergence of political sociology has gone hand in hand with the development of contemporary approach to political phenomena which involves a systematic, empirical and causal explanation of the inter-relationships between political and socio-cultural variables—an approach that obviously stands in great contrast to the traditional one which referred to moral or philosophical prescriptions and was interchangeable with political philosophy rather than down-to-earth social psychology and sociology.

Needless to say that the behavioural movement has come to be recognized as a dominant force in the realm of social sciences in general and in political science in particular[9]. However, its success has not gone unchallenged. Many political scientists have expressed doubt whether 'behavioural' political science reflects the proper focus of the subject. Such doubt is based on the adequacy of its fundamental principles of theory construction on the basis of observed and observable behaviour of individuals and their collective entitles coupled with their verification procedures to matters of value and to the question whether or not behavioural empirical approach can meet them satisfactorily. Furthermore, it is based on the general intention that a theory based on pure empiricism is sterile and that imaginative or speculative and, for that reason, 'non-empirical' hypotheses are necessary for the presentation of an adequate theory of politics. Thus behavioural movement in politics has had its own limitations that smack of its points of weaknesses which may be enumerated hereafter.

In the first plan, a student of political theory is at a loss to know as to what the advocates of this theory mean by the word 'political' that precedes the word 'behaviour'. If we examine the views of eminent political behaviouralists in this direction, we find that all of then have defined the term 'politics' in their own way ranging from Easton's thesis of authoritative allocation of values' to Lasswell's dictum of the 'influence and the influential'. It is atleast doubtful whether it is possible to define the term 'political' without reference to the purposes or the goals of groups engaged in the struggle for power. For instance, the purposes or goals of anarchists or syndicalists are fundamentally different from others like socialists and communists in view of the fact that whether they stand for the abolition of the state government and authority root and branch, or they look at them as instruments for achieving the desired goal. Hence, it becomes a problem to understand as to what constitutes 'political' in the individual or group behaviour in the strict sense of the term.[10]

Second, the behaviouralists sacrifice values at the altar of facts and thereby present a barren political theory. They can be, for this reason, charged with committing the crime of vulgar reductionism.[11] They exclude the norms of human teleology in so faras it is not concerned with the basic problems of 'political good' that remained a matter of prominent concern with great political thinkers like Plato, Aristotle, Cicero, St. Augustine, St. Thomas, Kant, Rousseau, Green and a host of others who subscribed to the stock of normative political theory. The contributions of the behaviouralists are, therefore, criticised for reducing norms and values into facts, quality into quantity, reason into unreason, and human components of personality into the animal or the sub-human.[12]

Thrid, the behavioural political theory has also been accused of being reactionary or an intellectual exercise in the direction of justifying and preserving the status-quo. Instead of working in the direction of analysing the forces of social change or offering the principles of a social revolution, the aim of the behaviouralists is to collect data and analyse it to depend and protect democracy in the world. Thus, Leo Strauss describes them as being 'biased' in favour of a particular form of political system. The result is that the contributions of the behaviouralists may be treated as 'methodologies and not at all designated as theories. Keeping this attention confined to the systems analysis of a great behaviouralist like Easton, a critic observes that at best his theories can be expected to produce reasonably well organised information of comparative sort, and perhaps to suggest areas in which further research is needed. They are too weak to be considered theories and they perform none of the essential function of theory.[13]

Finally, what has been described as the greatest weakness of the behavioural movement is its mad craze for 'scientism' evident from their placing total reliance on 'facts'. It may, however, be asked 'that there is 'more to seeing than meet the eyeball.[14] The facts take their place and meaning only after they have been selected and organized not before. Therefore, one man's fact is another's fiction. For example, the Buddhists do not see right angles and western intimations that right angles are part of the warp and woof of reality which may well strike the average south East Asian as more than little impious. In emphasizing the behavioural approach beyond all other approaches and the exclusive reliance on 'scientific methods', political science has been reduced to "a device invented by the university teachers for avoiding that dangerous subject of 'politics', without achieving a science'. A learned critic has observed that behaviouralists are a frustrated group of intellectuals who want to make science out of politics but cannot. The increase in the literature of quasi—theories is a manifestation of their untiring efforts, and lack of deductive theories that are meaningful is a proof of their dilemma.[15]

Notwithstanding these lines of attack, it may be conceded that behaviouralists have made significant contributions by furnishing valuable predictions about the likely and unlikely acts of man or by making us aware of the significant correlations and also by laying different emphases on the bases enabling us to think in terms of new categories.[16] In recent years, some of the essential weakness have been overcome in the phase of post-behaviouralism keeping which in view an American writer has hopefully visualized that the behavioural movement of protest will disappear by slowly decaying as a distinctive mood and outlook as it will become and in fact already is becoming, incorporated into the main body of the discipline.[17] The astonishing point is that it will disappear not because it has failed, but because it has succeeded and as a separate, somewhat sectarian, slightly factional outlook, it will be the first victim of its own triumph.[18]

While the controversial debate about the nature and scope of behaviouralism in political science continues, we may, for an specific purpose, confine ourselves to its 'visible' methodological effects on the discipline. The critics of behavioural movement in political science have generally ignored the fact that it has been a part and parcel of the enlightenment tradition of social sciences, which represents a general mood to test the existing theories about political phenomena in terms of observation, evidence, and inference in varying conditions. In fact, behaviouralism does not essentially represent an antithetical trend to classical tradition of political science; it simply reflects a 'new vision' or a 'new perspective' about political behaviour of man, which is characterized by a desirability to buttress the existing normative frameworks in political science by the hard-care of testifiable inferences or laws. It is this perspective which has been responsible for arousing willingness among political scientists to seek new theories and methods of enquiry from other social sciences, including sociology.

Here, we need to remember one thing while exposure to behaviouralism has been an entirely new trend in political science, the case of sociology is altogether different. At no stage has sociology needed to reach outside for new ideas, techniques and inspirations to anything like the extent of political science. This is mainly because it had has the privilege of being a universal science of social life that may embrace all aspects of social relations, economic behaviour, deviance, stratification of political life, family, urban life, and so on. This privilege has often led sociologists to the erroneous pre-supposition that other social sciences are in a sense, 'derivatives' of their own discipline. It is for this reason that the development of political sociology which is claimed by the sociologists as a specialized branch of their descipline, has created a sense of unfounded score among conventional political scientists that they will lose their own identity. The assertive claim of socio-logists or the unnecessary scare among the political scientists reflects, in the ultimate analysis, perceptual barrenness in the case of the former and a lack of conceptual dynamism in the case of the latter. This is evident from the fact that all compartmentalization in social sciences is now-a-days breaking down. Social scientists generally are becoming more receptive to the idea and conclusions of their colleagues from the different areas of interests. Witness the historian's use of the formal models of economic development, the social psychologists who concern themselves with the psychological predispositions conducive to economic growth, the development of interests among some economists in the psychological basis of consumer behaviour, and so on. Similarly in political science dissatisfaction with the traditional interest in law, constitutional history and political theory is also evident. In the last decade the teaching curriculum of most departments of political science has been fundamentally changed. Briefly, but not accurately, thus has been a move towards the so-called 'behavioural style' of political enquiry.[19]

While sociology with its behavioural ethos, has continued to grow in the fertile land of political science, opinions have been divided as to whether this newly emerging discipline should be called 'political sociology' or 'sociology of politics'. A number of questions have been raised with regard to the usage of the term, i.e., whether the two terms are the same or different in expression.

With the passage of time, the distance between the users of the term has tended to increase as they hardly seem to be decided on a uniform use of a single term, i.e., either of the already existing terms or a third one which could unanimously be coined. As for the distinction between two terms, we can hardly find an answer in definite terms. We may use terms like political science and science of politics without knowing how to distinguish the two or without being certain about the distinction between the two. There appears a similar case with regard to the distinction between political sociology and sociology of politics.

Sociology of politics implies sociology of the phenomenon or process of politics. Thus we may say that, it implies a systematic study of the sociological background of the political system, the non-political institutions, political process, political communication and political results and consequences. But these are the areas of study which are covered by political sociology also. Hence the difference between the two terms does not appear very clear or well-established for all political purposes, we may say the political sociology and sociology of politics are more or less the same. It is possible that in specific contexts scholars or writers prefer the term political sociology or sociology of politics or the other way round. But such particular uses or references may not go against the general trend of taking these two terms as more or less synonymous. Further, the term political sociology seems to be used more frequently than the term sociology of politics. As has happened in case of several other sciences, one particular term, in this subject too, will come to be stabilized or standardized with the passage of time.

Political sociology, as we have earlier explained, did not emerge in all suddenness. It has had a long history of conceptual development behind it. This history hints at a sociological ethos in contemporary political thinking. This, however, remained confined to what can be called a sociological explanation of politics, that was intended to analyze relationship between the state and the society and the way they provide contextual meaningfulness to each other. In fact, it is in the course of such explanation which is largely responsible for the contemporary controversy about the primordiality of the state or the society, that the term sociology of politics has emerged. This new discipline was also devoted to a systematic analysis of the impact of new social conditions on the traditional functions of the state which underwent significant alterations and adjustments over time. Thus sociology of politics symbolized more than acceptance of a new perspective of or approach to political phenomena rather than development of an autonomous discipline. In other words, it was a sociological version of conventional discipline of political science, which derived its strength, in the main, from the inter-disciplinary revolution in social sciences of our time.

The rise of political sociology, although it has tended to derive its historical strength from the contextual debates about the autonomy of or inter-dependence between social and political phenomena, refers to the crystallization of a specialized discipline. In fact, political sociology starts where sociology of politics ends. This is because the fundamental assumptions of political sociology is that social conditions are responsible for both causes and consequences of political phenomena. This statement implies that all political processes presuppose social contexts, a systematic understanding of which provides them with a fuller meaning and, exactly in the same manner, changes in structure and cultural matrix of society can, to a great extent, be explained in the light of knowledge about the level and range of political processes.[20]

Thus with the development of political sociology the controversy about primordiality of the state of the society has been buried and a new framework of analysis has been developed for allowing either of them or its component elements treated as both independent and dependent variables in the explanation of social and political processes and the patterns of their concomitance. This position is further clarified when Lipset and Beudix assert that.

The error lay in trying to deal with state and society or two independent organisms, and that one should not ask which is more important and preferable. Political sociologists came to argue that the state is just one of many political institutions, and that political institutions are one of many clusters of social institutions; that the relationship among these institutions is the subject of sociology in general, and that other institutions in the special province of political sociology. In debating with political scientists about the credibility of political sociology, sociologists have argued that the independent study of the state and other political institutions does not make a theoretical source.

If we accept the above position, we can safely assume that while sociology of politics tends to start with the state as an all encompassing political institution and measure its impact on society, political sociology tends to start with society and explain the way it influences and, in turn, influenced by the state as a powerful political institutions. Such difference between academic positions of the two disciplines is on account of the conceptutal limitation in the case of the former and a full-fledged methodological autonomy, in the case of the latter. It is probably this differences which explains why sociology of politics has tended to remain as an offshoot of political science, whereas political sociology with its unlimited analytical potentiality has come to acquire an academic status which, even if it tends to combine the two within its realm independent of both political science and sociology. Political sociology, therefore, far from being merely a sociological explanation of politics is the systematic study of the impact of political institutions on the structure and culture of society and vice versa. This view is supported by S.M. Lipset when he observes that political sociology is the study of interrelationship between society and political institutions; and that political sociology is not solely the study of the factors that condition the political order. Indeed political institutions are themselves social structures and hence or often the independent factors that affect non-political social structure. Basically, it studies the nature, scope, and implications of human relations in the context of political processes. This includes among other things, the analysis of social power and social progress in the light of the patterns of political development and culture.

**References**

1. Symon Chodak, *Societal Development*, Talcott Parsons, *Social Structure and Politics*, R.M. MacIver, *Politics and Society*.
2. Talcott Parsons, Ibid.
3. Runciman, W.G., *Social Science and Political Theory*, Cambridge University Press (sec. Ed.), 1975, p. 34.

4. S.A. Rice, *Quantitative Methods in Politics*, Knspt, New York, 1928; H. Tingsten, *Political Behaviour; Studies in Evolution Statistics*, PS. King, London, 1937, C.E. Merriam and H.F. Gasnell, *Non-Voting*, University of Chicago Press, Chicago 1924; P.M. Rossi, 'From Land Marks in Voting Research, in E. Burdick and A.S. Broadbeck (eds.) *American Voting Behaviour* Free Press, Glencoe, 1959.
5. A Soniet and J. Tanenhaus, "Trends in American Political Science", *American Political Science Review*, 62: 9, 33-947.
6. Don R. Bowen, *Political Behaviour of the American Public*, Columbia, Ghio; C.E. Merril Pub. 1968 p. 4.
7. Robert A. Dahl: "The Behavioural Approach in Political Science: Epitaph for a monument to a successful Protest", in *American Political Science Review* (December 1961). p.p.763-72 and reproduced in Gould and Thursby (eds) *Contemporary Political Thought: Issues in Scope, Values and Direction*, (New York; Holt, Rinehart and Winston, 1969) pp. 118-36.
8. Don R. Bowen: *Political Behaviour of the America Public* (Columbia, Ohio: CE. Merril Pub. 1968) p.4.
9. B. Crick, *The American Science of Politics*, Routhdge and Kegan Paul? London, 1959; MQ. Subley in J.C. Charles worth (ed) *Contemporary political analysis*, Free Press, New York, 1967, pp.51-71; S. Walin, *Politics and Vision*, Little Brown, Boston, 1960, pp. 434-552.
10. Christian Bay, a critic of behavioural politics, designates it as 'pseudo-politics' or 'counterpart politics'. "A critical Evaluation of Behavioural Literature, *American Political Science Review* (March, 1965, pp. 39-51).
11. S.S. Akinchan, "Sociological Theory and Social Determinism Towards a Dialecticised Perspective of Research", *Journal of Social and Economic Studies*, 1976.
12. V.P. Verma, "The Behavioural Research and Political Philosophy: Some aspects," *Indian Journal of Political* Studies, Jodhpur, Vol. No,. 1976, p. 27.
13. Mechan: *The Theory and Method of Political Analysis* (Homei Wood III: Dorsey Press, 1965).
14. N. R. Hansen: *Patterns of Discovery* (Cambridge: Cambridge University Press, 1961).
15. P.S.C. Northrop: *Logic of the Science and Humanities*, (New York: Meridian Books. 1959) pp. 40-49.
16. See Alfred Cohham, "Ethics and the Decline of Political theory", *Political Science Quarterly* (Sept., 1953) p. 335.
17. Mechavn, *op cit*, p. 161.
18. Dahl in Gould and Tuesly, *op cit*, p. 132.
19. Robert Edowse and John Hughes, *Political Sociology*, (John Wiley and Sons, London 1972) pp. 2-3.
20. Lipset and Reinhard Bendix, *The Field of Political Sociology*, p. 26.

# Chapter - 2

# Nature of Political Sociology

## What is Political Sociology

Political Sociology, as we have observed earlier, has basically emerged out of the growing necessity to analyse social structure and cultural order of society in the context of political system and its underlying institutional and normative ingredients. Giovanni Sarton has treated political sociology as a strange blend of sociology of politics and political science. This view seems to be a little erroneous, because although political sociology had something in common with sociology of politics in the initial phases of its development, it has, by virtue of developing its own concepts, methods and theories which are fundamentally different from that of sociology of politics and of conventional political science, come to acquire an autonomous and distinct discipline that has tended to revolutionize both general sociology and conventional political science.

Political sociology may be defined as an application of sociology to the study of political phenomena and process and their implications for society, culture and human behaviour. This is to say that if the individuals are exposed to the same set of experiences, the degree of uniformity in their behaviour will also be increased. As a corrolary to this, people belonging to similar groups are more in conformity with each other than that of dissimilar groups. That is, the varying socio-economic and organizational factors modify the individual behaviour. Moreover, the sociological theory postulates that social system and its articulating processes themselves constitute the forceful determinants of human behaviour. Hence any behaviour, be it religious, political, economic or moral has to be understood from a sociological perspective. This approach reveals the causative phenomena embedded in the social system. This is in essence the rationale for the application of sociology to the study of politics.

If we accept the above set of propositions, the study of politics, traditionally speaking, has been restricted to investigations of documents of treaties, analysis and interpretations of constitutional and international law, types of government with their detailed characteristics and ideologies, such as communism, democracy, etc. But with the acceptance of what can be called a sociological rationale, the study of politics has shifted in countries like U.S.A. from the library type studies to empirical investigations. Already, several successful attempts have been made to impose the rigorous concepts, models, systems and some of the methodological techniques of sociology for the study of political phenomena. To cite a few instances the studies by Agger and Goldrich,[1] Arendt,[2] Brotz,[3] Eldersveld,[4] Hyman[5] Axelord,[6] Wright and Hayman,[7] and many others, are significant attempts in this direction. These and other works emphasized an 'interdisciplinary urge' in the analysis of social and political phenomena, which was largely responsible for the emergence of political sociology as a specialized discipline for the study of multifaceted interplay and relationship between social and political phenomena. Political sociology thus offers an inclusive and comprehensive perspective for the study of interdependence between social and political structures in the light of which alone we can understand not only the ongoing process of change in economic and cultural orders of society but also significant shifts in the attitude and orientations of people due to the inclination of new values and ideologies that emerge out of changing social, economic, and political conditions. This is why political sociology has tended to become a conceptual as well as methodological link between political science and general sociology which appear to have shunned their academic bias for being bound by meaningful relationship in the study of society, culture, and polity. Mukhopadhyaya[8] has rightly observed that political sociology is the product of a cross fertilization between sociology and political science that studies the impact of society on politics and also the reverse, although viewing the substance of politics in a social form. In fact, this view is commensurate with what has hither to been called a 'behavioural persuasion' in politics which stresses the need to study not only what man does politically, but also the social and cultural meaning he attaches to his behaviour.[9] It is this perspective which characterizes most of the pioneering works[10] which constituted the background for the emergence of political sociology as a specialized and full-fledged discipline.

Some political scientists have maintained that the heart and soul of political sociology may be said to lie in the capture and exercise of power in political contexts against the sociological background. This stand is apparently based on their conventional view that the subject of politics tends to geer round the process of capturing and exercising power for certain ends and goals. As a matter of fact, the main preoccupation of political sociology consists in description, categorization, and analysis of the relationship of political phenomena to the social system. This suggests an investigation into the process of political representations and participation and the impact of economic and social development in all these aspects. Considerable research has already been conducted in U.S.A. in testing the key concepts, such as 'legitimatization', 'consensus', 'pressure groups' and others. To illustrate, legitimatization is generally meant to suggest political norms that motivate and guide behaviour, the rules that prescribe what ought to be right rather than what is and the sustenance and transmission of these norms, i.e., political symbols, definitions, etc., from one generation to the other. The mechanism of consensus are aimed at the articulation of the process of legitimatization. For example, studies conducted by Axelrod,[11] Wright and Hyman[12] in 1958 and others, confirm that political articulation is made in the context of reference groups.

## Reviewing the Available Literature

A brief review of the current literature in the area of political sociology will enable us to clearly conceptualize the concepts and the variables employed for the comprehension of the political process. This will also enable us to develop a conceptual scheme, which can be utilized as a guidance for further research. The scope of the present review is restricted to suggest the range of interests exhibited in research studies, relating to political behaviour. As a matter of fact, such studies as voting behaviour have attracted the attention of many social scientists for two reasons. First, voting statistics are readily available for different regions and countries over a period of time. Second, these patterns can be easily compared over a period of time, within a community and among different communities. Such comparison helps to establish certain recurrent regularities in voting behaviour and also enables us to relate to the theories of organizational change. The literature on voting behaviour shows certain recurrent patterns and relationships in the voter turnout as associated with various social, economic, and demographic variables. Some of the specific areas of study constituting the actual scope of political sociology are influence of family on socialization; reference groups and political articulation; the role concept; participation, orientation and voting fluctuations; study of elite; political, social and economic factors in voter participation; ecological factors in the explanation of political behaviour; rural/urban differentials in voter participation; patterns of voting behaviour; leadership and social change; political socialization; interest groups and political processes; resource groups and resource networks; political development and structural linkages, their implications for the society; political attitude and ideologies in the context of nation building; and so on. We can deal with these specific areas of political sociology in a precise manner separately.

The evidence from the current literature point that 1. participation and involvement of the individual in politics and 2. the types of political goals or policies sought is a function of socialization which is reflected in the process of pre-adolescence differentiation. For example, several studies have shown that boys are more likely than girls to select public figures as "ego-ideals", girls are more interested in fiction and less interested in news and public affairs, etc. Likewise, it has been demonstrated that left right ideological changes and dissensions of different adult groups have their correspondence in childhood differences. These and several other factors support that the child learns at an early age to intimate politics in a manner similar to that of adults. Hyman[13] has demonstrated how families act as agents of political socialization. Gupta's study further corroborates Hyman's contentions in the Indian context. Lipset, Trow and Colman,[14] Maccoby, Mathews and Merton,[15] and several others correlated the political attitudes of children with those of parents.

The concept of 'reference group' has been extensively used by political scientists as well as sociologists in a number of studies. Hence, an elaboration of this concept and its implications constitute a significant area of political sociology. The motives, attitudes, pattern of interaction and the stereotypes to a large extent are a function of an individual's belongingness or association to a group or groups. That is what an individual learns from a group-mode of thought, standards of evaluation and goal perspective. People with common interest or characteristic interact more often than with members of dissimilar interests. Hence, for any action of an individual the 'group' for which he belongs becomes a 'referents object'. These objects may be caste and kinship groups, religious symbols, books, newspapers, movies etc. Robert Merton has classified reference groups into 'normative' and 'comparative' groups. The 'normative group' sets, maintains and transmits behaviour or standards for the individual, whereas the comparative group acts as a frame of reference with which one evaluates and compares himself with others. These two analytical distinctions are very important to the core of sociological theory. Further, the 'normative' and 'comparative' groups may serve either as a positive or a negative frame of reference.

The influence of socialization on politicization, political articulation as shaped through reference groups, the interaction of political, economic and social elite in the formulation of political decisions and many other aspects have been subjected to serious investigations. A brief presentation of some of the pre-occupations has been made to enable scholars to perceive the nature of interaction between the political and social variables. In fact, many studies have shown that political behaviour is shaped through the interaction of interpersonal relations that manifest in the research groups. Merton[16] found that opinion leaders interpret the media to the members of group. They act as 'gate keepers' in the flow of information. Hence this role in shaping the opinions of the people has been studies. Jonousitz,[17] Katz and Lazarsfeld[18] also studied how the mass media and the patterns of interpersonal relations interact to shape the political opinions and analysed the patterns and types of opinion leadership.

Analysis of political behaviour in the 'context of role concept is another important area in political sociology. There is an amazing diversity of definitions in this regard, however. This can alsc be attributed partly to the theoretical focus that one has approached. Each one of the several contextual meanings as provided by different disciplines like sociology, anthropology, and social psychology, have undoubtedly served to tackle the type of problems for which they were designed. Which type of definition is more suited is dependent on the nature of problem chosen for investigation. However, these definitions may roughly be classified under three or four broad categories.

The definition given by Ralph Linton consist of "attitudes, values and behaviour ascribed by the society to any and all persons occupying a position". This approach has also been taken by Theodore Newcomb and others. This definition implies consensus among the members of society as to the expectations for incumbents of a position. It is rarely possible to have such a consensus on any role expectations in a given society. This definition does not imply what a person actually does in a position but indicate the behaviour expectations ascribed to him by others. The second type of definition has been concretely formulated by Talcott Parsons who has observed that 'roles' are situationally determined. He further elaborates that 'the actor' develops a system of 'expectations' relative to the various objects of the situation. These objects may be 'social' 'physical' and 'cultural'. A role constitutes "a sector of total orientation system. It is organized about expectations in relation to a particular interaction context. These expectations are integrated with a particular set of value standards which govern, interact with one or more alters in the appropriate complementary roles". "What an actor is expected to do in a given situation both by himself and by other constitutes the expectation of that role. What the relevant alters are expected to do, contingent on ego's action, constitutes the sanctions. Role expectations and sanctions are, therefore, in terms of the content of action, the reciprocal to each other. What are sanctions to ego are also role expectation to alters, and vice versa. Parsons' definition as distinguished from the above pursuits the measurement of the degree of consensus on the role-expectation in interaction systems.

The definition by Kinsley Davis falls into the third category. He defined that a role "is the manner in which a person actually carries out the requirements of his polition". His and other definitions are sufficient to indicate the importance of this area within the scope of political sociology, even if there persists a lack of agreement to the precise definition of a concept. Researches in the area with the help of a commonly acceptable operational definition will enable us to reappraise the concepts in current use of sociology like role expectation, role orientation, role dissonance, role-set and role strain in the context of change taking place in political structure, and political institutions.

Then comes the area of relationship between voting fluctuations and the levels of participation. For example, Glaser[19] found that fluctuations among some groups are more high than other. Hastings[20] concluded that 'non-values' are the least politicized elements of the electorate. Few more studies concluded that high levels of voter turn-out in local elections may not be attributed to high political consciousness. Instead, they may be due to a large segment of what is called as 'protest vote'. Political sociology can obviously highlight the social and cultural dimension of such voting fluctuations, especially in the context of changing bases of role expectation and orientations.

The study of elite has come to be reorganized as the most challenging dimension of political sociology. Elites are those persons who are in a position to exercise considerable influence to shape the policies in an area of given social, religious, political or other systems. These, elites can be found in all societies and in all strata of human activity. 'Circulation of elite', a concept frequently used in political sociology borrowed from Pareto, implies the inflow and outflow of people into positions of political control. For example, in a transitional and developing economy, the traditional leadership based on caste, kinship and landed aristocracy is being fast replaced by the emerging elite, i.e., the newly rich, businessman, graduate engineer, lawyer, etc. In the past 20-30 years, these different types of elites have been subjected to intense investigations. The economic elite of America have been studied by Rogo[21], Bendix and Lipset,[22] and several others. Likewise, the role of the power elite has been studied by Warner and Abegglen.[23] But field relating to the composition, interchange and the function of political elite has not yet been fully cultivated.

In recent years political, social, and economic factors in voter participation have also been studied by political sociologists. The study by Berelson[24] for example stressed the role of political influence upon constituents as contributing factor in voter participation. He discusses how the social, political, and psychological forces influence individuals and groups in their choices. For example, he reports that the intensity of religious background in Elmira, a small community in up state of New York, determines the political affiliation. Likewise, the Republicans had a higher rate of voter turnout than the Democrats. Another study conducted by Berelson and others focussed on certain social factors, that influence the voting process. They found that voting is homogenous in almost all familiar, and people in the same organizations tend to vote similarly. In other words, family group, and organizational affiliation influence the voting behaviour of an individua! as well as groups.

Another study by Merriam and Goshell[25]dealt with the act of non-voting itself. They found that certain groups in the Chicago area voted more than other group and political apathy was predominantly greater among certain section than others. They tried to explain the factors involved in 'non-voting' rather than the voting patterns. Some studies have pointed out that occupation is one of the important factors which account for voting turn-out. Tingsten and others[26]found that government employees have a higher rate of voter turn-out than other occupational groups. Farmers now enjoy wider support from various governmental policies. For this and other seasons, they predicted that more farmers were expected to vote and have more organizational activities.[27]

Voting participation seems to increase as one rises on the ladder of occupational structure in any society. A number of reasons, such as social and economic factors and amount of leisure available contribute to the continued interest of these groups in social and political affairs and policies. Members of these groups usually have good educational background and acquire technical skills in the discharge in their economic, legal, and interpersonal relationships with various strata of the population. They are also widely exposed to mass media and to opposing opinions on various political and economic issues, to acquire themselves with the issues and problems involved. Therefore, the upper occupational groups have a higher voter-turnout than manual or clerical workers. In other words, social stratification, organizational diversity, and hierarchy of role performances in any society enhances the voter participation of certain groups as compared with others. Besides occupation, there are other economic factors that influence the voter turn-out.[28] Even in a relatively less controlled capitalistic society like the U.S.A., business corporations are increasingly dependent on the policies of the federal and local governments in the allocation of research funds for industrial and defence projects, price controls, and the tax structure. In other parts of the world like Canada, England and India, where the government controls the key industries, the influence of government on business groups is very high. In view of these facts and others, we expect a high rate of turn-out among various business groups.

In addition to economic factors, religious factors also are considered to motivate political action and voting behaviour. The majority of the catholics in Kerala for example helped to overthrow the communist controlled state government in 1956. Likewise, the highest turn-out among the Jews in certain parts of the world is considered to be reaction against anti-semitism in different parts of the world. It was agreed that prohibition as an issue in the general elections of 1952, 1957 and 1962 in India helped the ruling Congress party to gain more support from the women folk. It was stated by Harris[29] that the issues of 'corruption' and 'communism' in the 1952 American presidential elections accounted for the estimated 55 percent turn-out of female voters.

Many studies support the theory that voter turn-out is highest in the situations of economic, political, and international crisis.[30] These social factors affecting the voting behaviour have been corroborated by empirical evidences.[31] Societies that have low rate of social and economic mobility are expected to have higher rates of voters turn-out than societies where mobility is maximal. The threat of the use of coercion are expected to produce very high voter turn-out to avoid anticipated deprivations and punishments. The turn-out of as much as 99.7 per cent in certain elections in the Soviet Union is attributed to perceived threats.

The studies, discussed here-in before, indicate the extent of association between various political, social, economic, religious categories and the patterns of voter turn-out. Similarly, these are studies which indicate relationship between voting behaviour and such ecological factors as size, distance, and urbanity. Some of these studies were ecological categories for a general explanation of political behaviour, others have empirical evidence to support the hypothesis that residents of urban areas vote more than those of rural areas, and still others make assertion that residents of rural areas vote more than those residing in urban areas.[32]

Eulan[33] postulates a direct relationship between the character of an area's ecological structure and the structure of the party system. He argues that urban environment is more complicated in its social, economic, and functional structure, and, as such, is more propitious for party competitiveness than rural areas. Therefore, he hypothesizes that "urban structure is conducive to the existence of competitive party systems and that there is a progressive transition to semi-competitive and non-competitive systems as areas are located along the urban-rural ecological continuum. To test this hypothesis, he arranged Ohias eighty eight countries on a rural-urban continuum. The data support the propositions that urban areas are more favourable for competitive political structure. In contrast, when Schmidhauser[34] analysed the nintey nine countries of lowa, he failed to find any association between certainty and political competitiveness. This does not invalidate the Ohio study, however, since urbanity may be only one of the factors involved in the development of a competitive atmosphere.

Cantril[35] has argued that growth of urbanization favours the rapid economic development through industrialization. Urbanization and industrialization together create new socio-economic classes which lead to economic and political cleavages. Non-urban societies, tend to be more homogeneous in their social and ethnic composition and are likely to conform to the norms of prevailing social and political systems. Hawley[36] has pointed out that the extent of 'differentiation is contingent to a large degree on its size. Size determines the range of physio-psychological variation and also the extent of territorial scatter. Increase in number produces a corresponding increase in the number of intrinsic differences in the population, though not necessarily a corresponding increase in the functional variation.

The differences between metropolis, town and rural area in terms of political participation have also been discussed. Investigations of Key states that the metropolis, towns and villages differ not so much in their corporate concerns but vary to large extent in the views of those types of people that predominate in these areas. The difference relates to variations in occupational distribution, economic status, and ethnic composition, among others. Hence all such characteristics contribute to establish different patterns of political behaviour in these areas. He has also argued that people of small towns, villages and countryside stand between those of metropolis and cities, if they are arranged on a liberal to conservative scale, on certain domestic issues like trade union influence, medical case, job guarantee and tax structure. Hence, the people in rural areas and small town, according to Key are not as conservative as people usually suppose them to be on many domestic and international issues. On the other hand, people in small cities seem to be more conservative on such issues.[37]

The above mentioned studies thus have tried to relate urbanity to the degree of political competitiveness. Thus the general conclusion is that urban areas have different patterns of social, economic, and political composition and also that they tend to be more heterogeneous in their political characteristics. Alongside the investigations into the ecological differences and political behaviour, several studies have been conducted, in the Indian context, to show that the social and cultural impact of urbanization account for significant shifts in the political attitudes and behaviour.

The works of Kini,[38] Akinchan,[39] and Ashraf[40] show that while urbanization has not only brought about changes in social texture and cultural ethos of urban communities but it has been responsible for gradual secularization of political behaviour including the bases, patterns, and attributes of leadership. Thus urbanization has been paralleled by the emergence of a new political culture which may conform to the democratic urge of society. The new political culture involves significant shifts in value preferences and changes in political behaviour, particularly in those areas which have been communicationally accessible to and under constant influences of the urban centre. Crystallization of this culture has been contingent upon further extension and viability of modern political and social frameworks and institutions in rural area, literacy or exposure to mass media, diversification of occupational structure, development of interest groups and networks, value orientation and behavioural changes in more differentiated and specialized institutional settings. This is precisely because these conditions have created the prerequisite cultural condition for the political socialization of people not only of urban areas but also of the remote rural communities, which have been exposed to new condition of social life.

The majority of attempts to explain voting behaviour in an ecological framework support the proposition that urban areas have a higher rate of voter turn-out than rural areas. While discussing the demographic characteristics related to voting behaviour, Lipset[41] states that urban residents vote in larger proportions than residents of rural areas. Lane[42] has advanced several reasons for expecting a higher rate of voter turn-out in metropolitan and urban areas as against small towns and rural areas. These explanations are based on the research findings, by other social scientists. Some of the reasons he has cited are:

(i) In urban areas the working classes have an opportunity to organize and lead their members in social and political activities. The ever present conflict or tension between the working classes organizations and the managerial organizations in urban areas enhances the voter participation, whereas in rural areas, the working classes are likely to accept the leadership of the upper classes and hence no conflict is possible. In other words, organizations competitiveness in the sphere of politics increases voter participation.

(ii) Even though there are political and social cleavages in rural areas, they tend to be less sharp than in urban areas. The ethnic composition of rural areas is relatively more homogeneous. Hence any type of ethnic tension is absent. The predominant ethnic tension in urban areas is one of the factors for the higher rate of voter turn-out.

(iii) Sense of citizenship and civic norms are more strongly internalized in metropolitan areas than in rural areas.

(iv) Exposure to political, social and economic issues, and the levels of education are higher in urban areas than in rural areas.

(v) And, political activity increases with the density of population of an areas because factors making for higher participation have a higher incidence and prevail over counter faces in this area. Similarly Campbell, Gurin and Miller[43] have concluded that residents of urban areas vote in larger proportions than residents of rural areas. They analysed the extent of voter participation for the presidential elections of 1948, 1952 and 1960, using a survey research technique for the whole of the United States. Their results show that metropolitan areas had higher rates of voters turn-out than rural area in the 1948, 1952, 1956 and 1960 presidential elections. The following table for 1948 and 1952 presidential elections was obtained by the Survey Research Centre. The same pattern are repeated in 1956 and 1960, hence the result of these two elections are not reported here:

| *Sl. No.* | *Type of Community* | *Total voting* | |
|---|---|---|---|
| | | *1948* | *1952* |
| 1. | Metropolitan Area | 79% | 83% |
| 2. | Town and Cities | 73% | 63% |
| 3. | Rural Areas | 68% | 68% |

Myron Weiner[44] has also corroborated these conclusions by advancing empirical evidences in this regard. Analysing the voting averages of the general Elections in various states of India, of period between 1952 and 1972, Weiner Osgoodfield[45] showed significant rural urban variations of voting in the context of different political parties. The following table gives a clear view of the pattern of voting behaviour in India in terms of rural—urban background:

**Distribution of the vote among the radical parties, Congress, and other parties and Independents in urban-rural constituencies: All India (1952-1972).**

| | *1952a* % | *1957a* % | *1962* % | *1967* % | *1972b* % |
|---|---|---|---|---|---|
| *Urban* | | | | | |
| Communists and Jansangh | 11.7 | 16.7 | 22.0 | 26.5 | 24.9 |
| Congress | 45.6 | 46.8 | 45.3 | 38.2 | 48.7 |
| Other parties and Independents | 42.7 | 36.5 | 32.7 | 35.3 | 26.4 |
| *Rural* | | | | | |
| Communist and Jansangh | 6.1 | 9.3 | 12.6 | 16.0 | 16.6 |
| Congress | 43.2 | 45.1 | 43.4 | 41.6 | 46.2 |
| Other parties and Independents | 50.7 | 45.6 | 44.0 | 42.4 | 37.2 |

(a) Single Member Constituencies only.
(b) Figures represent the average of state percentages. Polling for the constituency size of Jammu and Kashmir, Goa and Rajasthan are excluded from the calculation.

Similar treatments of data have led the investigators to conclude, among many other important things, that there is evidence to show electoral changes in rural areas are often preceded by changes in urban areas. Virtually in every state, the rise in turn-out in rural constituencies was preceded by substantial increase in urban turn-out. Similarly, in almost every state in which the Jansangh and Communist parties are active, disparity in votes between the urban and rural areas (with the communists or Jansangh having a higher urban vote) is followed by a rise in rural support in the next elections. Many explanations have been suggested for the growth of radical protest parties in urban India: the discontent of urban employed, the social and economic frustrations of younger voters, the increasing dissatisfaction of the middle class, the slow pace of economic growth, and in the case of the growing vote for Jansangh, an increase in anti-Muslim sentiment among Hindus. These hypotheses require more evidences for validation in the actual context, however.

There are studies which show just the reverse side of the trend, i.e., rural areas have a higher rate of voter turn-out than their urban counterparts. For example, Robinson and Standing[46] found that in India, residents of rural areas out-voted those of urban areas. These researches ranked the ninety-two countries of India by population density in 1940. The countries were again ranked on average percentage vote in the presidential elections of 1936, 1940, and 1944. A similar rank order correlation between population density and average votes polled for prosecuting attorneys in the non-presidential election year 1934, 1938, and 1942 was arranged. The results in both period yielded negative correlations, confirming the hypothesis that rural areas have a higher rate of voter participation. Interestingly, they also found that the most rural countries had the highest rate of voter participation. Likewise, most urban countries had the lowest rate of voter turn-out.

Key[47] has argued that in the larger cities of the south there is lower electoral interest than among the small town and farm people. He states that non-voting is higher in the larger cities. Countries having a city of 1,00,000 or more have remarkably a lower rate than the remaining ones. Likewise, countries having a city of 1,00,000 vote in smaller proportions than the countries not having a city or a town. Scarrow[48] has analysed the voter participation in the federal and provincial elections of Canada based on aggregate voting of data. The results support the proposition that political competitiveness and voter participation are higher in rural than in urban areas. He also reports that Boer farmers in South Africa have a higher rate of voter participation and efficient organizational activity that the residents of the urban areas.

Thus, the studies based on the aggregate voting do not support the results obtained by the survey research samples. This may be because studies conducted by the survey research are based on national samples whereas the studies based on the aggregate voting data are restricted mainly to a regional or a local area. Therefore, a real comparison of these two approaches cannot be made until more studies based on aggregate voting data for large areas or survey studies made of similar areas have been conducted.

## Political Sociology as a Science

Having delineated the field or the scope of political sociology, we are confronted with the problem of defining its status and nature, i.e., whether it is a scientific discipline because of its inherent adherence to the norms of science or alternatively, it is an art. Judging it from the scientific standards, we can say that political sociology is a science because it possesses the major characteristics and fulfils all requirements to attain such as sociology, psychology, economics, and political science. In other words, political sociology abides by those scientific cannons of knowledge which emerged out of the enlightenment tradition/observation of fact, interpretation of evidence, and generalizable inference and which form the core of positivist thinking in the empirical tradition of social sciences. In accordance with this principle the nature of political sociology can be demonstrated not on the basis of the subject matter it studies but on the basis of the methodology it adopts in approaching the social and political phenomena. This is in consonance with the commonly admitted opinion that the unity of all science consists along in its method and not in its material.[49] It has therefore been observed that the true sign of science is a certain type of approach towards the field which one intends to investigate[50]or that "science is a certain way of looking at the world"[51]. Therefore, we can say that if science is, in essence, an attitude toward the world, a point of view, a systematic body of knowledge and a way of finding, then political sociology, like other social sciences, represents a scientific discipline which endeavours to formulate theories about the relationship between polity and society with the help of a body testable evidences and generalizable inferences which are arrived at through a systematic study of social and political behaviour in representative contexts of human society.

Broadly speaking, political sociology adopts the same scientific methodology as adopted by general sociology for the theorization about social facts. This methodology has been founded on Comtian positivism and elaborated by Emile Durkheim, the father of modern sociology, in his well-known classic entitled "The Rules of Sociological Method". Since it would not be possible to go in detail of the positivist tradition of general sociology, we may identify the major steps in scientific method and examine whether or not poli-tical sociology abide by them. These steps are:

1. Selection of the problem of universal implications.
2. Specific hypothesization or formulating a set of tentative propositions.
3. Collection of data or information from representative categories or classes of the universe.
4. Empirical Testing through organisation and interpretation of data such as classification description and explanation.
5. Identifying a body of principles about concomitance of facts, causal relationships leading to laws or generalizable evidences.
6. Predictive capability about the occurrence of events or phenomena with specification of contextual limits or deterministic transcendence.

The above steps is a scientific methodology represents characteristics or pre-conditions, on the basis of which a certain body of information or branch of knowledge can be called science. Obviously, political sociology is capable of abiding by all these preconditions. It offers a wide scope for scientific investigation in the context of constant interplay on the one hand, between the social and cultural order and the political organizations and institutions, and between social attitudes and political outlook and behaviour, on the other. It endeavours to identify those problems or events which emerge out of such display and which have universal and even global implications for the social and political systems. Once such problems are identified, it is in a position to formulate specific hypothesis or tentative propositions which could act as torch bearer in the intricate course of scientific investigation. For example, a typical hypothesis in the realm of political sociology could state whether or not there exists positive or negative relationship between the extent of cultural change in the course of urbanization and the extent of political socialization i.e., the individuals' or groups' involvement of and commitment to democratic norms and values in their political behaviour. Since a given polity consists of such classes or categories of people which are characterized by their typical ideas and orientations, a political sociologist engaged in scientific investigation could collect relevant data or information from the representative segments of society so as to cover the whole or the part of the universe about which patterns of uniformities are sought. The information so collected could be organized and classified in manner which could help the researcher in the domain of political sociology to arrive at certain conclusions about the inter-relationship between the various classes of information or facts. This is what can be known as pattern of concomitance of the social and political facts. Interpretation of such relationship among a given set of variables could constitute the basis for identification of not only simple causal relationship but also laws for explaining the conditions in which such events generally occur. These tested laws tend to constitute the solid step towards generalization of empirical inference in hand. However, such generalization of the inferences could either be restricted to specific contexts or could be allowed to have a global range of its operationability. Political sociology possesses a soung body of information or data upon which testable hypothesis could be formulated or even the existing body of laws and principle could be further tested for enlarging the scope of their generalisability or predictability. Those who are familier with the science of political sociology know that it possesses a very impressive body of data or information with regard to the nature of phenomena of power, classes, groups, leaderships, elections, planning, developments, modernization, acculturations, electoral behaviour, patterns of leadership, public opinion, movements and so on. This body of information mostly obtained by actual practitioners of sociology, anthropology and behavioural political science is already well-organized rather than haphazard or chaotic, so as to constitute the ground for erecting commonly acceptable laws and theories about the relationship between polity and society. The role of caste in determining the outcome and implications of Indian elections is a well acknowledged fact. Emergence of middle castes as class i.e., through inter-caste organizations in rural areas and the changing pattern of leadership at all levels of polity represent yet another important domain of research in political sociology. These changes have tended to bring forth important shifts in the traditional agrarian structure which is characterized by growing more weaker and disadvantaged sections. In urban areas, accelerated pace of urbanization and industrialization has resulted in large-scale migration of people from villages to the cities in search of non-traditional employment and occupation which reflect significant shifts not only in the social texture and cultural pattern of urban communities but also their susceptibility to new values and ideologies in political life. There are but a few of those important issues on which political sociology as a behavioural discipline can focus its attention and by drawing useful conclusions, can substantially add to the body of existing social-scientific knowledge. Political sociology is already in possession of the concepts and constructs of immense scientific value which, if utilized in appropriate manner, could help in drawing empirical conclusions of universal applicability.

## Political Sociology as an Art

Political sociology can be treated, atleast in the sense of the practical application of its principles as an art. Art means skilful execution of an object in itself so as to yield desirable results which could satisfy individual as well as collective needs. It also means, the obtaining of a certain standard of efficiency in a given activity or work through practical application of a set of experiences coupled with reasoning and intuition. Obviously, it implies the acquisition of a capacity to foretell or anticipate the events and implement the generalizable experiences or inferences in terms of these events or phenomena. Political sociology offers ample scope for utilization of its principles or generalizations which could help an individual or a group in influencing and even conditioning a social and political situation in tiding over its day-to-day problems, and is giving a desirable direction of growth to the system as a whole. The political sociology as an art enables its practitioner to master a situation by skilful execution of its plans which he formulates on the basis of his experiences, judgement, strategies, and with the help of his selected tools and techniques that provide him the relative freedom from chance and its generally unpalatable consequnces. To succeed in an effective coordination between the available resources, the environmental factors, and the personal aspirations on the one hand and to take those timely decisions and judgements which enable one to face the odds in the way of achievements is essentially to succeed as an artist. And from this point of view, political sociology can be taken as an art also. Our opinions may vary as to whether its utilitarian art or an art in the sense of craftmanship. But the vary fact that the principles of political sociology can become, when cautiously utilized, an instrument of personal or collective gains, it acquires the status of an art. And the political sociologist or the practitioner of the principles of political sociology can be treated as an artist. However we cannot say that the newly emerging discipline of political sociology is more an art than a scientific discipline. Its relevance as an art matters only for those who find it instrumental to the attainment of thier desired goals. With such restricted relevance, political sociology has nothing to do with its scientific status which make it a challenging domain of human knowledge.

**References**

1. Agger, R.E. and Goldrich, D. "Community Power structure and Partnership" *American Sociological Review,*1938, 23, pp. 383-92.
2. Arendt, H. *The Origins of Totalitarianism,* New York, Harcount 1954.
3. Brotz, H.I: "Social stratification and Political order" *American Journal of Sociology,* May, 1957-64(6), pp.571-78.
4. Eldersveld, S.J. "Theory and Method in Voting Behaviour Research, in H. Eulaw, S.J. Eldersveld and M. Jantritz (eds) *Political Behaviour; A reader in Theory and Research,* Glencoe III. Free Press, 1956 pp. 276-77.
5. Hyman, H.H., *Political Socialization: A study in the Psychology of Political Behaviour,* Glencoe III., Free Press, 1954.
6. Axelrod, M., "Urban structure and Social Participation". *American Sociological Review,* 1965, 21, pp. 13-18.
7. Wright, CR and Hayman, HR "Voluntary Association Memberships of American Adults: Evidence from *National Sample Survey.*
8. Mukhopadhyaya, AK, *Political Sociology.*
9. Heinz Eulou,*The Behavioural Persuasion in Politics,* 1963.
10. Some of these works are: Arthur F. Bently, *The process of government;* David B. Trueman, *The Governmental Process;* Charges E Merriman, *New Aspects of Politics;* Harold Lasswell, *Who gets what, when and why?* David Easton, *The Political System;* E.C. Banfield *Politics, Planning* and ; Robert; *Public Interest;* Dahl,

*Modern Political Analysis;* William Bluhm, *The Theories of Political system;* J.B.D. Milhu, *The nature of Politics.*

11. Axelrod, M. "Urban structure and social participation *American Sociological Review,* 1965, 21, pp. 13-18.
12. Wright C.R. and Hyman H.R., "Voluntary Association Membership of American Adults: Evidence from National Sample Surveys," *American Sociological Review,* 1958, 33, pp. 284-94.
13. Hyman, *op, cit.*
14. Lipset SM, Trow, and Coliman, J., *Union Democracy,* Glunce, III, Free Press, 1956.
15. Maccoby, EE, Mathews, R.E. and Merton, As. "Youth and Political change" *Public opinion Quarterly,*1954, 15, pp. 23-29.
16. Merton R.K., *Social Theory and Social Structure* (Rev. Ent. Ed.) Glencoe III. Free Press, 1957.
17. Jonousitz M., *The Community Press in an Urban Setting,* Glencoe III., Free Press 1952.
18. Katz E. and Lazarsfeld, P.F., *Personal Influence,* Glencoe III. Free Press, 1955.
19. Glasser, W.A., "Fluctuations in Turn-out" in W.N. McPhee and W.A. Glaser (Eds.), *Public opinion and congressional Elections,* New York, The Free Press of Glencoe, 1962, pp. 19-51.
20. Hastings, P.K. "The voter and the Non-Voter", *American Journal of Sociology,* 1956, 62, pp. 302-307.
21. Rogo N., *Recent Trends in Occupational Mobility* Glencoe III. Free Press, 1953.
22. Lipset, S.M. and Benedix R., *Social Mobility in Industrial Society,* Berkeley, University of California Press, 1960.
23. Warner, W.L. and Abegglen, JC, *Big Business Leaders in America* New York, Harper, 1955.
24. Lazassfeld, P.F., B. Berelson and Hazel claudet, *The Peoples Choice,* New York, Dwell Sloan and Peace 1944; and B. Berelson, P.F., Lassarsfeld and W.N. Mc Phea, *Voting,* Chicago, University of Chicago Press, 1954.
25. Merriom C.E. and H.F. Goshell, *Non-voting, Causes and Methods of control,* Chicago, University of Chicago Press 1924.
26. Tingsten, H. "Political Behaviour" in Studies in Election *Statistics Stockholm Economic Studies,* No.7., London P.S. King. 1937.
27. Lipset, S.M., *Agrarian Socialism,* Berkeley, University of California Press, 1950.
28. Campbell A. and Khan R.L. *The People Elect a President,* Ann Arbor, University of Michigan, Sinves Research Centre Publication-9, 1952.
29. Harris L., *Is there a Republican Majority,* New York, Harper, 1954.
30. Key, V. Jr., *Politics, Parties, and Pressure groups,* New York, T.Y. Growell, 1952.
31. Campbell and Khan, *op. cit.*
32. Hawley, Amos H, *Human Ecology,* New York, Ronald Press, 1950, p. 204.
33. Eulan, Heizz, "The Ecological Basis of party System, The case of Ohio", Midwest Journal of Political Science, Vol. I, 1957, pp. 225-35.
34. David Gold and J. Schmidhauser, "Urbanization and party Competitiveness", *Midwest Journal of Political Science.* Vol. 4, 1960, pp. 62-75.
35. Cantril, H, "Why we vote the way 'we do', *New York Times Magazine,* September 24, 1944, p.12.
36. Hawley, Amos H., *Human Ecology,* New York, Ronald Press, 1950 pp. 204-505.

37. Kay V.O., *Public Opinion and American Democracy,* New York Knopft, 1960, pp. 110-18.
38. Kini, N.G.N., *The Urban voter in India.*
39. Akinchan, S. *Urban Growth and Political Socialization in India,* Janaki Prakashan, New Delhi, 1981.
40. Ashraf, Ali, *op. cit.*
41. Lipset S.M. *Political Man,* New York, Doubleday, 1960 p. 187.
42. Lane Robert, *Political Life,* Glencoe, III. Free Press, 1959.
43. Campbell A., Gerald G., W.E. Miller, *The voter decides Evanston,* Illinois, Row Peterson.
44. Weiner, Myron, and John Osgood Field (eds.) *Electoral Politics in the Indian States* Manmohan Books, 1975.
45. Weiner Osgoodfield, *op. cit,* pp. 31-35.
46. Robinson, James A. and William St. Standing, 'The case of Indians' *Journal of Politics,* vol. 22, Feb. 1949, pp. 96-111.
47. O. Key, Jr., *Southern Politics in State and National,* New York, Knopf 1949, p. 5, 11-13.
48. Howard A. Scaprow, "Voter turn-out in Canada", *Midwest Journal of Political Sciences,* 5, November 1961 pp. 351-364.
49. Karl Peascon, *The Grammar of Science.*
50. Gillin, and Gillin, *Cultural Anthropology.*
51. Weinberg and Shabat, *Society and Man.* Prentice/Hall Inc, 1976 p.7, p.u.p.l

# Chapter - 3

# Scope and Approaches of Political Sociology

## Delineating the Scope

A review of the major trends of research in political process allows us to construct a tentative scheme of analysis or a conceptual model which can provide a theoretical focus and methodological rigour that are generally lacking in a number of studies conducted in India. This model however, is subject to alterations according to imperatives of a situation. The various elements of the model, as indicated below, are logically interconnected so that their combination and permutation may yield a number of testable hypotheses. Strictly speaking, all such logical derivations are supposed to be universally valid. But for empirical testing the conditioning variables will have to be identified for establishing operational range of some of the hypotheses in specific contexts. The model is as follows:

| 1 | 2 | 3 | 4 |
|---|---|---|---|
| Society | Community | Mass Media | Opinion Leaders |
| 5 | 6 | 7 | 8 |
| Elite | Interest groups | Reference groups | Family |
| 9 | 10 | 11 | 12 |
| Structural change | Social control and consensus | Change in cultural order | Cultural adoption |

**Interaction**

| 1 | 2 | 3 | 4 |
|---|---|---|---|
| Voting<br>(*a*) Pattern of voting<br>(*b*) Fluctuations in voting | Partisan preferences<br>(*a*) Left<br>(*b*) Right | Formal and Informal Political organizations, i.e., Party organizations Legislatives, Parliament | Political Articulation |
| 5 | 6 | 7 | 8 |
| Interest Aggregation | Political Roles | Power: control exercise and change of power | (Communication) Issues on which cleavages and dissensions occur |
| 9 | 10 | 11 | 12 |
| Mechanisms of consensus and the process of legitimization | Structural differentiatives and Political capabilities | Political culture including the including the norms and standard of political behaviour | Political orientation and socialization |

After a brief review of the available literature, we can draw a few important conclusions in the context of voting behaviour and its relationship with social, economic, and cultural and ecological variables.

1. Voting patterns and fluctuations can be related to the type of community, i.e, rural, urban or metropolitan, to the type of family, belongingness to a particular group and to many other socio-economic and demographic variables.
2. The role of opinion leaders in shaping the process of political articulation, interest aggregation, legitimization the mechanisms of consensus and cleavages may be investigated.
3. The structure and functions of political institutions like parties, legislatures, local governments, pattern and rate of elite circulation in these institutions, identifications and manipulations of channels of political control and the role of interest groups in the process of this manipulation can be subjected to intensive analysis.

In order to further classify these propositions: (a) What is the structure and function of party organizations? (b) Who are the active members of these organizations? (c) What is this socio-cultural and economic background? (d) What are their objectives and goals for the nation? (e) What is the level of their political articulation and interest awareness ? (f) What are the chances for recruitment into the Parliament and legislatures? (g) And how are the candidates selected?

We have so far highlighted, with the help of a careful review of recent empirical researches, the behavioural dimensions of politics in the context of different socio-cultural economic, demographic, and ecological variables. Obviously, these dimensions refer, among many others, to the patterns and fluctuations in voting behaviour which constitute the core of empirical ethos of political sociology. However, political sociologists are required to develop useful constructs and theories about political system in the social context. For this political sociology utilizes the basic assumption in general sociology that political system represents one of the crucial dimensions of the whole social order.

In the words of David Easton,[1] the pioneer of systematic approach to politics, the political scientists have been acting on the unexpressed premise that the phenomena of politics tend to cohere and to be mutually related. Such phenomena form, in other words, a system which is part of the total social system and yet which, for the purpose of analysis and research, is temporarily set apart. Thus although system view in political science tries to isolate the area of politics as an independent system, this has been mainly for the sake of methodological convenience. For clear recognition of the fact that societies and other social groups are to be treated as relatively persistent entitles functioning within large environments. However, such entity, involving interdependent variables or elements which are its properties enjoy relative functional anatomy and, as such, have clearly distinguishable boundaries which set them apart from their environments. Each of these has a tendency towards a state of equilibrium, i.e, the system tends to maintain itself through various processes whenever it is disturbed either from within or from extraneous forces. Thus each entity representing a system tends to be structured in acccordance with certain invariant problems—characteristic of all social systems. Internal differentiation takes place with specific structures and process being developed to handle specific kinds of problems, and as a result, various sub-systems evolve, such as the economic system, the political system, the societal system, the cultural system, etc. In the case of political systems, the major task and function, or contribution to society is that of selecting societal goals, mobilizing resources for their attainment, and making societal decisions.[2]

Keeping this in view, Parsons treated political system as one of the crucial sub-systems of an inclusive social system. Political system, according to him, represents the 'goal attainment' system of society which functions in coordination with other sub-systems that could be called as 'adaptative' system. Representing economic structures and institutions 'pattern maintenance' system, representing social structures, and finally integrative system that entails the whole normative order of society. Thus political system cannot be fully understood unless we explain it in the context of social, cultural and economic phenomena which together constitute its indispensable boundary and, as such, affect its internal process and forces. From this point of view, the political groups and institutions have to be necessarily viewed in the perspective of other social groups and institutions which constitute the social order. This is because the form and the content of political system tend to vary from one society to the other, apparently because of the variations in cultural, religious, stratification, and family systems in different societies.

Hence there is the necessity of studying political processes, as special cases of more general sociological and psychological relationships. Thus sociological factors like groups behaviour, demographic and ecological characteristics, class composition and conflict, cultural homogeneity and heterogeneity, and the norms and values in collective life tend to bear upon the nature of the government, legal order and the power structure.

Political sociology, by keeping the objective of analysing the ongoing and inevitable relationship between society and polity as the uppermost, tries to explain the manner in which social phenomena determine the nature of government and politics. This does not mean that it invariably treats the political institutions and legal order as dependent variables. There may be so only in the initial phases of sociological explanation of political phenomena. But at later stages, when the perspective is related for allowing the measurement of the impact of political structure and institutions on social attitudes and behaviour, politics may assume the role of independent variables. Thus the distinct task of political sociology is to explain, in a macroscopic way not only the social foundation or context of political institutions power-structure, leadership, and ideologies which constitute and characterize a polity but also to explain their relevance for the maintenance of social order in general, and for social mobilization of the masses in view of the attainment as collective goals, in particular.

At microscopic level, it tries to analyse political processes, attitudes and behaviour in terms of the social structures and cultural values and institutions which characterize a society. Thus it has been rightly observed that the state is just one of many political institutions and political institutions are one of many clusters of social institutions; and that the relationship among these institutions and cluster of institutions is subject of sociology in general, and that the relationship between political institutions and other institutions is the special province of political sociology.[3]

Broadly speaking, political sociology is concerned with social basis of power in all institutional sectors of society. In this tradition it deals with the pattern of social stratification and their consequences in organized politics. It is one particular approach to the study of social organization and societal change. In narrower terms, political sociology focuses on the organizational analysis of political groups and political leadership. In this perspective, the core of political sociology involves the study of both formal and informal party organization, with its linkages with the governmental bureaucracy, the legal system, interest groups and the electorate, at large.

As societies strive to become modernized and the role of formally organized political parties become more and more dominant, it appears difficult to make a sharp distinction between the social stratification and the institutional approaches to political sociology. Nevertheless, these perspectives assume persistently different conceptions about the political process and the reflections of the basic writings of Karl Marx and Max Weber, respectively, both of whom had deeply influenced the emergence of a sociology of politics and later to the actual discipline of political sociology.

From the formulations of Karl Marx has come the pervasive view that class conflict and social stratification derive from economic factors or from social relations generated by the mode of production. But Marx's fundamental contribution is not limited to or even dependent upon the orientation that political behaviour is an expression of economic interests. To the contrary, his essential contribution was that he made the study of political sociology equivalent to the study of social structure, or macro-sociology, as it has come to be called. Marx's view that the political system derives from the pattern of social stratification, rather than his specific emphasis on the primacy of economic factors in fashioning social relations, has been a dominant theme in the development of an empirical analysis of politics. Nevertheless, such an orientation has been criticized, both by political scientists and sociologists because it reduced political events to social by-product and fails to consider the consequences of different types of political institution on societal change. The social stratification point of view has been described as a form of sociological reductionism that has inherent limitations because of the institutional and cultural factors which are excluded. The economic determinants view of social stratification is also seen as barrier to comparative analyses because, by implications, it assumes the universality of a historical pattern of industralism which holds at the most in Western-Europe and does not apply to the United States. Moreover it is appropriate to an understanding of the developing nation, where new forms of political organizations are crucial to economic growth.

It is from the writings of Weber that political sociologists received an 'intellectual' impetus for a more autonomous and more institutional view of politics. As sociologist Weber adopted reasoning which converged with that of Marx, in that he held a comprehensive view of social structure as a basis for analysing politics. However, he saw social stratification encompassing both economic relation and social status-prestige and honour. Furthermore in his essay 'Class, Status and Party' (1921) Weber postulated that the emergence of modern society implies a historical process of separation of political institutions from economic and social structure. Political institution thereby emerges as worthy of direct sociological enquiry because they are independent source of social change. These classic formulation of social stratification view and an institutional view of politics have persisted despite their reformulation in the light of historical events and intellectual criticism. As the division of labour has become more complex, social stratification theories have been reformulated as interest group theories. Politics is still seen as derived from struggle and conflict of social strata, but these are viewed as more differential and as expressing the demands of specific interest groups-economic, professional, organizational and even ethico-religious. Social stratification theories of politics have been broadened to include the view the governmental bureaucracy and the political party itself have emerged as new strata and thereby as element in the theory of interest groups.

The institutional approach has come to be reformulated as theory of 'social strain'. Political parties are seen as mechanism for accommodating the strains that exist in modern society. Thus the identification of the conditions of effectiveness of political organization in performing the mediating function becomes a central topic of this sociological enquiry. Because the political party penetrates all sections of society and because quasi-political institutions develop to assist the party in this mediating function, the strain theory of political sociology must extend widely beyond the internal structure of party organization. The political sociologists address themselves to a range of overlapping empirical problem, whether to begin with a concern for underlying social stratification or with a direct investigation of political party organization.

Often the differences between these theoretical positions involve which the differences of social values and conceptions of political philosophy. It is much too crude to label social stratification theory as radical and institutional theories as moderate in their orietations to political change. It can be stated that some theorists who emphasize social stratification in their view of political sociology are also committed to comprehensive and ideological positions of political change. By contrast, the exponents of institutional thinking often tend to be concerned with pragmatist and incrementalist strategies of political change.

The current interest of political sociology transcends dogmatic instance of its early precursors whether it is stratificational approach to or institutional view of politics. As a matter of fact political sociology today does not hesitate to often combine the two approaches for explaining the social context of political phenomena in both evolutionary and dialectical perspectives—former involving orthogenous development of social and political structures and the latter conflict and integration among the elements of society and polity. This itself is a product of what has been known as the 'end of ideology area'. Political sociology has tended to develop a pragmatic approach to political facts. As a result the contemporary practitioners of the discipline focus their research on a variety of questions which concern down-to-earth realities. These questions are: What conditions in society promote political systems regarded as legitimate, others as illegitimate, by citizens? Why are some governments democratic, others totalitarian, still others a mixture of the two? What determines variations in party system, levels of political participation, and rate of voting, etc.?[4]

Perhaps it is this fact which has led S.M. Lipset[5] to observe that one of political sociology's prime concerns is an analysis of the social conditions making for democracy. This view is shared by Gabril Almond who has tried to describe, with the help of the examples taken from various European and non-European societies, the nature and causes of a particular kind of democracy. He has by contrast presented a sketch of a general theory of the 'final', 'formal', 'efficient' and material causes of all political systems and has utilized it for a comparative analysis of the changing politics of Asia, sub-Saharan Africa, the North-East, and the Latin America. In his study, Almond has replaced the conventional terms like state, power, office, institutions, public opinion and citizenship training by such terms as political system, tunitions, roles, structure and political socialization, respectively, with a view to creating new set of analytical categories and for developing new tools of analysis of non-democratic societies in contrast to those which are narrowly legalistic, practical and which were developed out of pre-democratic political experience. Adopting a functional approach to political phenomenon he has tried to demonstrate that ultimate objective of political systems is to verify the society either by transforming it into another or by maintaining the existing ways of life. This has led Almond to identify five important out of seven functional areas of the political system. These are: the socialization and recruitment function, i.e., 'educating the members of society in the spirit of the regime and in the performance of political role; 2. interest articulation i.e., developing the mechanism for expressing claims or demands for political action; 3. interest aggregation, i.e., devices for consolidating individual claims in group of claims, such as parties and pressure groups; 4. political communication, i.e., communication system must exist to facilitate all other functions; 5. rule making and rule adjudication and i.e., the system must have procedures for making authoritative rule, applying them to particular cases, and dealing with conflicts about the specific meaning and application of the rules. These functional areas of the political system must be studied in order to know about the 'capabilities' of the regime. The best regime is one that is the last in producing unity because integration of society is the ultimate purpose of a political system. This view has led political sociologists like Organiski to conclude that the process of political development symbolizes increasing governmental efficiency in utilizing the human and material resources of the nation for national goals. Such efficiency would be measured in terms of four stages of political development, viz, the politics of primitive unification, the politics of industrialization, the politics of national development and the politics of abundance.[6] For Samuel P. Huntington[7] political development involves institutionalization or existing structures and norms which produces stability. The more political organization is a complicated (constituted of multiple organization sub-units, hierarchically and functionally, autonomous differentiated and separated from other spheres of activity), and coherent. The more it is instititutionalized, the more it is considered developed. Gabriel Almond[8] has viewed it as growing characterization of the system or structures by 'capabilities' which are five-fold:

1. Extractive moblizing material and human resources, 2. Regulative control of the behaviour of individuals and groups through management of conflict and consensus 3. Distributive (allocation of goods, services and status), 4. symbolic and 5. Responsible (relationship between inputs and outputs).

Another important theory about the structural diversification characterizing the process of political development is adumbrated by Kar W. Deutch.[9] He has proposed six criteria: 1. for evaluation of the diverse aspects of growth of the decision making system and its potential capability for action, 2. its economic strength with a special consideration of the rate of economic growth, 3. the growth of operational resources, or the availability of material and human resources capable of introducing relevant changes in response to new challenge, 4. the rate of growth of autonomy of self-determination; stronger cohesion, expanding network of internal channels of communication producing a better steering performance of the system, 5. the ability of the structure to overcome internally its problem of enlargement in scale through self transformation, 6. goal—changing ability. He has further pointed out the fact that the growth of "decision system" in all these aspects has to be balanced by a growing autonomy of the composite units of the whole generating within the society or state an integrative behaviour based on the awareness of existence of an internal muliple economy. Thus several authors have tried to see the process of political development in the context of structural differentiation and institutional diversification of a given society.

From the above discussion, it is clear that the main endeavour of political sociology is to explain, in a non-political way, the political phenomena in their social contexts. The political structure and institutions are viewed, not as an autonomous or socio-generis elements but essentially deep rooted in social, cultural, economic, and demographic processes which tend to determine their nature and directions of growth. This should not however lead us to infer that political structures and institutions are merely by-product of social processes and that they hardly bear upon the social fabric and cultural pattern of community life. Quite on the contrary, these structures and institutions, representing what has been termed by sociologists as political sub-system of society, constitute not only a functional framework for co-ordination of the various elements of society but an institutional basis for the very stability and continuity of society. It is only through them that society ensures social mobilization of the masses at all levels in view of fulfilling its cultural and economic goals. And finally it is only through them that society elaborates its effective mechanism of social control for ensuring an equilibrium among the divergent structures which must be characterized by mutual complementarity and an optimum level of consensus. From development seems to be contingent upon the character and operational range of the political structures and institutions. This is why the issues involved in the process of political development have been the issues involved in the process of development of society as a whole. This is to say that the very process of development of political structures and institutions affect and, in turn, are affected by the increasing scale of society which involves at the same time, structural differentiation and institutional diversification at all level of collective life.

Keeping in view of the above perspective, we can delineate the scope of political sociology in the context of three major political processes which involve constant interaction between social structure and political institutions. These are: political communication, political participation and political socialization. We shall briefly deal with these processes in order to show their relevance as specific dimensions of the scope of political sociology.

### Political Communication

If we treat 'communication' as any transmission of signs, signal, or symbols between persons and 'political' as a process whereby desired changes are affected in the rules governing the relations between the individuals, then 'political communication' will represent a category that includes a large production of all deliberative and hortatory activities that take place outside of the household.[10] And by a narrow definition it will refer only to the activity of some specialized institutions that have been set up to disseminate information, ideas, and attitudes about governmental affairs. In a broad sense, it will imply the flow of desired information from the centre to the periphery of politic-administrative structure so that various elements of the political system are coordinated and controlled in an effective way. It will also imply the modes of conditioning or influencing political behaviour through propaganda and persuasion so as to arouse a widespread sense of conformity to the available political norms and institution.

In fact, political communications presupposes changes in societal conditions which may be due to the process of urbanization, industrialization, and modernization, and the new imperatives of controlling the behaviour of social groups and organizations. Here, the most important role is played by the media of mass communications which comprises the institutions and techniques by which specialised social groups employ technological devices to disseminate symbolic content to large heterogeneous and widely dispersed audiences. Such communication when related to social and political structures play the most crucial role in the context of the transmission of a society's heritage from one generation to another, the collection of information for the surveillance of environment, the correlation of various posts of society in response to the changes to environment, and the inducement of individuals and groups for necessary adjustment with the changing social, economic, and political conditions.

The politically specialized means of communications generally entail identification of seven phases of political decision making. These are: intelligence and planning, or the use of persuasion (or other means) of affecting results; prescription, or law-making innovation, or the preliminary characterization of a concrete situation in terms of prescriptions, application, or the putting of prescriptions into effect in concrete circumstances, appraisal, or the characterizing of the trend of events according to the policy objectives achieved or rustrated; and termination, or the ending of a prescription and the adjustment of claims based on expectations created during the period when the prescription way in effect.[11] The importance of political communication at these levels of decision making assumes special significance in the context of the political elite who for the purpose of social and political mobilization of the masses have to depend on a common stream of information. This is because "they are in need of a stable map of the context; likewise, they require access to information, that nourishes fundamental perspectives of faith, belief, and loyalty.[12] From this view point unless the focus of attention of elite members is reached and perspectives are patterned by media of communication, common experience fade, common goal values are in confusion, and common identities dissolve. As the ideological structures that confer a measure of continuity on the problem-solving process lose coherence, behavioural maladaptations are frequent and more threatening to public order.[13]

Political communication, when conceived in a systemic perspective, has come to be recognized as synonymous to political cybernatics. Originally known as a system of control and communication in animals and machines, the cybernatic approach to political communication is now called as 'political cybernatics', involving 'a body of theory and techniques for the study of probabilities in different but analogous universes such as certain types of machines, animals, individual human beings, societies and nation-states-and the ways in which message transaction function to control such universes"[14] W. Rass Ashby[15]' pioneer of cybernatic approach, refers to it as the study of all possible machines'—the word machine being construed to include men and animals as well as inanimate systems. Obviously, the most important concept in the cybernatics is that of a machine which recognises stimuli, 'learns, adjust itself automatically upon receiving feedback about its performance and mover through a determined number of possible status.[16] Thus political communication in the context of cybernatics consists of (i) a model drawn from the information theory and cybernatics, (ii) a theory of communication nets, and (iii) a set of proposition partially derived from other theoretical areas, such as democratic theory, organisation theory, and decision-theory, about the characteristics and effects of communications and their media on attitude change, public opinion formation, voting behaviour, maintenance and stability of a political system, consensus, correction, political development, perception and ideology, and political socialization.

Implicit in the process of political communication conceived within the framework of cybernatics is the view that all political structures and institutions represent the processes of some sets of goals.[17] It is within this framework that the basic mechanisms through which these processes manifest themselves affect decision. This approach, thus, may be taken as analogous to and also different from the decision-making approach since it 'devotes particular attention to the processes of making decision as contrasted with the actual consequences of decisions. Such an interpretation leads to three circulations that this approach involves: first, it emphasizes at all points problems of dynamics and of the various information flows attendant upon communication flow constitutes the basic unit of analysis—the actual flow arising from the movement of the bits of information through the relevant system; and thirdly, there are various structures that shape this flow of information with important consequences for the resultant decisions. It is clear from the above discussion that political communication constitutes an important domain of political sociology. It is more so, because the political systems it strives to study necessarily presuppose boundaries of larger social systems which constantly influences their nature and behaviour. The end product of political communication is a body of decision which determine the systems' functional range in terms of the pre-defined goals. In fact, the goals of political systems are same as those of the larger society. In view of this political communication represents the formal aspect of social communication, which is vital for coordination and control of its various component elements and which is usually assumed through institutionalized modes and mechanisms of information diffusion including mass media.

However, it is necessary to make a distinction between communication as a general term and political communication as a process which ensures vitality and dynamism in a political system. The former essentially involves the means and channels of communications like press, radio, and television which are only marginally referred to in the wider study of political communication, whereas the latter involves a dynamic movement of demands and decisions from one part of the political system to another as no operation of the political system can take place unless parts of the system can communicate with each other. Thus whereas social influence basically involves exchange, reciprocity, mutual awareness and influence in the context of individuals and groups which together constitute the society,[18] political communication is a process of establishing linkages between the various parts of the system and also the present with the past and the future so that demands are followed by policies —This is why a researcher is required to study political communication in the same way as he does in the case of the study of political system as a whole, i.e. in terms of the inter-penetration and reciprocal influences between structures and behaviour. This perspective entails three basic questions; first, what consequences follow from the general principle that the study of communication is truly the study of the dynamics of political system? Second, what is the nature and characteristics of these processes and structures? Third, what are the effects of these structures and processses on the communication levels of a given polity. Answers of these fundamental questions, however, cannot be found by looking at political system as an isolated or a fully autonomous entity. Quite on the contrary they require an integral view for highlighting the no-political vari-ables which influence various dimensions of political commu-nication. And it is here that political sociology is supposed to assume its analytical role for explaining constant interplay between the elements of political system and those of the larger society which surround them.

## Significance of Political Sociology

The value of political sociology can be indicated from different angles. First, as a scientific discipline having its well-defined area of specialization, political sociology not only represents a specific domain of human knowledge but also enjoys in the names of other social—scientific disciplines a relatively autonomous academic status.

Secondly, as a body scientific principles and laws which are verifiable and testable in empirical situations, it helps us understand socio-cultural context of political processes that ensure allocation of power and authority among the members of a group, a community or society. It helps us discover the conditions and processes through which power is exercised within the framework of certain social structures which assume political significance and constitute a distinct sub-system of society. Besides, it also helps us to understand, in a systematic way, participation of people in politics and the bases of status and esteem of leadership so as to highlight its qualities and limitations in the context of social and political mobilization of the masses.

Thirdly, since laws and theories of political sociology many, in the manner of other behavioural disciplines, vary in terms of their operational range, i.e., they may be of middle range or global validity and they can help us to predict the intricate human situations which, if not redeemed in time through correction measures, may threaten the community life and by stalling the process of development and progress may threaten the society as a whole.

For example, if power is allowed to be concentrated in the hands of a few who because of their traditionally dominant position or economic strength, misappropriate the resources of the nation and come in the way of the percolation of the benefit of planning and production to the last man, it will render all efforts of development meaningless, encourage conflict between the classes of 'haves' and 'have-not', and render the social life dilapidated by cultural and economic distortions and absurdities which will bring the whole society at the brink of chaos and anarchy.

Similarly if leadership does not grow its roots in the common masses who because of faulty implementation of national policies of welfare and reconstruction are left to remain in the appalling conditions of poverty and ignorance, politics will become an abnoxious game of a few, who in connivance with administration machinery will encourage nepotism and corruption in all spheres of society.

Fourthly, political sociology will enable us to establish whether or not the process of economic development whatsover has been paralleled by a corresponding pace of political development and whether or not the breeeze of modernity blowing from the urban and industrial centres, has been adequately inhaled by the common masses of the remote and distant villages where thrives the heart of nation. Similarly, many short or middle range predictions can be made in the context of electoral behaviour, functioning and effects of politico-administrative structures at grass root level, and ideas, attitudes, and orientations of the individuals who are involved in the political process at micro-levels. In the global perspective too, political sociology has tended to be recognized as a useful disceptive. Asian colonial states which have emerged as independent nations, political sociology, as a science studying the process of political modernization in developing societies, has tended to assume special significance. Until the end of second World War, the value of political sociology for the study of election behaviour in the Asian or Indian context was not well realized. However, with the gradual emancipation of the colonies from the clutches of economic exploitation by the wealthy nations and their increasing realization and awareness of the imperatives of national building and economic growth, political sociology has been accepted as a discipline of great utility.

In India, after independence which heralded an era of social and economic reconstruction and acceptance of adult franchise as political modus operandi for determining the priorities and 'commitments' of the nation, political sociology, as a science to study the indispensable reciprocity between the social and political processes, has tended to assume unprecedented importance. Studies in political sociology, in recent years, have led the researchers to discover and formulate valuable principles or generalizations in the context of voting behaviour of Indian people. Thus, ever since the First and the subsequent General Elections were held in India, specializing courses in political sociology have been introduced in Indian universtities, projects of studies sponsored at various levels to unfold the social and cultural mysteries of political behaviour, and an extremely, rich body of literature built in specific as well as inter-disciplinary perspectives. These trends have tended to popularize political sociology as a potential discipline and elevate scientific status. Similarly with the growing interest in studying and observing the trends of social, economic, and political change in the context of specific groups, classes, and communities with distinct cultural and lingual identity, and their implications on political attitudes and behaviour, have brought into focus the tremendous importance of political sociology.

Again in the context of developing countries like India, with the more organized efforts of the local populations and the government for an all sided and rapid development, such as Five-Year-Plans in India and Seven-Year-Plans in Indonesia, scholars have resorted to the methods and principles of political sociology for measuring and examining the nature, consequences, and scope of such growth. Thus political sociology as a discipline affording a body of principles and generalizations and activity seeking to discover uniformities and norms, etc., in social, economic, and political life of groups, communities, and nations, has come to establish itself and grow in its capability and scope for the study of political behaviour.

## Approaches to Political Sociology

Political sociology, as we have explained herein before, has the unique privilege of enjoying many options in so far as approaches to political behaviour and its varying dimensions are concerned. These options refer to various forms of methods and techniques which represent different approaches to the political phenomena. We may discuss, briefly although, the major approaches that have come to charac-terize the emergence and growth of political sociology as a scientific discipline. These approaches are behavioural view, structural view, structural functional analysis, systems approach, and input-output analysis.

**Behavioural Perspective**

Behavioural perspective in political science involved our effort to combine theoretical rigour and empirical research and to test generalizations through systematic inter-group and even cross-national comparisons. The desire for theoretical rigour led the political scientists to take over and adopt from the leading contemporary school of sociological analysis such concepts as culture, structure, function, input, outputs feed-back and system. These concepts gave political sceintists a systematic framework of analysis and comparison of political behaviour in different communities and societies. The behavioural perspective involved a major effort to make precise and qualitative measurements of political phenomena. This enabled to amass a large quantity of data on social, demographic, economic, cultural, and political characteristics of societies. The development of survey research and its widespread acceptance as a major strategy or research, created substantial data files on the background characteristics, attitudes, values, and behaviour pattern of individuals. The refinement of more sophisticated means of mathematical analysis (factor analysis, regression, path analysis) plus the emergence of the high speed computer as a standard tool of social science research made it possible to analyse the relationship among a variety of variables inways that had been totally impossible. The potentialities of survey research for the study of political behaviour were first exploited significantly by Davniel Berner in his analysis of the Passing of Traditional Society, published in 1958. The ways in which aggregate cross national-data could be used were dramatically suggested by Karl Denteh in his path breaking article on "Social Mobilization and Political Development" which popularized behavioural perspective in political science.[19]

The term behaviouralism involving a reinvigorated spirit of scientism, as discussed earlier, had several sources. Well before mid century "behaviouralism" was a well developed point of view and method in psychology, stressing observable behaviour over 'introspection' and 'subjectivism'. Behaviour was the focus of attention, especially after World War II, for those social scientists who wanted to observe what could be studied objectively. This was in consonance with spirit of 'behavioural science' that conveyed a scientific intent to focus on observable behaviour.[20] Likewise the adjective 'behavioural' was converted in the course of events into the noun "behaviouralism" and within political science it came to designate the movement toward a harder and sharper methodological stance toward the social political phenomena.

Although, there is a lack of clarity and consensus about the meaning of the term, we can indicate its main tendencies and tenets which guide empirical studies of political phenomena. As a matter of fact behavioural perspective has emerged out of a reaction against mere description which was intended to be replaced by plain empiricism of simple factualism. It represented a discontent and the subsequent intellectual revolt against speculation, deduction from the 'first principles' against a ground interpretation of history, the contemporary world, and future reproduction; against legalistic modes of thought and "institutional" modes of analysis; against entangling political science with moral or ethical matters with a preoccupation to "prescribe". Thus, the new approach favoured attempts to learn and know how to apply proper scientific modes of thought and methods of research, focussing attention on actual, observable behaviour thereby seeking to appraise and test available theories in the behavioural contexts with the help of scrupulously collected data and through vigorous application of statistical and quantitative methodology. This perspective alone could enable the research to proceed toward attainment of a high level generalization involving a capability to explain phenomena with clarity, simplicity, and economy, and toward the classified goals of prediction and control.

In a way, behavioural perspective in political sciences are the refined version of simple behaviourism which itself had arisen against the "subjectivism of interospectionist psychology". To tell it plainly, since overt movements are the only human events which are publicly observable, psychology, as simple behaviourists believed, was to concern itself with the external behaviour only.

The application of behavioural perspective within the realm of political science involves many explanation of political phenomena which will be outside the normative framework of the study of government so as to take into consideration the social, psychological, and economic factors which are both the causes and consequence of the struggle for power. As a result more and more emphasis has been laid on the study of the roles and functions of political behaviour involving the study of psychology of political parties, or elections and behaviour of voting as well as the study of propaganda, pressure groups, and revolutions.[21] Study of three phenomena in behavioural perspective enable us to discover regular and uniform political behaviour and, as such, permit us to establish generalizations of explanatory and predictive value.

The behavioural ethos in political studies is reflected in the pioneering works of Harold Lasswell, David Easton, Gabriel Almond and, more recently in those of Myron Weiner, Joseph Palembora, Sidney Verba, Karl Dentefe, G.B. Powell, R.A. Dahl, David, After, Edward Shils, and a host of others who have tried to seek explanation of political issues in the context of non-political behaviouralism as a strategy of research has been outlined by David Easton. These assumptions refer to such features as regularities in political behaviour and verifiability of propositions, in this regard, with the help of empirical data, specific techniques adopted for acquiring and interpreting data, replacement of qualitative judgements by quantification of data through rigorous measurement of relationship between variables of crucial importance, capacity to distinguish between value and facts or between ethical and empirical dimensions of research, systematization of empirical inferences in term of 'short' 'middle', and 'long' range theories about political behaviour, a balanced combination of theory and research so as to ensure accuracy and precision in analysis, explanation, and prediction in the context of interrelated political and social phenomena, capacity to utilize knowledge derived from analysis and explanation of political behaviour for the solution of urgent practical problem of society, and finally, integration of political science as a scientific discipline with other social sciences like sociology, psychology, and economics, in terms of the principles guiding the fundamental unity of science. Thus the important characteristics of behavioural perspective of research can be summarized as follows:

1. In the first place, the political behaviour approach specifies the bahaviour of persons and social groups rather than events, structure, institutions or ideologies, as the unit or object of both theoretical and empirical analysis. It is of course, concerned with these latter phenomena, but only as categories of analysis in terms of which social interaction takes place in the typically political situations.

2. It seeks to place political theory and research in the frame of reference common to that of social psychology, sociology and cultural anthropology. This interdisciplinary focus follows inevitably from a concern with behaviour-overt and symbolic. Even though the particular transactions studied are limited to those carried out in pursuit of political roles and political goals, political behaviour is assumed to be a function of personality, social organization, and society.

3. It stresses the mutual inter-dependence of theory and research. Theoretical questions need to be studied in operational terms for purposes of empirical research. And, in turn, empirical findings should have a hearing on the development of political theory. Its empiricism, is therefore, quite unlike the 'brute facts' approach of an earlier descriptive empiricism. It is self-consciously theory oriented.

4. In general, behaviourists reject the institution as the basic unit of analysis and centre their attention on the behaviours of individuals or their groups. To them strictly speaking, some of the most interesting phenomena with which political scientists deal cannot be classified as institutions. For example, interest groups and political parties are not parts of the formal institutions of government. Similar is the case with other areas of inquiry like public opinion, propaganda and other channels

of political socialization. The attention of a political scientist should not remain confined to the formal institution of state and government. Instead, he should start with this assumption that any act which involves the use of power is a political act and, therefore, is properly defined as part of the province of political science.

5. The ultimate purpose of political scientist is the construction of a systematic empirical theory of politics—a theory that constitutes reliable knowledge. On the one hand, it means a critique of the traditional methods of gathering and analysing information. On the other hand, it has been used to ignore 'values' and rely on 'facts'. Value judgements which go beyond the realm of objectivity cannot be tested by criterian open to all.

6. This approach cultivates a belief in the unity of the social sciences. It is in view of the fact that all social sciences have a common subject matter—human behaviour. The division among the social sciences are matters of analytic and practical convenience. They are not, as if more, an eternal configuration of social reality. The boundary line among the social sciences is based on the role that an individual plays as a parent, a consumer, a voter and the like. Obviously, like a social scientist, the political scientist is concerned with a particular or specific role of the individual. Such an assumption has led to an immense cross fertilization of theories and techniques. In good point, political science has been the beneficiary and not the source of these trends.

7. It tries to develop rigorous research designs and to apply precise methods of analysis to political behaviour problems. It is concerned with the formulation and derivation of testable hypotheses, operational definitions, problems of experimental or post-faction design, reliability of instruments and criteria of validation, and other features of scientific procedure. It is in this respect that the political behaviour approach differs from the more conventional approaches of political science. But, it does not assume that the procedures of the scientific method can be simplifically and mechanically applied to the analysis of the political process.

Thus, what distinguishes the behavioural approach from other approaches, is the advocacy of development and utlilization of more precise techniques of observing, classifying and measuring data and the employment of the most sophisticated available means of mathematical analysis. Although this approach involves unprecedented sophistication and precision in the analysis of the elements of political behaviour, especially to the context of other dimensions of human behaviour, several objections have been raised against its unscrupulous application. These objections are as follows:

(i) Political phenomena by this very nature cannot be subjected to any rigorous study. Human behaviour, whether individual or social, cannot be studies with objectivity which is necessary in the acquisition of scientific knowledge.
(ii) Political phenomena is not amenable to experimental enquiry. There are far too many variables and historical contingencies to permit anything but a very general kind of statement of regularities which could hardly lead to generalization or the discovery of the laws of human behaviour.
(iii) Even if such laws could be discovered, human ingenuity was always capable of evading them in which they would lose their validity.
(iv) While one may not object to one starting with a hypothesis at the early stage of research, the very purpose of research could be defeated if an attempt was made to adhere to it very rigidly.
(v) A purely descriptive approach was also not without its advantages. Many an analysis of political phenomenon, based on minute description and arrangement of its various aspects in a sequence of development has shed valuable light on events in the past and has been an important factor in our understanding of political phenomenon in the historical perspective.

These and other objections, however, have come from the traditionalist practitioners of political science who have been opposed to the very application of scientific principles in the study of political and social behaviour. In other words, they have expressed preference for philosophising stance towards the government and other political institutions to a behavioural concern with the observed and the observable elements of social and political life and institutions. Such preference has been certified by indicating the sterile nature of scientific objectivity and by re-emphasizing value laden rather then value-neutral approach to social and political reality. Such objections have not, however, inhibited the growth and widespread acceptance of behavioural approach as a promising strategy of scientific inquiry within the realm of political behaviour.

In fact, there are several dimensions of human behaviour which do not necessarily evoke value judgements by the social scientists, and, as such they can be studied in a scientific manner so as to demonstrate standardized patterns, uniformities, and regularities in social and political life. In fact in a certain way behavioural approach, far from being entirely opposed to the normative stance can be treated as complementary to it. The scientific social knowledge derived from the behavioural analysis of political phenomena can serve as a solid foundation on which normative or institutional theories of conventional political science can be rendered more meaningful in the actual contexts of social and political life. From the point of view, behaviour perspective can enable us to add to the existing theories of political science the strength of precision, generalization, and prediction. And for this not only the traditional practitioners of political science are required to show their unnecessary and unwarranted scepticism towards the behavioural approach but the users of behavioural strategy too are required to avoid what Abraham Kaplan called 'crudities and errors' which have remained curiously resistant to the so-called self correction techniques of science, especially in view of the changing imperatives of social conditions.

**References**


1. David Easton, The Political System; *An Enquiry into the state of Political Science,* Alfred A Knopt, Chicago 1953, pp. 96-97.
2. William Mitchell, 'Systems Analysis' in *International Encylopaedia of the Social Sciences,* vol. 15, The Macmillan Company and the Free Press 1968, p. 473.
3. Merton R.K., Broom. K., and Cortell, L.S. (Eds.) *Sociology Today, Problems and Prospects,* Harper Torch Books, New York, 1953, p. 83.

4. Smelser N.J. and Davis A.J. (eds.) *Sociology*, Prentice Hall New Jersey, 1969, pp. 85-86.
5. Lipset, S.M., *Political Man,* Mercury Book, London, 1960, p. 21.
6. Organiski, A.F.K. *The Stages of Political Development*, Alfred and Knopt, New York, 1965.
7. Huntington, Samuel P. *Political Order in Changing Society* Yale University, New Hever, 1968.
8. Almond Gabriel, and James Colman, *The Politics of Developing Areas,* Princeton University Press, Princeton, 1960.
9. Deutch Karl W, *The Nerves of the Government: Models of Political communication and control,* The Free Press, 1966, Also see '*The Growth of Nations:* some Recurrent Patterns of Political and social integration; *World Politics,* Vol. V., January, 1953.
10. Ithiel de sola Pool, "Political Communication", in *International Encyclopaedia of the social sciences. op. cit.* pp. 91-95.
11. Lasswell H.D., *The Future of Political Science,* Athron Press New York, 1963.
12. Arora Satish K, *Political communication. The Public Language of Political Elites in India and the United States,* Holt Ringhart and Winston, Inc., New York, 1969.
13. Ibid, p. 5.
14. Wiener Norbert, *The Human Uses of Human Beings,* Doubleday, Garden city, 1956, p. 15.
15. Ashby, W.R. *Design for a Brain,* Widley, New York, 1960, p. 87.
16. Waxby, Stephen, L. *Political Science: The Discipline and its Dimensions: An introduction,* Scientific Book Agency, Calcutta, 1970, p. 170.
17. Young O.R. *System of Political Science* (Englewood Clifts, New Jersey, Prentice Hall, 1968, p. 50.
18. Jean Blondel, *An introduction to comparative Government,* London-Weidefeld and Nicholson, 1969. p. 223.
19. Samuel Huntington and Jorge Daminguez, "Political Development in Science" in *Handbook of Political Science,* Vol. 3., *op. cit.* p. 2.
20. Dwight Waldo, "The Recent Period: Political science since World War II, *Handbook of Political Science, op. cit.,* p. 58.
21. Johri J.C., *Contemporary Political Theory,* Sterling Publishing House, New Delhi, 1972, p. 336.

# Chapter - 4

# Political Participation and Political Socialization

## The Forms and Bases of Political Participation

As societies modernize, changes presumably take place not only in the levels of political participation but also in its forms and bases. In a traditional society electoral lobbying, and organizational activity at the national level are presumably rather limited. Government decisions at all levels tend to deal with individual benefits and particularistic issues. Contacting activities are consequently, of critical importance for both higher and lower status individuals. The development of a more complex society tends to involve the creation of a bureaucracy and routinized procedures for handling many of these issues and hence creation of obstacles to contacting by lower-status individuals. At the same time decision-making tends to become more generalized, dealing with collective benefits and costs, which facilitates action by those higher-status individuals and highly conscious groups capable of engaging in concerted lobbying efforts to achieve their objectives.

A simple theory of modernization would suggest a shift in relative importance from more traditional bases of participation (patrons-client and communal groups) to more modern ones (class, interest, groups, party). In fact, however, modernization does not necessarily decrease the role of patron-client relationship and communal groups. Instead, it is more likely to supplement these with other bases. In a more modern society, in short, the bases of participation will be more complex and diverse than they are on traditional society. Patron-client relationship provides a means for the vertical mobilization of down-status individuals by the established elites in traditional societies. [1] In purely traditional societies, patron-client relations may exist with little overt political context. The introduction of competitive elections gives the clients one additional resource-the role-which he can exchange with his patron for other benefits. Patron-client politics can lead to high levels of political participation in rural areas.

Migration to cities removes political clients from the patron-client system. However, it may also reinforce the stability of that system in the country-side by draining of surplus population, which might otherwise lead to class and radical politics, and it can also lead to patron-client patterns in urban environment. This is especially likely to be the case where rural elites also move into city. Beyond that, the relation between the migrant and urban *cacique,* or ward boss, often resembles that of the rural pattern clients. There are however, two differences: (1) the urban *cacique*-client relationship is more explicitly and primarily political in character and (2) the status differences between *cacique*-client are likely to be less than between rural patron-client system.

In a traditional society political participation at the national level is limited to the members of the upper class, and consequently the units of participation are primarily intra-class cliques supplemented in some measure by patron-client groupings. As the scope of participation broadens, however, the opportunities for class and interest-group participation multiply in both the rural and the urban areas. In some circumstances, peasants may be mobilized on a horizontal or class basis for electoral or lobbying purposes. Rural class-based politics, however, is often likely to involve violence and to take revolutionary forums. In urban areas class based politics is more typical of industrial workers and white collar middle-class groups than of the poorest urban dwellers who, if organized at all, are likely to be organized on a neighbourhood basis. Class-consciousness is rare among all low income groups.

Neighbourhood participation can be used on either the rural village of the urban ward or barrio. In cities, the neighbourhood is probably more important for political organization than any other base. This is particularly true for new settlements within the city. Many of the most important services that the city government provides are distributed on geographical basis: votes supply, sewage disposal, police and fire protection. Neighbourhood organizes to demand these services. New settlement may also have to establish their collective individual rights to land and to legal recognition. In rural areas, the villages may be a base for political organization, but, except in some circumstances, the competition among the villages is less intense than that among urbanites. By and large, a higher percentage of urbanites than of rural villages is organized for political demand-making.

Socio-economic change more often increases than decreases communal group consciousness, political activity, and intergroup violence. The extent to which communal groups become the base for political participation depends, in large measure, on the relations among the groups. These in turn reflect the number, size, location, and power of the groups. Different patterns of communal participation reflect the extent to which:

1. There is a large number of small communal groups in the society or a small number of large ones;
2. Different groups have different sources of power (education, wealth, coercion, external affiliations, organization);
3. The government is controlled by a majority, plurality, or minority communal groups;
4. Communal groups are geographically segregated in different regions and between rural and urban areas or one intermixed in close proximity;
5. Some groups that have been viewed as "backward" "traditional" improve their socio-economic status and threaten to produce a "status reversal" vis-a-vis traditionally dominant groups.

It would appear from the above discussion, that the structuring of politics on communal lines tend to produce higher levels of political participation than the structuring of politics in terms of patron-client relations, class, or neighbourhood. Structuring politics on communal bases, of course, can also lead to a breakdown of cooperative relations among communal groups, increased communal hostility and antagonism, communal violence, and potentially serious threats to national integration. Hence governments may attempt to reduce both political participation and communal group hostility, because of the close relationship between the two.

Modernization presumably does lead to increased socio-economic differentiations within a communal group.[2]. But these tendencies have often been exaggerated. The number of a communal group who significantly improve their socio-economic status above the average levels of the group may cease to identify primarily with the group and decreases their interactions with their group members. To the extent that they do detract themselves from the group, they also deprive the group of more sophisticated and moderate leadership and intensify the homogeneity of those who continue to identify with the group. In this instance, individual socio-economic mobility by some may reinforce tendencies toward collective political action by others.

The political party is the distinctive organization of modern, participant politics. It is relatively unknown in societies with low levels of political participation. More frequently, the party is a supplementary overlay that serves as a vehicle of political expression for some other type of group or as a way of coordinating and integrating the political activities of two or more groups. Other bases of political organization typically reflect more specialized motives and interests on the part of this members. The party in some measure, is often different because it attempts to unite together for particular political objectives mobilized and autonomous participants with a variety of different motives. In general, the greater the extent to which parties are tied in closely with traditional patron-client groupings, communal groups or occupational class groups like peasant organizations and labour unions, the more important role they tend to play in fostering political participation and to some extent its forms will be set by the extent to which the cleavages between two or more bases of participation coincide and thus appeals to one base are reinforced by the appeals to other bases.[3]

## Political Socialization

An individual's behaviour is normally analysed as a joint function of historical and contemporaneous influences. Research on political socialization is intended to deal with historical influences on adult political attitudes and behaviour at least that part of history that has fallen within the individuals' life span and bears some proximal relation to his life space. Thus the field of political socialization has been anticipated in political theory of almost every era, form Plato through Rouasseauto, to Mao. Its current incarnation date mainly from American studies of civic education in the 1920s and 1930s.[4] However, it had somewhat delayed entry into the empirically oriented political behaviour literature mostly in the context of electoral attitudes.[5] Research in this area suddenly began to spurt in the late 1950s and early 1960s, inspired mainly by Hyman's monumental monograph[6] and by pioneering empirical studies of children's attitude conducted by Fred Greenstein[7] and by David Easton and Jack Dennis.[8] And since then the research output has increased at a geometric rate, resulting recently in the publication of several texts and readers.[9]

The contents of politcal socialization fall into three broad categories. 1. Attachment to political system, 2. Partisan attitudes, aand 3. Political participation. Attachment normally is defined as focusing on institutions, structures, and norms of the political system or 'regime', and partisanship focusses on the current incumbent "authorities" and other persons, groups, policy stances, and ideologies, competing for power and influence. The distinction between attachment and partisanship, though intuitively pleasing at first glance, turns out to be a displeasingly fuzzy one empirically. The third content—political participation has already been discussed in detail. Attachment and partisanship mainly involve attitudes, whereas participation involves good behavioural acts to a greater extent, so it is hard to fit any very united theoretical organization to both sets of phenomena. In particular, the development may be related in very different ways to the life cycle.

Political socialization has been defined in a wide variety of ways, though the variety boils down to two main alternatives. The most conventional defintion implies society's moulding of the child to some a priori model, usually one perpetuating the status quo. Such terms as 'modoctrination', 'acculturation', 'civilizing', 'cultural transmission', and adopting 'cultural norms' are common synonyms for this usage. Langton has put it in this way: "Political socialization, in the broadest sense, refers to the way society transmits its political culture from generation to generation. More often overlooked is an alternative definition emphasizing the child's idiosyncratic personal growth, in which the developing human being gradually attains his own personal identity, which allows him to express himself and to seek to meet his own idiosyncratic needs and values in his own way. Neither is necessary perquisite to or consequence of an effort to look at children's political dispositions, or at how they change through life. The study of political socialization is not necessarily the study of conformity and the maintenance of the status quo, despite what some critics have written. Thus the available theories of political socialization take either of the two forms, as Easton and Dennis[10] have noted "psychological' or 'political'. The former theories treat individual dispositions (e.g. the child's political attitudes, level of political involvement, etc.) as the primary output variables of interest, whereas 'political' theories treat them as a mere expresssion of the key output variables which involve some aspects of political system or political policy.

In other words, political scientists find fundamental justification for studying political socialization in the fact that early attitude acquisition ultimately has some consequences in the political system. Psychologists, of course have a more intrinsic interest in the process of development itself, and thus may lead to some interestingly puzzling dialogues. The political contents that occupy political scientists (e.g. party-identification) can seem psychologically peripheral and thus of hardly any interest to developmental psychologists, whereas esoteric psychological theories without any obvious relevance to adult behaviour (i.e. those of Piaget) may seem irrelevant to political scientists. In fact, the age range during which political development is presumed to occur has undergone many changes over years. Today there is tendency to identify political socialization with the study of pre-adult or even of pre-adolescent political behaviour. This is in contrast to the earlier convi-ction that citizen bossomed full-blown upon entry into the electorate since children had no political thoughts. Much of the interesting research on political attachment has focused on pre-adolescents, though in recent studies adolescents and young adults have been paid greater attention. With partisanship, however, it is apparent that development can potentially take quite different forms at a number of crucial points scattered across the entire life span. Broadly speaking political socialization can be studied in two phases: 1. Childhood political socialization which may range from simple chauvinism consisting, in the main, child's own concept of his nationality and his personalizing and idealizing of the objects symbolizing the government or 'the regime' to the 'main' distinctions between the 'malevolent' and the 'fallible' body and the ideas and reactions reflecting the process of transformation of early postivity to later partisanship.[11]

The most concerted effort to design a distinctive political theory to relate childhood political socialization to variations in the persistence of political systems.[12]. According to this theory early political socialization proceeds as follows: The child first becomes aware of the political system (politicization), chiefly through the proximal figure with whom he has personal contact and the remote personal symbol of the government. He thus views the government as symbolized by these two persons (personalization) who he views as powerful and benevolent (idealization). As the child matures, this early idealized and personalized view of government gradually evolves into view in which government is symbolized by institutions, which the child gradually approves and likes. This kind of diffuse system support among the citizenry is seen as critical to system persistence, at least in the long run. The undergoing proposition in this theory is that early idealization and personalization are necessary conditions for diffuse system support later. One implication is that such contingency should neither hold individual children. However, none of these data on children or on adults deal directly with the key developmental proposition of the theory, that early idealization should anticipate later adulthood attachment to the political regime. Some recent researches have tried to show that persistence of all kinds of early socialization reduces into through adulthood. They have tried to highlight partisan predispositions which, existing in a wide variety, focus on various political, social, nationality, and religious, groups, on various issues positions, and toward historical events, and thus establish that partisan dispositions have their origins in childhood, though it has been difficult to answer precisely how persistent these childhood predispositions are and what role the family plays in their formation in the context of nationality, race, social classes and other groups and party identification. In this context, the scholars have attached great importance to parental transmission implying that children's partisan attitudes were largely copies of parental attitudes, and this rapidly became collective wisdom.[13]

Question arises as to what determines the degree of parental influence over offspring attitude. The simplest and most helpful socio-psychological theories in trying to account for family influence seem to come broadly from the reference group approach. This primarily concerns the communication of the group norms and the identification of the group. Translated into the terms of family such an approach would converge particularly on the communication of parental political attitudes, effective ties to the parents, and the extra-financial influences. In fact, frequent and consistent communication of a parental position should depend on several contingencies. First, there must be a 'real' parental attitude to communicate, and presumably this depends on (1) a simple and stable attitude object, (2) stability of parental attitude over time and (3) aggreement between parents on political issues, (4) the normal level of political involvement of family members, and (5) the occurrence of public events that provoke communication, and finally, (6) full and unbiased reception by the child, which will be a significant thing. All these factors ought to affect accurate reception of stable parental attitudes by the child. Thus it is generally held that political socialization is largely complete by early adolescene or so, and little attitude change takes place thereafter. Socialization proceeds gradually from middle childhood through adolescence and is complete only when young adults either have or have not been resocialized. Researches in this context have led to four major findings which represent the burden of evidence or persistence: (1) adults steadily resist any systematic pressure to change their partisan attitudes, nevertheless (2) erosion of political trust with aging; (3) any socialization, even in early adulthood, apparently demand, exacting and usually powerful social situation; (4) the major systematic defections from initial childhood socializations appears to be limited to the age period during and immediately following adolescence. However, more plausible has been a revisionist position taking account of continuing socialization and occasional resocialization through adolescence and into early childhood. However, a close scrutiny of literature in this context reveals that persistence of early socialization has generally been underestimated in most empirical studies because of (1) changes in attitude items across time in longitudinal perspectives, (2) changes in the connotations of attitude objects overtime. If indeed socialization residues tend to be rather specific and do not generalize readily to other contents, they may be highly persistent in their original form, which is of continuing political relevance as long as the same political and social conflicts persist.

While research on persistence of early socialization continues to grow rapidly, some scholars have expressed serious doubts about the validity of their findings. Their criticisms of the over reliance on the persistence of early socialization has been based on several carefully examined propositions which warrant further empirical investigation. Among these propositions are (1) early political attitudes are whimsical and unreal; (2) they have been only superficially and improperly measured, principally with the questionnaire method; (3) sampling has been so inadequate as to invalidate the research results; (4) early political attitudes do not persist beyond childhood or adolescence (5) they have little or no influence on adult attitude and behaviour; (6) they have little or no importance within the political system; and (7) research on political socialization has a conservative bias because it investigates pattern maintenance rather than attitude change.[14]

Early socialization residues on adults political behaviour is rather an intricate issue. It has proved to be a thorny thickel to both social psychologists and the political scientists. Some political scientists have quite reasonably questioned the powers of early socialized attitudes to contrast later behaviours such as are involved in active political participations. It has however been generally agreed that situational variables play a large role in determining over and behavioural acts, though certainly not to the exclusion of attitudes. There is no dearth of evidence to show the role of pre-adult socialization in promoting the partisan commitments and behaviour of the individuals.

Political socialization, as discussed earlier, represents a process through which individuals are inducted into the political culture so that their orientation towards political objects are formed. It usually implies a bearing process by which norms and behaviour acceptable to a well functioning political system are transmitted from one generation to the other. The aim of the process is to train or develop the individuals in a way that they become well-functioning members of a political community. Obviously, this definition emphasizes the psychological dimension of the individuals gradual learning of the norms, attitudes and behaviour which may be acceptable to an on-going political system. Thus, the process involves constant acquisition of political values by the individuals during the course of their participation in social and political life. In other words, political socialization is gradual inculcation of values, norms and orientations in the minds of the individuals so that they develop trust in this political system and thereby keep themselves like well functioning citizens and also leave their indelible imprints on the minds of their successors. In fact, it is through this process that a given system seeks its institutional legitimacy as well as structural stability for no system can function smoothly unless the process of the internalization of political norms and values takes place in a desirable way. Here, it may be pointed out that though political socialization invariably involves imperativeness of stabilization in political structures and behaviour, it should not be constructed as 'anti/change' concept. It actually lays stress on the point that any change in the political system must, in the manner of other sub-system of the society, be institutionalized gradually and peacefully. This means that if the attitudes, orientations and values of the people change through time, due to internal transmutations or external pressures, a simultaneous change in the sphere of political culture must take place in order to avoid the risks of sudden changes that may upset the system and eventually bring it to the brink of chaos. In order to avoid such situation, the system ensures that the shaping of political values and the process of change should run in conformity with each other.

In fact, out concern with the process and implications of political socialization arises out of a multi-dimensional, contextual and interactive view of human behaviour which seems to be a precondition for a proper analysis of political life. The available literature on the subject, however, indicates that the perspective of political behaviour has been too much fragmented to provide a basis for avoiding divergences in the conceptualization of the process. Various explorations of political socialization generally focuss on either the process or the 'outcomes'. Typical of the former is Easton and Dennis'[15] definition of political socialization as those development processes through which persons acquire political orientations; or, Dawson and Premitt's[16] on those processes through which the citizen matures politically. Thus, more often than not, political socialization has been conceived as a process which moulds individuals to a prior set of norms and conventions, rather than one which enables him to become an active innovator and modifier of political learning through socialization process. The latter aspect has been highlighted by Piaget[17] in his distinction between 'accommodation' and 'assimilation', the latter referring to individual's action upon and modification of environmental transmisssions, and the former stressing individuals' modification of himself to meet the demand of the environment. Viewed in the Piagetian perspective, the concept of political socialization will entail an analysis of the development of political consciousness in terms of 'accommodation' as 'assimilation'. Recent studies when closely examined seem to be little inspired by the Piagetian model, as most of them conducted in the context of 'developing human', have been confined to psychosomatic aspect of the process which has led to only herristically valuable, if not idiosyneratic inferences about personal growth in the context of political learning. As a result of this, research in this promising domain has, for the most part limited itself to political content of early socialization which throws little light on adult political socialization, especially in the context of acquisition of political values through interaction with the environment.

Rightly has Siegal remarked that 'what we have is a vast body of literature on the manifestations of adult political involvement and a dearth of literature on the causes or antecedents of involvements. Hence we know more about political behaviour than we do about political socialization.[18] As a matter of fact, pre-adulthood acquisition of values and behaviour patterns mostly relate to political lessons rather than crystallization of political attitudes as an outcome of conscious adjustment with the environment. For instance, orientation toward such values as equality, freedom of initiative, social justice, secularity, adaptativeness, and action-disposition symbolize environmental imperatives of value assimilation rather than implications of early socialization.

It would be worthwhile to remember that the term value is central in all types of conceptualization of the process of political socialization. From this point of view, it is both necessary and desirable to understand the various dimensions, overt and covert, of value, especially in the context political outlook and behaviour. The term value 'implies' an individual's concept of an ideal relationship between him and his environment, which he uses to assess the goodness or badness, the rightness and wrongness of actual relationships that he observes or contemplates, and acquisition of political values in the process of socialization, essentially involves his awareness about the available range of choices of varying saliency in political behaviour.[19] The individual's value system: an organization of these choices or preferences which are hierarchially arranged according to a system of priorities which varies situationally. In fact, Hyman the conceptual father of political socialization, has emphasized the fact that social institutions were to be treated as the inculcators of culturally shared political values whose transmission acted as a conserving force for the political system.

Any variation in the individuals system of priorities could be accounted for in terms of shifts in the social environment itself, which tended to condition the crystallization of political orientations. This view can be confirmed by many empirical studies which suggest that social environment exerted pressure toward conforming values and that values changed because of external changes in degree and the kind of information and social and political ideology. Values may become irrelevant or be affected by economic-technological change or change in demographic factors.[20] It follows from this that value change depends more upon the mechanism of broad social processes and less upon individual psychodynamics which itself appears, in the ultimate analysis, to be the outcome of environmental constraints on motivational adjustment.

The study of political socialization in a developing country like India can be seen as the sum total of the ongoing relationship between the modernizing effects of the process of urbanization and industrialization and the changing bases of political participation. The whole gamut of changes entailed by these processes has not only provided the much needed institutional base for political participation of the masses but it has also brought forth significant shifts in the socio-cultural environment which have resulted in wider awareness of national goals in economy and politics.

Being essentially the process of social mobilization, both urbanization and industrialization have involved large scale movement of people from one sphere of life to the other: from villages to cities, from farms to factories, and from families to the schools and colleges. An unprecedented scale of mobilization both in physical and psychological terms, has made people aware of the fact that the institutions affecting their social life could, in turn, be affected by them. Large number of people who had participated only in village politics are now looking at things in the perspective of national politics in which they feel constantly involved. New political movements, sporadic or episodic, which have been aimed at affecting the nature and the course of national politics, have brought various groups and organizations together which, inspite of this competing interests have tended to cost their tribal, caste and religious characters.

As a result of this, a new socio-political order seems to be in the offing, the major characteristics of which are (a) considerable degree of congruence between the cultural and the political identities of a population scattered on a wide territory: (b) functional linkages between the centre and the periphery; and (c) growing commitment to the norms and values of a national community. This, a study of the process of political socialization in the Indian context will require measurement of the value preferences which symbolize patterns of political socialization among the leaders and the voters of both rural and urban background. In a study, conducted in the above perspective, a set of eleven values which symbolized changing value preferences in the political context, were identified for the purpose of measuring the extent of political socialization of the rural as well as urban electorate and leaders in a dychronic perspective. These values were: concern for national goals of socio-economic prosperity, acceptance of democratic institutions, conflict avoidence and conciliation, participation in decision making, willingness for making sacrifices, democratic decentralization of power, righteousness and sincerity, change orientation and adaptativeness, abatement of social distance and removal of economic disparity, secular outlook in politics and action propensity.

The results of the study showed, among other things, positive shifts in attitudinal syndrome, in the context of political modernity which symbolized movement of the individuals, in psychic terms, from 1. caste attachment to class consciousness, 2. from localism to universalism, 3. from nationalism to trans-nationalism, 4. from indifferent involvement to conscious participation in the political process, 5. from diffusion to specific expectations, 6. from affectivity to personal affectiveness, 7. from fatalistic resignation to rational orientation and 8. from traditional authoritarianism to democratic disposition.[21]

The three processes which we have explained herein before, constitute the core of political sociology. It is through a clear understanding of these processes that we can know the intricate relationship between society and polity, i.e., the way in which political organization and institutions tend to find their ultimate expression in the structure and culture of a society. Thus the central concern of political sociology is to highlight those processes which relate the political structures and institutions to the social and cultural order of a society. It is this relationship 'encompassed' in the case of the former and 'encompassing' in the case of the latter —which render political behaviour as ultimate expression of social life of members of a group, community or society. Keeping in view of this perspective, the field of political sociology can be divided into four major areas:

(i) Social foundations of power structures; **i.e., the**way in which political power and authority and the structures associated with them fall within the purview of social organizations and cultural values, especially in the context of their legitimatizations at various levels of social order within which they tend to be embedded for finding a meaningful expression. In other words, while conventional political science is concerned with formal aspects of government and authority, political sociology endeavours to highlight the system of built-in social and cultural support for the political institutions. Furthermore, the political order is concerned, in the main, with the regulation of allocation of and even struggle for power, political sociology, inherently transcendental in its focus, tries to highlight their social and cultural determinants as well as consequences. Thus, this area of political sociology includes a systematic explanation of the interplay between social structure and politics, political institutions and social change, social dimensions of the problems of legitimacy, social organization and political systems, social hierarchy and allocation of political power and authority, and intermediary structures as linkage between social groups and political organizations.

(ii) Social dimensions of political process i.e. social channels of political communication. It includes a systematic analysis of the interaction between various organized or semi-organized groups (in politics) such as interest groups and pressure groups, political parties and the masses, and the social determinants of stability and change in political order and institutions.

(iii) Social aspects of political culture i.e. cultural constraints of political development. This area includes political implications of urbanization and industrialization, education and political socialization of the masses, social change and political modernization, caste, class and politics, democracy, political change and social institutions, social roots of ideology and party politics, and social disssent, mass movement, and politics; and

(iv) Social aspects of political behaviour i.e. the relationship between social conditions and political outlook and behaviour. It will also include explanation of the pattern of voting behaviour and the group life, involvement and participation in political organizations and institutions, social constraints of interest articulation, recruitment, delegation and social organization, social consequences of political movements, elite politics and society, social stratification and crystallization of political roles, social mobilization and political personality, and social determination of political leadership.

**Political Participation**

The process of political participation refers to those voluntary activities by which members of a society show in the selection of rulers and, directly or indirectly, in the formation of public policy. It refers to the activities of private citizens designed to influence government decision-making. These activities include voting, seeking information, discussing and proselytizing, attending meetings, contributing financially, and communicating with the respresentatives, enrolment in a party, convassing and registering voters, speech-writing and speech making, working in campaigns and competing for public and private office are considered to be the more active forms of political participation. It is clear that term political participation draws our attention to political activity rather than attitudes and behaviour of private citizen to those who are professionally involved in public affairs. It includes all efforts to influence government decision, legal or illegal, violent or peaceful, successful or unsuccessful. Moreover, it also includes not only activity designed by others. Former may be called as autonomous participation and the latter as mobilized participation. The fact that most of these activities characterize every society with more or less differentiated and elaborate political structures, indicates that participation is our ingredient of every polity, large or small. Whether the society is an oligarchy or a democracy, some one must make political decisions and appoint, uphold, and remove leaders. Failure to participate obviously leads to deprivation of a certain share in power which the politically conscious individuals aspire for.

Participation is an essential ingredient of democratic societies which are characterized by such attributes as consent, accountability, majority rule, equality, and popular sovereignty. Indeed the growth of democratic government is in part measured by the extension of suffrage and the correlative rights to hold office and to associate for political purposes. This is in contrast to traditional societies in which power and participation is restricted to a limited group of people who may constitute mobility or traditionally privileged section of society who claim to possess superior mental faculties and competence. With gradual democratizations of power structure, these prerogatives and privileges tend to be transferred into common man's rights and duties.

The expansion of participation in democratic societies was partly stimulated by the desire to give meaning and force to the principles of consent, accountability, and political opposition. Participation in the principle means by which consent is granted or withdrawn in a democracy and rules are made accountable to the ruled. Since man can be equal and free only if they share in the determination of their own affairs, participation has been viewed as a means for realizing these democratic objectives as well.[22]

Despite its crucial importance, very little effect has been made to develop general theories of political participation in terms of smallest number of assumptions and explanatory variables. Although participation is apparently a complex phenomenon that depends on very many variables of different weights, one cannot rule out the possibility of developing a general conceptual model for explaining it.

The variables which determine the pattern of political participation can atleast be grouped into two broad categories: those influences which are essentially internal and those which form the individuals external environment, social and political. This categorisation will lead up to infer that (1) individuals are embedded in matrix of social forces (i.e. status, income, education, occupation, religion etc.) that orient them toward or away from political participation; (2) characteristic differences in drives and capacities will account from individual variations in the context of political stimuli; and (3) the degree to which social and psycological predispositions find expression as political activity depends partly on the nature of political environment itself including the political structure and institutions, the party system, and the pattern of social and political values and beliefs. The three sets of variables are closely interlinked and intermingled. A change in any of them can, therefore, increase or decrease participation and an analysis on the basis of any one of them is bound to be misleading.

Political participation is constantly influenced by social environment. The elements that compose the social environment include education, occupation income, age, race, religion, sex, mobility, and residence. There are empirical evidences to show, as we have seen earlier, that most of these variables correlate to some degree with participation. In general participation tends to be higher among the better educated, members of higher occupational and income groups, the middle aged, the dominant ethnic and religious groups, the settled migrants, people living in urban areas and those having membership of voluntary associations and organization. Usually, education involves high and reliable correlations with participation, partly because it helps to develop a sense of civic duty, political competence, interest, and responsibility, as well as personality attributes of self-confidence, dominance, and articulateness.

Furthermore, the school environment itself serves as settings to which the skill of participation is acquired, viz., joining organizations, performing organizationally assigned duties, participating in meeting, discussing social, economic, and political issues of collective importance, and taking initiatives for organizing people in view of achieving collective goals, and finally learning the ways to transcript their political interest and knowledge to the kith and kins. Then, education involving the attributes of articulateness, sensitivity to self interest, and effective socialization by political culture, tends to account for frequencies and variation in political participation. Similarly high frequency is observed among the middle aged compared with young adults reflects the need for time and experience for politicization to take effect; and the same participle applies to the greater turn-out and activity of settled residents against transients.

The greater political activity in the cities, compared with rural areas testifies to a higher level of articulateness there. The greater political activity of voluntary association reflects in some measure the effects of all three influences; articulateness, awareness of self-interest, and greater exposure to the agencies of socialization. Similarly, other variables of the varying strength can be pointed out, such as power influence, motives, pressure, drives, etc. To these we may add some crucial psychological variables, like competition, achievement, affiliation, aggression, money, prestige, status, recognition, approval, manipulation, sympathy and responsibility which impel human behaviour. The influence of these variables can be understood in terms of the individual's personality traits and the cognitive structures which in this context represent certain characteristic ways of conceptualizing the self and the surrounding socio-political world.

In any case, it is worthwhile to remember that political participations however influenced by the psychological attributes mostly refers to a group activity and is typically organized on the basis of social class, interest groups, communal groups, neighbourhood, face to face relations, the political parties and ideological predilections. This is why small levels of political participation obviously vary greatly from one society to another and change over time within a particular society.

The most important premise of political sociology in the context of political participation is that individuals and groups in societies which are undergoing socio-economic modernization, are essentially characterized by a wide range of political activity and as such a high level of participation in political processes. Daniel Learner who correlated literacy and urbanization with general modernization concluded that the traditional society is non-participant whereas modern society is participant. Now it has become commonly accepted position that the principle political difference between traditional and modern societies concerns the scope and intensity of political participation.

As the societies are more industrialized, urbanized, and differentiated more people become involved in politics in more ways than they do in less developed, agricultural, rural, more primitive economic and social systems. Hence the general conclusion that a national level of political participation varies with its level of social, political and economic development.[23] Increased in socio-economic modernity and the expansion of political participation seemingly march hand in hand through history. The higher level of socio-economic development in society, the higher the level of its political participation and, presumably, the higher the ratio of autonomous participation to mobilized participation. The relationship between the socio-economic development and political participation can be summarized as follows:

(1) Within a society, levels of political participation tend to vary with socio-economic status. Those who have more education and income and are in high status occupations usually are more participant than those who are poor, uneducated, and in low status occupations. Economic development expands the proportion of higher status roles in society; more people become literate, educated, better off financially and engaged in middle class occupations. These factors obviously correlate with each other very strongly. But studies indicate that each also tends to have independent effect of varying strength in different societies of political participation, appears to be strongly related to political participations and educations even more so.

In his cross national study Inkels[24] found education to have consistently high relation to active citizenship when other variables, such as factory experience, rural or urban origin, media exposure, and length of urban residence even held constant. Length of factory experience also had a consistent, if less strong, relation to active citizenship in all six countries of the study. On the average each additional year education added about 2.5 points to an individual's active participation score (rated from 0 to 100). While each additional year of factory experience added about 1.25 points. Similarly, Almond and Verba[25] concluded that among the demographic variables usually investigated —sex, place of residence, occupation income, age, and so on—none compares with the educational variables in the extent to which it seems to determine political attitudes. Education and other status variables are, however, more clearly related to some form of political participation than to others. In the Verba-Nic five-nation study,[26] for instance, education had a strong relation with both campaign activity and communal activity, a weak relation with voting, and virtually no relation with particularized contacting.[27]

Let us examine the reasons for which status variables tend to produce greater political participation. Evidences from a variety of studies show that high status is associated with feelings of political efficacy and competence and that those who feel politically efficacious are much more likely to participate in politics than those who do not. The status variables, in short, are related to participation through attitudinal variables. Indeed high status individuals who do not feel politically efficacious do not participate significantly more in politics than similarly efficacious low status individuals. Higher status people, particularly more highly educated individuals, are more likely than lower-status people to feel that it is duty of a citizen to participate in politics, and people who have this sense of duty are, in fact, characterized by high degree of political participation.

(2) Socio-economic development also promotes political participation because it leads to a multiplication of organization and associations and the involvement of larger number of people to such groups. Business organizations, farmer associations, labour unions, community organizations as well as cultural, recreational, and even religious organizations are more characteristic of more highly developed societies. Individuals who belong to and participate in such organizations are much more likely to participate in politics than individuals who do not belong to such organizations. Indeed, an increasing amount of evidence has suggested that organizational involvement may be a more important factor than socio-economic status in explaining differences in political participation. A careful analysis of the Almond-Verba data for the United States, Great Britian, Germany, Italy and Mexico showed that socio-economic status explained roughly 10 per cent of the variance in participation and organizational involvement explained roughly 25 per cent of that variance. Similar conclusions have been drawn by a mumber of other studies also.[28] As for increased participation of individuals in organized groups, the variables of economic development seem to play crucial role. Such participation is either by socio-economic participation or directly through group consciousness. Studies show that people with higher education, income, and occupational status tend to be more involved in organization than people less endowed with these attributes. Erbes[29] study of three Iowa communities found social states and

organizational involvement to be more closely related to each other than was to political participation. Others have drawn similar conclusions.[30] Nie and his associates found the following product moment correlation coefficients between social status and organizational involvement in their five countries.

| | | |
|---|---|---|
| United States | - | 435 |
| United Kingdom | - | 313 |
| Italy | - | 304 |
| Mexico | - | 227 |
| Germany | - | 213 |

A close relationship between organizational involvement and social status tends to reinforce class distinctions in participation. Class and group consciousness may produce high levels of organizational involvement and of political participation. For instance the less rigid the class structure of a society, the more important are class and status variables in explaining differences in participation. The more rigid class structure of a society and hence the class or group consciousness of lower status population, the less the extent to which political participation to be related to socioeconomic status, provided that low status group participation is not held down by either political repression or a 'negative' self-image of the group that it should not participate in politics. Class rigidity thus promotes groups consciousness and political participation only in societies in which other conditions permit political activity by low status groups.

(3) Economic modernization produces tensions and strains among social groups, new groups emerge, established groups are threatened, low-status groups seize opportunities to improve thier lot. As conflict multiplies between social classes, regions and communal groups, social conflict intensifies and, in some cases, virtually creates groups consciousness, which in turn leads to collective action by the group to develop and protect its claims vis-a-vis other groups. The collective experiences that generate group consciousness may stimulate a political culture or style favourable to participation, which will continue beyond the generation that underwent the experiences. Sustained high-level group

identification and political participation may also require, in some cases, sustained external conflict. The slum dwellers, when politicized, more often than not find, particularly in big metropolitan cities, that they have to engage in collective political action to seize land, to depend on their settlement against eviction, or to secure elementary civil services. In a study of Mexico city, it was found that the migrants from rural areas were more politically active than both natives generally and their own sons particularly, despite the fact that the two latter groups had more of the attitudinal and psychological orientations normally associated with political participation.[31] Among the migrants, however, continued perception of external threat or outer group hostility to the survival of the community or the security of the individual land tenure had produced high levels of community identification and participation.

(4) Economic development in the past produced a notable expansion of the functions of government while the scope of governmental activity, was clearly influenced by the political values and ideologies of the dominant groups in the society. It is highly influenced even by the level of economic development in that society. Highly industrialized societies run by governments devoted to free-enterprise capitalism typically have more highly socialized economies than the agrarian societies run by committed socialists. The form simply requires more governmental, regulatory, and redistributional activity. The more the governmental active influence over the social groups in society, the more those groups see the relevance of government to their own ends and the more active they become in their efforts to influence governmental decision-making. Groups often become politically active in order to stop government from making increasing demands on them in the form of taxes, services and regulations.

(5) Socio-economic modernization normally takes place in the context of national development. The nation-state is the vehicle of socio-economic modernization. Consequently, the relationship between the individual and the nation. State becomes critical for him and his identity with the state tends to override his other loyalties. That identity is theoretically expressed in the context of citizenship, which presumably override distinctions of social class and communal group and which furnishes the basis for mass

political participation. Socio-economic modernization thus implies the emergence of a political culture and a world-view that, in some measure, legitimizes and hence facilitates political participation. And this is the case in both democratic and communist, industrialized and industrializing societies of the world.

We have seen that significant variations in overall levels of political participation exist among the societies. The reasons are varied. Many of those factors related to socio-economic modernization are affected by it which in turn promote political participation may themselves have other causes in addition to the process of socio-economic modernization. Group conflict and consciousness, organizational involvement, and the expansion of governmental activities tend to be promoted by the process of economic development. But they may also result from migration, exploitation, war, aggression, political leadership, ideological and religious differences which can in turn occur quite independently from economic development. The one factor promoting political participation independently from socio-economic modernization is the status structure in society. As societies become more developed, however, variations in political participation may be shaped less by status structures than by political and organizational factors that are not necessarily determined by the level of political development. Besides, some aspects of socio-economic modernization may have little direct impact themselves on political participation. This is the most notable case with respect to urbanization. Lerner, as we have earlier discussed, assigned a primary role to urbanization in the context of political participation. His hypothesized data seemed to support the proposition that urbanization had led to literacy, onto mass media exposure or consumption, which in turn was related to political participation.[32]

Subsequently other scholars analysed these presumed casual relationships and came up with somewhat different patterns, but they still attributed a major primary role to urbanization. Alker[33] for instance, tended to downgrade the role of media consumption, and instead had stressed a more direct line from urbanization to literacy to participation. Tanter[34] argued that the causal path was from urbanization to literacy to media consumption and then from both literacy and media consumption to participation. However, there does not appear to be any consistent global difference in the levels of rural and urban participations. In some societies votings are high in rural areas, compared to other societies in urban areas. Tingsten, for example, had concluded that while in several countries the urban population was "politically the more active", it was, none-the-less a fact that no general rule could be followed for political participation in rural and urban areas.[35]

Another reason for variation from the prevailing relationship between socio-economic modernization and patricipation is that there are some ways in which the former may tend to reduce the latter. The expansion of the scope of governmental activity, for instance, may have negative as well as positive consequences for the levels of political participation. People are likely to perceive government as relevent to their own concerns, but they need not be accompanied by increases in the feeling of political efficacy. The increasing concentration of governmental activities of the national level and away from the local level may have just the reverse effect. So also increased specialization in governmental activities, the professionalization of governmental personnel, and the increase in the proportion of complex and technical programmes and policies within the total assortment of governmental activities.

In traditional societies, governmental decisions are more likely to deal with individual benefits or particularistic issues. Socio-economic modernization causes a relative decline in particularistic decision-making, marked expansion of more generalized decision-making, dealing with collective benefits, and the development of more routinized procedures for handing individual needs. The incentives for personal contacting and small group lobbying, particularly by low status individuals and groups, may consequently be reduced. Modernization may also increase the social distance between governmental officials and low status individuals. The peasant who could appeal to and even negotiate with the village chief and local landlord may be totally incapable of dealing with the urban trained agrarian reform official sent out from the capital city.[36]

The process of modernization also tends to increase the functional specificity of relationships and organizations, including those related to politics. In a traditional agrarian society, the elite and the men are presumably related to each other through diffuse ties, which encompass economic, social, religious and political relationships. Thus multi-functionality of relationships make it easier for the village elite to mobilize his followers for the political purposes. In a modern society, the political organizers attempt to create parties of integration designed to provide comparable diffuse multi-functional relationships and also high level of political participation.

In fact, in Turkey, India, Thailand, and elsewhere the highest voting turnouts are precisely in those areas where the local leaders can capitalize on their social prestige and cultural superiority and on economic incentives and implicit or explicit coercion to mobilize their supporters to the polls. Similarly, modern parties of integration, combining cultural and welfare functions with purely political ones, tend to be very successful in producing substantial voting turnout. Political organizations and leaders that are only political, in contrast, are not likely to produce comparable rates of participation. In short, organizational multi-functionality correlates positively with political participation. The overall tendency in modernizing societies, however, is toward more specific functional relationships. To the extent that this occurs in politics, that is, to the extent that organs of political participation become distinct and specialized purely in political participation, they will become less successful of it. The expansion of political participation leads, paradoxically, to the development of professional political class, which, by segregating off political relationship from other relationships, tend to reduce or limit political participation.

It is generally seen that social mobility is concomitantly associated with the process of economic development. Differentiation of economic structure implies gradual multiplication of social and economic opportunities, thereby paving the way for social mobility, both horizontal and vertical. In the short run, individual social mobility is likely to decrease political participation. If the individuals can achieve their goals by going to the city, by shifting to the higher-status occupations, and by improving their economic well-being, these may in some measure by a substitute for political participation-Economic development involving growing networks of transport and communication, roads, bus lines, urban services-reduce the uncertainties and costs of migration and hence keeps down the level of rural political participation. Where migration is impossible or difficult, peasants are more likely to resort to politics, despite its uncertainties and risks.

The fact that urban political participation rates are not, by and large, higher than rural rates, when education and occupation are controlled for, would suggest that there may be compensating features in the urban environment which act to keep participation down despite presumably more intense stimuli, from mass media and personal contacts. The broader opportunities for social and economic mobility will increase political participation in the long run but may tend to reduce it in a short run. Economic development may thus produce greater pressure and stimuli to participate in politics, but may also, other things being equal, lessen the incentive to do so by opening up more appealing opportunities to participate in other things.

### Ideology and Political Participation

An enormous literature has been produced on ideological preferences as related to various social, economic, political and demographic variables. Such literature can be divided into two categories: 1. Studies showing variety of interests exhibited in associating 'leftist' vote with a number of social and economic variables; and 2. studies that attempted to correlate ecological factors with leftist voting.

Explanation of voting behaviour in terms of left versus right is more complicated than a simple dictionary of voting and non-voting because dissensions and cleavages in political organizations result from the lack of consensus on the various divergent political social, and economic policies and issues. For instance, in some countries like Japan, India, Ceylon and others, political parties are classified as right versus left, more in terms of political ideologies such as democracy and totalitarianism whereas in countries like the United States and England the division is based on the concepts of change and equality and the issues involved rather than the basic differences as to the structure and constitution of the government.

In so far as the patterns of leftist voting is concerned, the general trend in many countries is that the lower income groups vote more for political parties with leftist ideological inclinations. This has been empirically corroborated in the United States, England, France, India and many other countries. This suggests that economic position is important in political preference. Within these, lower income groups employed in certain occupations like coal-mining, fishing, humberwork and employees of railroads, public works, etc., tend to support extreme leftist organizations more than those in other occupations. Many studies demonstrated correlation between areas of high employment and leftist voting in the United States, England, Canada, and Germany, Wiley[37] found a high correlation between high employment and leftist vote in Michigan. His study supports the proposition that voting is used to some extent as a means of searching for economic security.

Ethnic composition can be argued to influence the extent of leftist voting in a definite way. The members of the minority groups with a given income level are likely to vote leftists in large proportions than the majority groups. Status as an element fostering the growth of leftist voting was analysed by Aaenger[38] and by Sydnor and Dunningham.[39] They found that voting along class of status lines was more distinct in 1936 and 1940 than in other election periods. However, there is no unanimous agreement as to the importance of class and status in ideological preferences. For example, Gallup[40] has observed that pronounced differences in the class composition of republican and democratic voters, conspicuous in 1936 are slowly disappearing.

Brown[41] studied voting preferences in terms of output and total marginal and average costs. He states that a voter perceives the possible alternatives of action, and takes that course of action which costs him least but gives maximum personal satisfaction. These costs are expected to vary from region to region, hence one should be able to predict the voter turnout from an index of economic for various regions. Beale[42] made comparisons of voting preferences between 150 metropolitan areas and 293 non-metropolitan areas. He found that people in a given economic areas are likely to have a consistent different voting pattern than those in dissimilar economic areas. It is his thesis that economic areas will yield information on voting behaviour than political regions. Lazarsfeld and Berlson[43] developed, on the basis of their research data based on Elmira two important propositions, 1. the greater the ward the smaller the number of people voting democratic, and 2. people group themselves in homogeneous political environments. The study conducted by Arneson,[44] too in a typical Ohio community, developed the proposition that in general the percentage of voters in various social categories like religious application, neighbourhoods and occupations followed the same pattern in 1948 as in 1924. Thus their studies attempted to show relationship between leftist voting and the various social, economic and religious categories. They also tried to explain the occurrence of such and association between social categories and ideological orientation.

Aside from the social factors, ecological variables have also been examined to throw light on the pattern of leftist voting. In Germany two studies found that leftist vote increases with the increasing size of an industrial plant and the increasing size of a city. Wood's [45] analysis demonstrates that in the states of Illinois, Pennsylvania and New York nearly half of the American majorities was provided by the sub-urban countries. In 1952, 17 are of 24 sub-urban Congressional districts around the 20 largest metropolitan areas chose Republican Represantatives. Between 1948 and 1952, the sub-urban in the fifteen largest metropolitan areas increased their Republican plurality from 773,000 to 1,688,000. In 1956, the same trend continued except in Los Angles and San Fransisco. Epstein has summarised the patterns of Democratic voting in Wisconsin gubernatorial elections within the period of 1948 to 1954 and from the 1957 elections to the Senate. His findings may be summarised as follows:

1. Democratic maintained in metropolitan Milkwaukee county and in the category of other urbanized areas and cities over 50,000 were not generally extended to the class of cities below 50,000 during the years of Republican state-wide victories.
2. Republican majority while regular (1948-1954) in the category of medium sized cities (10,000-50,000) were strongest and most persistent in small cities and villages below 10,000.

The above mentioned studies have came to the general conclusion that leftist vote usually tends to be higher in large-sized industrial organizations, cities and metropolitan areas.

**References**


1. The interest of political societies in patron client relations blossomed in the late 1960. Among those works which can be mentioned here for ready reference are Lande, Carl H., *Leaders, Factions, and Parties. The structure of Philipine politics,* New Haven: Yale University South East Asian Studies Monograph No.6, 1965, Tarrow, Sydney G, *Peasant communism in Southern Italy,* New Haven: Yale University Press, 1967; Weingrad Alex, "Patrons, Patronage, and Political Parties, "*Comparative studies in society and History,* 10: 377-400, 1968; Scott, Laws C., "Corruption, Machine Politics and Political change", *American Political Science Review,* 63: 1142-58 1969, and Patron-client Politics and Political change in South East Asia "*American Political Science Review,* 66: 91-113, 1972; Powel John Duncan, "Peasant Society and clientalist Politics in *American Political Science Review,* 64: 411-25, 1970; Lemarchand Rene and Keith Legg, "Political Clienteism and Development: A Preliminary Analysis". *Comparative Politics,* 4: 149-78, 1972.
2. Rudolph Lioyd and Susonne H. Rudolph, *The modernity of tradition,* Chicago, University of Chicago Press, 1967.
3. Huntington, Samuel P, and Joan M Nelson, *Socio-Economic* Change and Political Participation, Cambridges Mass: Harvard University Press, 1976.
4. Merriam, Charles E. *The Making of Citizens,* Chicago: University of Chicago **Press 1931; Wilson, Howard E, *Education for Citizenship,* New York: Mc Graw** Hill 1938.
5. Lipset, Semour Martin, Paut F. Lazarefeld, A.H. Burton, and J. Linz, "The Psychology of Voting: An Analysis of Political Behaviour" in Gardener Lindzey (ed) *A Handbook of Social Psychology,* vol.2. Reading, Mass: Addison-Wesley.
6. Hyman, Herbert, *Political Socialization,* Glencoe, III, Free Press, 1959.
7. Creenstein, Fred I. *Children and Politics,* New Haven: Yale University Press, 1965 and *Personality and Politics* Chicago: Markhan 1969.
8. Easton, David and Jack Dennis, "The Child's Image of Government", *Annals of the American Academy of Political and Social Sciences* 1965. 361: 40-57.
9. Adler, Norman, and Charles Harrington, Learning of Political Behaviour Glencio, III: Scott, Foreman, 1970; Dawson, Richard E., and Kenneth, *Permit & Political Socialization.* Boston: Little Brown, 1969; Greenberg, Edward S., *Political Socialization,* New York, Acherton, 1970; Siegel, R.S. "An Exploration into some aspects of Political socialization, School Children's Reactions to the Death of a President in Mortha Walfenstein and G. Kliman (Ed.) Children and the Death of a President, Garden City, HY: Daubbday, 1965s, Weissberg, Robert, "Adolescents Perceptions of Political Authorities". Another look at Political virtue and power, *Midwest Journal of Political Science,* 1972, 16:147-68.
10. Easton, David, *A Systems Analysis of Political Life,* New York: Wiley, 1965.

11. Greenstein and Nelson to Rolsby, *Handbook of Political Science, vol. 2 Micropolitical theory*, Addison Wesley Publishing company, California, 1975. pp. 93-153.
12. Easton David and Jack Dennis, *Children in the political systems: Origins of Political Legitimacy*, New York, McGraw Hill, 1969.
13. Connel RW,*The child's construction of Politics*, Melbourne, Australia: Melbourne University Press, 1971; Jennings, M Kent, and Richard G Niemi, "The Transmission of Political values from Parent to child", *American Political Science Review* 1968, 62: 169-84, Sears, O David, "Review of the R Hess and J, Torney. The Development of Political Attitudes in children" *Harvard Educational Review*, 1968, 38: 571-78 Jenning, M Kent, and Richard Niemi, *op. cit.*
14. Marsh, David, "Political socialization: The implicit Assumptions Questioned", *British Journal of Political Science* 1971, 1:453-65; Earning, Donald D, Joel J, Schwartz and Alden E. Lind, The Structuring Principle. Political socialization and belief system", *American Political Science Review*, 1973, 67: 415-32; Vaillan C. Pautline Marie, *The Political Socialization of Young People: A panel survey of Youngsters in a San Fransisco Bay Area*, Berkely: University of California Ama, 1972.
15. Easton David "Theoritical Relevance of Political Socialization", *Canadian Journal of Political Science*, 1, 1968, pp. 125-46; J. Dennis, *Children in Political system*, McGraw Hill New York, 1969.
16. Dawson, Richard E., *Political Socialization*, Little Brown, 1969 Prewitt K, "Political socialization and Leadership selection", *Annals of the American Academy of Political and Social sciences* 1965, 361, pp. 86.111.
17. Piaget, J, *Structuralism*, Basic Books, New York, 1970.
18. Siegal R, "Assumptions about learning of political values", *Annals of the American Academy of Political and Social* Sciences Philidelphia, 361, 265, Sept. 1965, pp. 1-9.
19. R. Milton, *The nature of Human values*, Free Press New York, 1968.
20. Henschel, Ary, "Relationship between values and Behaviour: A Development 'Hypothesis', *Child Development*, 1971, 42 pp. 1977-2007.
21. Akinchan Sitaram, *Urban Growth and Political Socialization: A Study of Rural Urban Differentials in Value Preferences and Leadership Behaviour in Bihar*, Delhi, Janaki Prakashan 1982.
22. Herbert Mclowsky, 'Political Participation', *International Encyclopaedia of the Social Science*, Vol. 12, The McMillan and Co., the Free Press, 1968, pp. 253-65.
23. Nie, Norman H., G. Bingham Powell, Jr., and Kenneth Prewitt, "Social structure and Political participation: Developmental Relationships". *American Political Science Review*, 63 pp. 361-78; Milbrath, Lester W. (1965) *Political Participation*, Rand McNeilly, Chicago 1965; Dye Thomas R, Politics, *Economic and Public*, Rand McNeilly Chicago 1966; Akinchan S. *Urban Growth and Political Socialization, op. cit.*
24. Inkeles, Alex, "Participant Citizenship in six Developing Countries, *American Political Science Review*, 63, pp. 1120-41.
25. Almond, G. and Sidney Verba, *The Civic Culture*, Little Brown Boston, 1965.
26. Verba, Sidney, Norman H. Nie, and Jae-on Kim, *The modes of Democratic Participation: A cross national Comparison, Comparative politics Series*, No. 01-013, vol. 2. Sage, Beverly Hills, California, 1977.

27. Inkeles, Alex. "Participant citizenship in six developing Countires", *op. cit;* Almond G.—Sidney Verba, Civic Culture, *op, cit;* Verba Sidney, M.H. Mic and J, Kim, Civic Culture, *op. cit.*
28. Almond—Verba *op. cit.*
29. Nie, Norman H., G.B. Powell, Jr., and K. Prewitt, "Social structure and political Participation: Development Relationships", Part I, *American Political Science Review* 63, 1969, pp. 361-78; Erb, Witham, "Social Involvement and Political activity: A replication and Elaboration", *American Sociological Review,* 29: 1964 pp. 29: 198-215, Lipset, SM, and Stein Rokkan (ed), *Party System, and Voter Alignments: Cross National Perspective,* Free Press New York, 1967.
30. Erb, William, *op cit;* Lipset, SM, *op. cit;* Orum, Anthony M, *"A Reappraisal of social and Political* Participation of Negros", American Journal of Sociology, vol. 72, 1966, pp. 32-46 Rokkan, s. *op. cit.*
31. Cornelius, Wayne, "Principal Research Findings Relating to Political Participation Among low-income Rural Migrants to Mexico city." Harvard University Centre for International Affairs, Cambridge, Mass. 1972.
32. Lerner, Daniel, *The Passing of traditional Society, op. cit.*
33. Alkers Hayward, R., Jr., "Causal Inference and Political Analysis" in J.L. Bernal (ed) *Mathematical Applications in* Political Science, Sothern Methodist University Press, Dallas, 1966.
34. Tanter, Raymond, "Toward a Theory of Political Development" *Midwest Journal of Political Science,* II, 1967, pp. 145-72.
35. Tingsten Herbert, *Political Behaviour: Studies in Election Statistics,* Bedminister Press, Iowa, N.J., 1963.
36. Greenstein, F.I. M.W. Polsby, *Macro Political Theory, A Hand Book of Political Science,* Vol.3, Addison Wesley, London, 1975, p. 42.
37. Morbert Wiley 'Unemployment and the Vote' Michigane State University *(unpublished Masters Theses),* 1959.
38. G.H. Aaenger, "Social Status and Political Behaviour" *American Journal of Social Forces,* September 1945 pp. 103-13.
39. G.S. Sydnor and N.E. Dunningham Jr., "Voting in Early America" *America Heritage* No.4 September 1952, pp. 6-8.
40. G. Gallup. "How 55 Million vote', *U.S. News,* May 23, 1955 pp. 56-64.
41. H.R. Brown, "Interpretation of voting in the Allocation of Economic Resources", *Quarterly Journal of Economics,* No. 1943, Vol. 58, pp. 27-48.
42. Calvin Beale, "Economics Affects vote" *Science,* Vol. 58, 1950.
43. P.F. Lazarsfeld, B. Berelson and Hazal Gandet, *op. cit.*
44. B.A. Arneson and W.N. Willis, "Voting Behaviour in 1948 as compared with 1924 in a typical Ohio community" *American Political Sciences,* June 1950, pp. 432-34.
45. R.C. Wood "Important Sub-urban vote". *Nation,* March 26, 1960, pp. 271-74.

## Chapter - 5

# Structural Functional Approach to Political Phenomena

### Structural-Functional Approach

Although a widely acclaimed strategy of research that has been evolved in recent times, structural functional analysis has not been entirely unknown in social and natural science in that both 'structure' and 'function' represent the basic concepts for describing and explaining the persistence of groups and communities within organizational framework. If we carefully examine it, it will appear to be just a synonym for explicit scientific analysis in general. "In scientific fields, marked by greater theoretical development and association applications of mathematical form of expression, the increased verbal explicitness that has recommended the various concepts of structure and function to may in biological and social sciences is more cumbersome than available alternatives".[1]

Put in simple way, structural functional approach consists of nothing more complicated than phrasing empirical questions in specific ways, e.g. (1) what observable patterns can be discovered or alleged to exist in the phenomena studied? (2) What conditions (empirical states of affairs) resultant from previous operations can be discovered or alleged to exist in the phenomena studied? (3) When process (or action, i.e., changes in the patterns, conditions, or both, depending on one's point of view, are discernible between any to or more points in time, can be discovered or explained in terms of observable uniformities, what resultant conditions can be discovered. The first question may be asked, "what structures are involved? The second, "what functions have resulted (or have been performed? And the third, what functions take place in terms of a given structure or structures?"

These questions can be asked in variety of ways so as to elicit answers that are both useful and necessary for the analysis of different types of problems. For example one might search for the possibility of adjustment in terms of a system, its normative contents, its 'necessary' features, and the degree of planning or consciousness involved, and so on. In addition to the most general form of the concepts of structures and function, eight subsidiary sets of concepts most generally associated with the form of analysis, either explicitly or implicitly, can be indicated. These are: (1) structure and function, (2) function and structural requisites, (3) functional and structural pre-requisites, (4) eufunction, dysfunction, eustructure and dystructure, (5) latent, manifest, UIR (unintended but recognized) and IUR (intended but unrecognized) functions and structures, (6) concrete and analytic structures, (7) institutions, traditions, and utopian structures, and (8) ideal and actual structures.[2]

These concepts involve different sets of explanatory or analytical imperatives. For example, the first set concepts require that the most general form of the concepts "structure" and "function" used for the purpose of scientific analysis must be defined in such a way that the other use of the terms represent specific categories. For example, the term structure may be defined as a pattern, i.e., an observable unformity in terms of which action or operation take place. Similarly, the term function may be defined as any condition any state of affairs resultant from the operation of a unit of the type under consideration in terms of a structure.

The second category of concepts require the identifications of the conditions necessary for the maintenance of the type of the unit under consideration, given the level of generalization of the definition and the most general setting of such a unit. Removal of such conditions will result in (a) total dissolution of the unit, or (b) the change of one of the structural elements of the unit on the level under consideration. i.e. the structural requisite under consideration. Similarly, a structural requisite requires identification of a pattern of action with observable uniformity which is necessary for the continued existence of the type of unit under consideration, given the level of generalization of the definition and the most general setting of such a unit. Thus structural functional requisites include the following steps in any specific case of analysis: (1) define the unit of phenomena to be studied; (2) discover (or hypothesize about) the setting (i.e., those factors determining the limits within which the ranges of variations of the not concerned take place, (3) discover what general conditions must be met (that is the functional requisites) if the unit is to persist in its setting without change (i.e. alternative structures) on the level under consideration, (4) discover what structure must be present in the system, as the minimum, of action in terms of the system is to result in the persistence of the unit in its setting without any change on the level under consideration (i.e. structural requisites).

The third set of concepts makes it an imperative to bear in mind that requisite conditions, though related to development of systems of analysis are not in and themselves oriented to questions of change, whereas the concepts of functional and structural prerequisites are. Thus a functional pre-requisite require identification of a function that must pre-exist if a given unit is to come into being in a particular setting. Correspondingly, a structural pre-requsite requires the identification of a structure that must pre-exist if a given unit is to come into being in a particular setting. The closer two stages of a given unit under consideration are in point of time, the greater is the probability that the requisites and the pre-requisites of a given unit will be identical. Requisite analysis can be used for examining any two of the three stages-initial, transitional, and resultant—or other stages in terms of a constant frame of references.

The concepts of the fourth category focus attention on questions of adjustment and maladjustment of the unit under consideration. Eufunction involves any such function as increases or maintain adaptation or adjustment of the unit to the units setting, thus making for the persistence of the unit as defined in its setting. Dysfunction entails those functions which lessen the adaptation or adjustment of unit to its setting, thus making for lack of peristence (i.e., change or dissolution) of the unit as defined in its setting. Eustructures point at patterns of relations in terms of which operations result in eufunctions, and dystructures entail the those patterns of relations in terms of which operations result in dysfunction. There may be a fourth kind of situation which is designated as "non-function" involving neither an eufunction or a dysfunction. The concepts under fourth category have been adapted from Merton, the famous American sociologist. Following Merton's usage, an element will be termerd "manifest" if it is intended and recognized by the participants in the system of action concerned. It will be termed "latent" if it is neither intended nor recognized. It will be termed "UIR" if it is unintended but recognized and "IUR" if it is intended but unrecognized. These concepts enable us to discuss levels of implications and sensitivity of the members of a given system to the structures in term of which they operate. Such distinctions are of vital importance in the discussions involving rationality, planning, and so forth.

The fifth category of concepts are crucially important in empirical analysis. The distinction between concrete and analytic structures is oriented to the type of abstraction involved in specific discussion about empirical phenomena. Concrete structures represent those structures which define the units that are atleast in theoretical sense capable of physical separation, both in time and space, from other units of the same sort. In other words, concrete structures hint at membership units involved in social action, i.e., units in regard to which any given individual may be classified as included or excluded, or some combination of the two.

Society, for example, is a concrete structure considered in operation. So an organizational contexts, e.g., families, business, firms, government, etc. Analytic structures are defined as structures, (i.e., patterns) that define the aspects of units that are not even theoretically capable of concrete separation from other structured aspects. If one treats the economic aspect of action as involving the allocation of goods and services and political aspects as involving the allocation of power and responsibility, then economic and political structures are analytic structures, since there are no social systems that are totally devoid of either economic or political aspects.

The concepts of the last category, necessitate the distinction between the structures that members of a given system feel should be structured of their behaviour or those of others and those structure in terms of which the members of a system determine and shape their behaviour and which can be described by an observer in terms of his acquired scientific knowledge. The terms 'ideal' and 'actual' in these respects may be applied in other connections, but they are most generally applied to the concept of structures.

We can indicate a few generalization in terms of these two structures, which are required in an empirical analysis. These are: *one,* there is no individual who can not make some distinction between ideal and actual structures; *two,* ideal and acutal patterns of a given system never coincide perfectly; *three,* the members of the system concerned are always to some extent aware of the fact that the ideal and actual structures do not coincide perfectly; *four* some sources of trees and strain in any social system inhere in the fact that ideal and acutal structures do not coincide perfectly; *five,* some of the possibilities of integration in terms of any social system inhere in the fact that the ideal and actual structures do not coincide perfectly; *six,* failure of the ideal and actual structures coincide perfectly is never explicable in terms hypocrisy; *seven,* perfect coincidence of the ideal and actual structures would require both perfect knowledge and perfect motivation on the part of all of the members of the system concerned in all possible situations. This would (a) overload any known set of cognitive capacities of individuals, and (b) were it possible to have perfect coincidence of the ideal and actual structures, the resultant system would be totally brittle, since any change of besetting factors necessitating or causing any change internal to the system would require complete resetting of all of the cognitive capacities of the members of the system.[3]

Structural functional approach as strategy of research in political sociology involves a systematic endevaour to explain what political structures perform and what are the basic functions in political system.[4] It enables us to discuss different types of structure with specific functions that are indispensable for the continuance of society that requires a well knit and functionally coordinated patterns of human relations for fulfilling its institutionally defined objectives. If a given society were to be treated as a self contained system the various patterns of structures with specific function could be viewed as sub-systems that functioned for attaining specific goals of collective life. Thus the basic assumptions and postulates of the approach could be summarized as follows:

1. It takes the society as a single, well-coordinated system, each element of which performs a basic function. The basic feature of a sub-system is the interaction of its components for the maintenance of its equilibrium. As Hempel[5] syas: "The kind of phenomenon that a functional analysis is involved to explain is typically some recurrent activity or some behaviour pattern in an individual or a group. And the principle objective of the analysis is to exhibit the contribution which the behaviour patterns makes to the preservation or development of the individual or the group in which it occurs. Thus, functional analysis seeks to understand a behaviour pattern or a socio-cultural institution in terms of the role it plays in keeping the given system in proper working order and thus maintaining it as a good going concern.
2. If society is a system as whole, it has its parts that are interrelated. A social system has a dominant tendency towards stability that is maintained by virtue of built-in mechanism. If there are deviations or tensions they are resolved. Thus change in a system is not sudden or revolutionary but gradual and adjustive, and
3. Underlying the whole structure, there are broad aims and principles that are observed by the members of society. Thus comes the factor of value consensus with its on-going usefulness even if this was unrecognized by those who were involved in them.

It follows, from the above discussion, that structural functional approach to political reality, requires discernment of a 'political system with specific structures and functions and as such, lays stress on the relationship between political reality and society. It characterizes a certain structure—that is, the arrangement by which legitimal policy decisions are made—but with an eye to its functions in the whole context of social behaviour.[6] Social theorists subscribing to this approach lay imphasis on this point that indeed, no society can survive or develop unless it has a political system performing such a function, that is, we might hold that a political system is a functional requisite of a society. The survival and maintenance of a social system require that society must be having a well-functioning economic system, a legal system, a system of values, and so on. In this scheme, the political system "would appear as that subsystem performing the distinctive function of making legitimate policy decisions or, to use shorter expression, the function of goal-attainment, for the society of which it is a part".[7]

In fact, structural functional approach represents a refined version of functional analysis which characterizes the works of famous social anthropologists like B. Malinowski, Radcliffe Browne, and Cluckhohn, Evans Prichard and Edmond Leach. These scholars studied pre-literate and tribal societies and functionally justified the role of rituals, magic, and religion with special emphasis on their integrative role. The study was adopted in sociology with further refinements, especially in the context of relatively small and autonomous village communities. Subsequently in late forties, some political scientists started applying the functionalist principles to the study of political phenomena in terms of the inbuilt mechanism, of system maintenance and regulation. And, it is this background which has paved the way for wide-spread acceptance and application of structural functional approach, which implies an applied form of empirical functionalism to the study of political phenomena. Now the approach has come to be recognized as a potential research strategy which enables an observer to discuss a set of specific structures with a set of specific functions which are necessary and sufficient for the persistence of the system. Here we can examine though briefly some of the works of pioneering political sociologists who have adopted this approach for studying the relationship between social and political phenomena. They are Marion Levey, Jr., Robert Marton on the one hand, Tolcott Parsons, and Mitchell, Apter and Almond on the other.

Marion Levy, Jr., has defined structural-functional approach as an analysis which "proceeds from the definition of the unit and to the elaboration of its setting.[8] Primarily concerned with the problem of survival of the system, it has developed the concepts of functional requisites or requirements or conditions of survival necessary for the maintenance of the essential characteristics of the same. The considerations of Marion Levy "correspond very closely to the definition of a system and the discussion of its environment and boundary conditions that are characteristics of analysis under the general systems approach. In addition, both forms of analysis are very much concerned with questions focusing on differences between relevant system levels, the reciprocal influences of various system levels on one another, and the implications of these factors for the levels of generalization and abstraction at which particular analysis are formulated.[9]

However, the name of Merton is more important who, apart from leading with the data of structural—functionalism, suggested certain new directions to rescue the functionalist theory from the critics. According to him, the central orientation of functionalism "is expressed in the practice of interpreting date by establishing their consequences for larger structures in which they are implicated. It is in the study of Merton that we find not merely the use of terms like structures and functions in descriptions of social reality that differentiates functionalism from other approaches, but the special way in which these terms are employed. The unique characteristic of functionalist description may be illustrated by looking at what is one of the most frequently cited examples of a functional analysis, namely, Merton's treatment of the functions of the political meachine in a large city. As he says: The machine fulfils the important social function of humanizing and personalising all manner of assistance to those in need and that it 'serves the function of providing those political privilegs (to business) which entail immediate economic gains. It is the particular way that Merton describes reality in terms of structures and the needs (functions) of the system and the manner in which these concepts are used to explain the phenomena of the political machine that work as a functionalist description.

Merton's special contribution to the structural functional

approach finds its place in his conceptual identification of functions which may be 'manifest' or 'latent' and 'functions'and 'dysfunctions'. While the manifest functions are those whose purpose and consequences are both intended and recognized the latent functions are those whose purposes and consequences are covert, unintended and unrecognized. There may be an intermediate pattern also in the nature of unintended but recognized purposes and consequences. He however insists that it is more important for a research to recognize latent functions, which are highly complex and difficult to recognize than manifest functions which are clear and well recognized.[10] Mertons distinction between functions and dysfunctions is based on the issue of survival and disintegration of the system. Thus, while functions are those observed consequences which make for the adaptation or adjustment of a given system, 'dysfunctions are those observed consequences which lessen the adaptation or adjustment of the same.

One important point that enhance the reputation of Merton as compared to that of Marion Levy and Talcott Parsons is that he seeks to save the structural functional approach form the charge of being explicitly conservative and biased against social change. Merton's views are reflected in the works of Almond, Binder, Apter and others who have drawn upon structural functional approach for the light it could throw on the process of political modernization. Thus, a relatively dynamic perspective, as carved out by those thinkers, has, despite its emphasis upon the conditions for stability or maintenance, has come to look like not leading necessarily to a defence of the status quo or to a disregard for processes of change.[11]

It is worthwhile to discuss the pioneering ideas of Talcott Parsons, who for the first time, developed a comprehensive theoretical framework for the study of societies in the structural—functional perspective. The key concepts in the Parsonian scheme of analysis are system, primary sub-system of a society, pattern variables and concept of change. Parsons has emphasized the fact that the component parts in a society are to be understood only in the context of the whole, for it is whole which is important and the whole essentially represents a system. Parsons concern is to analyse society as an on-going set of recurrent and inter-related social actions.

As he himself observes: "The most essential condition of successful dynamic analysis is continual and systematic reference of every problem to the state of the system as a whole. Functional significance in this context is essentially teleological".[12] Parsons views in the context of structural functional approach are represented by the following diagram.

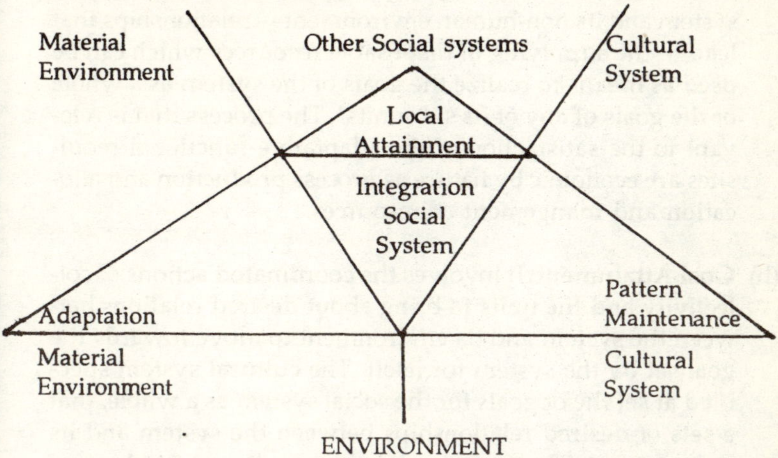


*Source*: See Robert Holt:"A proposed structural-Functional Framework in Charles Worth (ed) Contemporary Political Analysis, O. cit. p. 96.

Parsons has offered a model of his own system with its problems that it has to cope with, and a set of variables or dichotomous set of standards of preferences that the actors of the system are faced within a given social situation and are required to make explicit choices from these dichotomies for giving a definite shape to their orientation and behaviour. Parsons main concern is to study the needs of the system as a whole and its stability that is dependent upon their satisfaction. A system, according to him is an action framework inasmuch as all human actions occur within it. The individuals are the "actors" who play their "roles" in the context of the 'shared values' of the system. What is, therefore, of paramount necessity is that a state of equilibrium should be maintained on the basis of the fulfilment of the functional needs of society relating to four problems-allocation of resources; defining and sustaining the persuit of certain fundamental goals; maintenance of solidarity; and sustaining the motivations of the actors and of repairing any damage to those arising out of the performance of roles. These four problems are designated by him as:

(a) **Adaptation:** It indicated that the capacity of the system to meet the demands of the 'actors', must be increased. It is "concerned—with the relationships between the social system and its non-human environment— relationships that lead to the supplying of disposable resources which can be used as means to realize the goals of the system as a whole or the goals of any of its sub-units". The process that is relevant to the satisfaction of the adaptative functional requisites are economic by nature as process production and allocation and mangement of resources.

(b) **Goal Attainment:** It involves the coordinated actions of collectivity and the units to bring about desired relations between the system and its environment to move towards the goal set by the system for itself. The cultural system specified at set the of goals for the social system as a whole, that a sets of desired relationships between the system and its environment. The environment that is relevant for the goal attainment is complex, including an aspect of the cultural system and the non-human environment, and other societies. As one of the most important goals of the social system at the societal level is the preservation of the society itself, the defence of the realm involves a set of activities, that contribute to the satisfaction of the goal attainment functional requisite. In society, this function is performed by state of polity.

(c) **Pattern Maintenance and Tension Management:** It refers to the up-holding of the basic principles of the system with regard to both the values of such patterns and the commitment of the system units to them. Goal attainment is concerned with cultural components of a system and, pattern maintenance ŵith its social components. The role of the family or the homehold figures in. However, the role of other associations like schools, church, unions, etc. should also be emphasized in this connection. Three major premises are involved here. *First,* that major values must be passed on from one generation to another and it may be called acculturation process. *Second,* a social control process is concerned with the application of sanctions for violations of the prescriptions of the value system. *Third,* a tension management process attempts to prevent. The development of situations that increase the probability that large numbers of actors will violate basic norms.

(d) **Integration:** It is concerned with the adjustment of relations between and among the units of a system for establishing a level of solidarity among them to permit the system to function. It involves an aspect of the socio-control process. As a matter of fact, this functional requisite is basically concerned with the internal problem of coordination of differentiated, but independent roles. Parson admits that in every social system there may be some behaviour that is not prohibited by norms but is nevertheless mal-integrative. The integrative function is performed both by coercive mechanism (state) and non-coercive mechanisms (social institutions).[13]

Let us now examine the dichotomous set of much discussed pattern variables which involves dilemmas of orientation for behaviour.

### Pattern-Variables

#### (1) Affectivity Vs. Affective Neutrality

This set of polar preferences involves a dilemma of choice between gratification and discipline. It indicates whether the actors are interested in accepting immediate gratification or they want to prefer discipline in this context. It also indicates the extent to which the members of society are prepared to make sacrifices of their immediate gratifications in the interest of solidarity and integration. Thus the pattern—variable refers to a dilemma in the moral dispositions of the members of a given society. In other words the actor must choose whether to accept gratification from the immediately 'cognized' and collective objective or to evaluate such gratification in terms of its consequences for other aspects of the action system. The actor must therefore choose either to seek immediate gratification or to exercise self-restrain in the light of wider considerations which concern the collectively.[14]

### (2) Diffusion Vs. Specificity

This involves the capacity of the actors to choose specific contexts of action rather than a diffuse orientation towards unlimited traditional standards of behaviour. The choice of context is from amongst elements of personality system, cultural system, and social system. Thus it refers to scope or inclusiveness of relationships. The chosen elements define the scope of interest in the object. In other words, social objects are either functionally diffuse or specific. The actor must choose either to respond to selected aspects of social objects or without distinction to all possible objects.

### (3) Particularism Vs. Universalism

This involves difinition of scope of interest in the object. It refers in other words, it the actor decides to evaluate his choice in terms of wider implications, he must choose whether to give primacy to the moral standards of the social or sub-system. The actor must choose either to give primacy to self-interest or to the moral standards of a group to which he belongs.[15] The object may be judged in terms of some universal or general frame of references or in terms of a particular references scheme in which the ego is personally involved. In other words, whether or not the actor decides to grant primacy to such moral standards, he must choose cognitive or appreciative standards of behaviour. He must choose either to regard objects and persons as coming under some general principle or to consider them solely with respect to their particular relationship to the actor.

### (4) Quality Vs. Performance

This has also been referred to by Parson as ascription versvs achievement. In involves the dilemma whether the primary consideration, in defining a relationship, is given to ascriptive quality of the object or to some particular criteria of performances. In other words, it represents modalities of the social object which are treated as relevant for behaviour. In other words, social objects on relevant to a given choice situations are either quality complexes or performance complexes, depending on how the actor chooses to see them. The actor must choose either to treat objects and persons on the basis of their perceived qualities or in the light of their performances.

**(5) Self Orientation Vs. Collectively Orientations**

This set of pattern variable involves a dilemma of choice between the values of self interest or collective interest. If the chosen values concern the collective life they involves collective orientation. Likewise, if these values are related to a particular group or individual and is completely indifferent to the interest of others, it is to be treated as self-orientation.

These pattern-variables represent exhaustive analytical scheme to characterize social order in terms of the actual behavioural orientation of the individuals. As society evolves, the orientation of individual shifts from one end to the other of the pattern variables, thereby bringing about significant change in the nature of social relations and cultural order. The reål attempt of Parson is to describe and explain with the help of this analytical scheme, the manner in which units are adjusted with the whole so as to maintain on equilibrium in the system. The stability of a system is not possible without a general system of common cultural orientation. The sharing of value orientation is of special importance that makes the study of the attitudinal dilemmas of the actors as essential. One may say that as functionalist Parson does admit the factor of change as the total system is never at rest, it is always being pushed, prodded and knée-hauled, it is always subject to stresses and strains[16]and that he is for a change that is 'ordered' and for this reason, gradual and peaceful.[17]

**Structural Functionalism in Political Science**

The method of structural-functionalism was prevently adopted in political science by some leading American thinker in the sixties who came to realize that while analysing some political phenomena, they should be concerned with, among other things, their functions in the sense of the purpose served by it. Here it may be pointed out that function is treated as one and not necessarily a more significant one-among many relevant considerations that together comprise a comprehensive political analysis.[18] It is different thing that writers have described the meaning of this approach differently. For instance, while Hempel had little difficulty in identify this approach as 'special breed', he with others like Brown did distinguish functionalism from other approaches by sticking to the idea of its particular application. A subtle point of distinction between the two should be traced in this fact that while, according to Hempel, it is simply a particularly inconsequential type of explanation,[19] in the view of Brown, it is something different from an explanation on the basis of laws. Apart from some subtle points of distinction, it should be emphasized that structural functional analysis is a distinguishable approach primarily because of the selective aspects of social reality that it seeks to describe, explain and predict. It describes social reality largely in terms of structures, processes, mechanisms and functions, and these four aspects are of particular significance in the laws and theories that are developed.[20]

**References**

1. Marraipm J. Devy, Jr., *International Encyclopaedia of the social sciences,* Mac Millan and the Free Press, New York, 1968, pp. 21-28.
2. Marion, Levy, "Structural-Functional Analysis," *International Encyclopaedia of Social Sciences, op. cit.* 21-28.
3. Marion J. Levy, (Jr.), *op. cit.*
4. A.R. Ball, *Modern Politics and Government* (London:MacMillan 1971), p. 14
5. Carl G. Hempel: "The Logic of Functional Analysis"-Liewellyu Gross (ed.) *Symposium on Sociological Theory,* p.278.
6. Samuel H. Beer, and Adam B Ullan, *Patterns of Government* (New York: Random House, 1968), 8th Printing, p. 22.
7. Ibid. p. 23.
8. Marion Levy, Jr., *The Structure of Society* (Princeton Univ. Press, New Jersey, 1952) pp. 36-38.
9. Oran R. Young, *System or Political Science,* (Englewood Cliffs, New Jersey, Prentice Hall, 1968) p. 29.
10. Marton, R.K., *Social Theory and Social Structure, op. cit.* p. 105.

11. William Flaginan and Edwin Fougelman, "Functional Analysis" in James C. Charlesworth (ed) *Contemporary Political Analysis* (New York: Free Press, 1967) p. 72.
12. Robert Holt: "A Proposed Structural-Functional Framework in *Charles Worth (ed) Contemporary Political Analysis op. cit.* p. 96.
13. Holt, *op. cit.* p. 92.
14. Holt, *op. cit.* p. 94-95.
15. M.J. Mulkay, *Functionalise Exchange and theoretical strategy,* (London: Lighthedge Hegan Paul, 1971) p. 56.
16. Parsons, *Social system op. cit.* p. 482.
17. C.P. Bhambheri: "Functionalism in Politics", in *Indian Journal of Political Science,* Delhi, vol. XXXIV., No.4, Oct-Dec., 1973, p. 455.
18. Flanigan and Fougelmen, *op, cit.,* p. 72.
19. Hempel, *op, cit.,* p. 296.
20. Robert R. Brown, *Explanation in Social Science* (Chicago: Aldine 1963,) pp. 109-32.

## Chapter - 6

# Systems Approach in Political Sociology

### Systems Analysis

Systems analysis is yet another major strategy of research which can be fruitfully applied by political sociology. It has been derived from general systems theory which can be found in the realm of natural sciences. General systems theory as inspired by the methodology of natural sciences like biology, botany, physics, and mathematics can be best described not as a theory but rather a programme or direction in contemporary philosophy of science.[1] The classification of systems by nature of their relation to their environments and the search for laws governing the behaviour of each class can said to be the problems posed by a general systems theory. Once one has raised the general questions about possible laws governing the behaviour of systems, the problem of rigorous definition of a function comes to the fore.

In common usage, the term refers to widely separated concepts. Engineers are concerned with system as functionally related aggregates of technological devices. Physiologists single out functionally related portions of living organisms; social scientists speak of economic and political system, philosophers, about system of thought. Precisely speaking a system in terms of general systems theory is defined as (1) an ensemble of logically inter-related sets of entities (2) among which a set of relations in specified, so that

(3) deductions are possible from some relations to others or from the relations among the entities to the behaviour or the history of the system.

In the context of social sciences, the systems formulation of biologists carries special significance. One such important formulation has been that of Ralph W. Gerard (1958). According to him a "system" is primarily a living system and the process which defines it is the maintenance of an organization which we know as life. There is a hierarchy of systems, in which the larger ones frequently include the smaller ones as components or sub-systems. Thus, cells form organized aggregates known as tissues or organs; there in turn, are components of a biological individual. Similarly, individuals as component part of society stand in relation to each other as families or tribes signifying social arrangements or as species representing inter-breeding aggregates. Along the scale of social organization, we have aggregate characteristics of human beings —institutions, political units, and societies. Along the scale of biological organization, organisms and populations stand in symbiotic, predatory, or parasitic relation to each others forming ecological systems or "eco-systems". Thus in Gerard's scheme, the hierarchy of living systems from cell to society, or the entire biodata constitutes one dimension. The levels of organizations are horizontal rows of a matrix, of which the vertical columns have three aspects of living system: (1) structural, (2) behavioural, and (3) evolving. Structure can be viewed as inter-relations among the components of a system: the arrangement of its parts and the potential influence which they may have upon each other. Similarly, behaviour refers to a short term reversible changes of state of a living system, its immediate responses to environmental stimuli, the functions performed by its homeostasis devices in maintaining certain steady states, etc. And, finally, the third rubric deals with the long term, typically reversible changes—the development of embryo, the growth of an individual, the history of a society, and the evolution of species. This perspective can be applied with equal force to technological systems, social systems, cultural systems, and political systems.

From the systems perspective, societies and other social groups tend to be seen as relatively persistent entities functioning with larger environments. These entities qualify as system, because they are considered sets of inter-dependent elements or variables, which can be identified and measured. Systems have distiguishable boundary separating them from their environments, and each has a tendency toward a state of equilibrium, i.e., the system tends to maintain itself through various process in case of disturbance, either from within or from outside. Each system tends to be structured in accordance with certain invariant problems characteristic of all social systems. Internal differentiation takes place, with specific kinds of problems, and, as a result, various sub-systems will evolve, such as the economic system, the political system, the societal system etc. In the case of political system, the major task and function, or contribution to society, is that of selecting societal goals, mobilizing resources for their attainment and making societal decisions.

The concept of systems in political science is of relatively recent origin. Political scientists have growingly adopted it by drawing upon the work of other social scientists as well as biologists, physical scientists, and engineers. The physiologist Cannon, in the "Wisdom of the Body" (1932), influenced social scientists and particularly gave currency to the use of the term "homoestasis" to describe a crucial property of biological sub-systems and a highly suggestive one in the study of social systems. The writings of Bertalanffy on biology and general systems analysis have also had tremendous influence in this regard. Although very few political scientists turned to these writings directly, but there have been important linkages through the more widely known work of some sociologists like Parsons (1951;1958), Homans (1950) and Roethlisberger and Dickson (1939).

Parsons for the first time developed the technical idea of a social system and it has been through his work that several political scientists have come to employ the approach in the study of politics. Almond Easton, and Mitchell have based much of their conception of political system on Parsons own expositions in the realm of politics. However, a rigorous application of the system approach to political pehnomena has been obstructed by the lack of necessary mathematical sophistication and relatively less exposure to homologous social process and action. It is only through gradual development of qualitative sophistication in research methodology, especially in the wake of widespread acceptance of interdisciplinary research designs, that political scientists have admitted the fact that political behaviour could be specified in terms of a sharply delimited number of quantitatively linear variables in a system perspective.

Adoptions of systematic perspective has enabled the political scientists to describe and account for the internal structures of political system. The term structure is generally applied to those patterns of power and authority which characterize relationships between rulers and ruled - relationships which are more or less enduring and therefore more or less predictable. The unit of these power relationship is usually "role", which basically refers to those norms which prescribe behaviour in specific settings, relationships, and functions. Power and authority role pertain to the acquisition, maintenance and employment of powers and thereby constitute the building blocks from which the polity is constructed. Political roles are concerned with the making of decisions in the names of society and the performance of actions which achieve or implement these decisions and allocate scarce values and costs. The set of these roles and the behaviour which stem from there make up the political system. In analysing the internal structure of a polity, the political scientists describe these roles and persons taking them as they engage in interaction. The content of the roles, their origin, changes, and influences on behaviour fall with the purview of systemic thinking. Besides, it requires elaboration of the types of structures, such as the allocation of values and costs, the effective achievement of collective goals, and the maintenance of peace and order.

In order to characterize structures and distinguish them the political scientists have employed a variety of concepts and tools. Traditionally, the chief basis of classification has been distribution of power among the members of the system. The single base line has not proved adequate for descriptions of political systems, and even valid and reliable statements about the distribution of power are on insufficient basis upon which to compare political system. Many crucial similarities are missed when analysis proceeds on a single line dimension. System analysis have therefore devised more inclusive sets of variables and at the same time insisted that they be measurable. Parsons has advanced a set of dichotomous concepts called as pattern-variables to make possible more complete analysis of social and in the same manner, political structures. Similarly, Almond has suggested a classification scheme of structures that is based on the following basic dimensions of the political system: (1) the degree of differentiation; (2) the extent to which the system is "manifest" or "visible"; (3) the stability of the functions of various roles; (4) the distribution of power; and (5) the substitutability of roles.

The concept of boundaries is of crucial importance in systematic conceptualization. A system is thought of as being distinct from its environment or as being self-contained and therefore having observable boundaries. System analysis seeks to determine both the members of the systems—if they are concrete individuals—and the analytically distinct units of action which characterize the system. The former implies a member of the society or polity and the latter the actions that go into making up the political system of behaviour, not in terms of concrete individual but of the segments of their behaviour which are politically relevant. This entails arbitrary assigment of boundaries to the political systems, so as to distinguish political activities from a host of others.

Distinction of bounded systems and sub-system and the activities characterizing them constitutes the basis for an explicit distinction of the relations that are found between or among the system. Whether a given system is completely isolated or closed to specific kinds of external influences is established by detecting relationships across boundaries. This entails the problem of analysing the relationship between inputs and outputs. No firm agreement can be seen among the political scientists as to the appropriate labels or concepts to be used in designating such matters. Easton, for example, sees the inputs form society and its various sub-system to the polity as consisting of "demands and support", while Almond and Colman further divide and specify the inputs to the polity: "political socialization", "recruitment", "interest articulation", "interest aggregation", and "political communication." Easton calls the output of the polity as "decision concerning the authoritative allocation of values. Almond and Colman, on the other hand, describe these outputs as "rule-making", "rule application" and "rule adjudication". Mitchell uses the terms "expectations and demands", "resources", and 'support' to specify inputs; and "system goals", "values and costs" and "controls" to describe the political outputs. Notwithstanding these terminological differences, systems analysis is required to measures inputs and outputs, so that comparisons can be made between political systems. And thus its objective is to establish minimal ratio of these exchanges, as a basis for predicting stability systems and their capacity to achieve goals and to provide minimal levels of civic satisfaction for their members.

The ultimate concern of systems analysis is not to describe structures, but to explain the way in which internal functioning of the system is ensured. Before the systems perspective was adopted, political scientists knew a lot about political institutions and political behaviour, both in its individual and aggregate forms. Systematic knowledge about the basic means and processes through which inputs in different systems become transformed or converted into political outputs was rather inadequate. However, with the publication of Easton's political system and Dahl and Lindblom Politics, Economic, and Welfare: Planning and Politics—Economic systems resolved into basic Social Processes, Political scientist of the present generation should show interest in the elaboration of basic socio-political processes by which societies rationally calculate and control their collective actions—The processes which were to be observed in all societies. It is only because they are found in different combinations and environments, they produce different limits all of which can be evaluated.

We have seen that the search for new strategies, methods, and concepts for describing and understanding the political process has drawn the political scientists toward broader approaches to analysis. Systems analysis has offered a promising perspective in this regard. As a result, less attention is being devoted to the details of single political process, such as "judicial review", "legislative apportionment" or the "institutional analysis of the power—structures, while there is more concern for the characteristics and performance of entire political systems. Political analysis are recognizing that such things as voting behaviour or the legislative process cannot be fully understood without more exact information on how these processes function in various settings. Comparison lies at the core of scientific investigation, and political scientists are more concerned than over with developing suitable analytical framework which will permit sophisticated comparative studies in a variety of geographical areas. Systems analysis has tended to find wide acceptance in political science by providing the conceptual scheme so essential for placing political phenomena in this perspective. The pervasiveness of a system orientation to political analysis was suggested in Gabriel Almond's presidential address before the American Political Science Association in 1966.

The emerging analytical frameworks in contemporary political theory is the concept of system whether it is employed at the level of substantial, regional or structural units such as communities, legislative bodies or communities, at the level of national political units, or at the level of the international political system.

Although there was considerable awareness of the importance of systemic concepts among the political scientists, systems analysis of a distinct research perspective acquired its place only after the publication of David Easton's book entitled political system in 1953. As Easton continued to describe, amplify, and refine his particular approach to system analysis, a number of political analysts recorded to the concept of system as a research strategy and a variety of studies have embraced this analytical scheme in recent years.

A close scrutiny of the available literature reveals that the roots of systemic approach have been widely dispersed and its evolution attributable to many factors. One of these factors is primarily theoretical. For many years, conventional political scientist based their discipline upon a basic set of perscriptive or normative "theories" about the ideal polity. A number of modern political scientists realized that conventional approach suffered from methodological adsolescence and they increasingly shifted their focus from a normative perspective to empirical analysis. The subsequent emphasis on empirical measurement and data collection was also devoid of a substantial theoretical basis and, as such, serious questions were raised about collecting the facts and applying them to situation prematurely without theory. It is the increasing concern with a set empirical theories that has been responsible for new approaches and frameworks which are known under the category of systems analysis.

Whereas, a theory is a systematic statement of relationships between political phenomena, providing criteria of relevance, guiding the research for data and giving meaning to the real world. An approach is a less rigorous means for classifying, ordering, and structuring political information. When these classifications and conceptualizations are developed into models of the real world, theories begin to emerge. The ultimate goal is the explanation and prediction of political phenomena by relating them in ordered patterns. Modern political science is concerned with finding empirical regularities which cannot be adequately depicted or known without a mental framework. As such a framework, systems analysis developed as a consequence of out need to establish criteria for recognizing problems, define facts, and screen out irreleveat factors, and bring order to put perceptions of what is political.

Another influential factor in the development of systems analysis is related to an increased recognition of the continuity of nature and the interaction aspects of physical, biological, psychological, social, economic, cultural, and political phenomena. The approach as an outgrowth of cybernatics, the science of communication and control, developed as a reaction to compartmentalized knowledge and disciplinary boundaries. Emphasis was placed on interdisciplinary research, building a common language of science, a broad focus, and unifying theme.

A system view of politics can also be seen as a logically developed alternative to previous definitions of "political". For centuries, political philosophers explicated the meaning of politics and even more recent attempts in this process created mixed degrees of satisfaction and confusion. In many respects, Easton's definition of politics and the accompanying system components represent another progress in our search for what is political. This search has recently included emphasis on power, influence, and the influential, the legal environment of the government, decision making and non-decision making, the conflict of groups and interests, and politics as symbolism. The systems view point contends that the politics is the "authoritative allocation of values" and that political system is supposed to distribute and allocate a wide variety of values which the members of that system consider important (e.g., freedom, safety, resource, and skill) and it does so authoritatively. That is, the decisions of the political system are accepted as binding or legitimate, and despite the fact that government is only one of several agents of social control (family, church, school), it is the only legitimate societal institution with the ultimate sanction—the use of force.

The integral concept stemming from the development of general systems theory and its application to political science is that of a system. A system is any set of interrelated and interacting objects, elements, or variables. Furthermore, their interactions are usually characterized by predictable patterns or consequences—that is interactions are non-random. General systems concepts can be categorized as either descriptive, or as those dealing with dynamics, regulation, and breakdown. The descriptive components make distinctions about kinds of systems (e.g. open, closed) the hierarchical levels of systems (e.g. one system can be a sub-system of another), internal organization (e.g. interdependence, centralization) and the interaction of systems with their environments. Basically the components of any system can be reduced to its environment, inputs emanating from that environment, the conversion of inputs into outputs, and feedback of information through the environment back to the system.

Although the character of system components varies, this analogy holds for social as well as biological or physical systems. When the concepts are made politically specific, a political system is viewed as a bounded set of interdependent roles and structures, whose interactions authoritatively allocate values for society. The political system must not only make rules in the context of values to be allocated, but apply them and adjudicate them. Rule making, rule application, and rule adjudication are examples of functions which the political system must perform to assure its maintenance. Other functions frequently associated with any political system include the necesssity of expressing interests and desired (interest aggregation), including the values of the system (political socialization), training new leadership (political recruitment), and communicating in a system composed of information flows (political communication). Therefore, interaction in this system is any communication or information between actors, and political interactions are oriented toward the authoritatives, allocation of values.

Complexes of interactions create communication networks and information can flow from higher to lower status roles, such as elite to mass (downward communication), from lower to higher (upward communication), or between roles of generally equal status (horizontal communication). This information flow is the stuff of which decisions are made and the most influential members of the political systems are usually, by definition, ones that control the information flow process.[2] We have also seen that component sets of interactions and expectations held by actors in this system are roles. These role are defined by the actor and the expectation of others. Furthermore, every role has a status in the system and a structure is a set of interdependent roles. Many complex structures with legal bases are called institutions. For example, a bureaucracy is a structure with actors performing rather formalized roles.

Finally, there are those concepts which deal with the way system responds to stress. Stress is a disturbance which endangers the systems ability to persist or prevent the system from operating in its characteristic way. A characteristic of any system is its ability to cope with stress, and in this respect all political systems are adaptive systems. A basic process of cybernatics is homeostasis—that is, the ability of the system to achieve a steady state or maintain equilibrium. Like a thermostat in a beating system, the political system has homeostatic mechanisms which reduce stress. If they fail to operate effectively, the subsequent modification of roles creates a system transformation known as a step level-function, altering its characteristic behaviour. There is output failure when this system unsuccessfully generates outputs to cope with stress. One cause of such failure might be demand input overload, a situation in which demands are too numerous (volume stress) or too difficult (content stress) to process.

The components of the political system can be understood with the help of following diagram. The core of this system in the "black box" of authoritative decision makers and decision making agencies which are influenced by the inputs to the system evaluating from a diverse environment of other systems. These systems may be within the same society (intra-societal) or outside the society (extra societal). The inputs are demands placed on decision makers, and society which assures the decision makers freedom to interpret the meaning of inputs. Support for this system are either material (e.g. taxes), behavioural (obedience to laws), participating (e.g. voting) or defferential (e.g. respect for authority). Various structures such as political parties and interest groups transmit inputs by performing various functions (e.g. interest aggregating and interest articulation). The result of decision making is outputs or policy, which in turn influences new inputs from the environment through the process of feedback. Sometimes these outputs are substantive (e.g. a new tax) or symbolic (e.g. medal of honour). Since information and energy interchange is the basic component of any system, its boundary is defined by the fact that it requires more energy to transverse it than to travel an equivalent distance inside or outside that boundary. In a political system, the boundary is dependent upon the extent to which certain interaction lead to the authoritative allocation of values. In time of war for example, much of the economic system is infused into the political system. Furthermore, all political system are open systems in that they cannot function without environmental interaction.

**Components of a Political System**

A political system consists of several major attributes which may be distinguished analytically: inputs, outputs, decision making agencies or processes, feedback and boundary. Inputs consist of those activities emanating from the environment which get channeled into the decision making structures as the "raw material" to keep the system functioning. From another perspective inputs present themselves as stimuli to which decision makers react. The decision making or conversion portion of the systems paradigm can be viewed in two ways. In one sense, it represents those officials and agencies within a society charged with the legal responsibility for making public decisions and politics. Some system analysts, however, prefer to focus less on the official structures and more on the process of conversion itself; that is, the interaction which takes place as the inputs are transformed into outputs. Easton for example, comes within this latter category.

Outputs in the simplest sense, are decisions and acts of officials which may take the form of laws, administrative decrees, and count decisions. The feedback loop or process is what gives the political system its dynamic quality. The operation of the system does not stop with the production of outputs. Instead, governmental decisions and policies affect other systems surrounding the political system (the environment) which may in turn generated the focus of inputs for the political system to process. In addition, certain focus of outputs or policies might return as feedback directly to the decision makers as a new input without necessarily going through the outside environment. The environment was described as being made up of a network of other systems (e.g. economic, social, cultural), which surround and influence the political system. Since the political system is an open one, it constantly changes in a series of transactions and exchanges across the boundary which separates the system from its environment. We can discuss these elements separately.

**Environment or Boundary**

Boundary serves as major source of inputs to the system. Easton has suggested a broad two-fold divisions: intra societal and extra societal. For example, in the case of urban political systems, extra-societal forces would represent those occurrences taking place outside the community itself, such as in the national or regional economy, which eventually influence the local polity. The decisions or programmes of state or national level, which affect the cities are another example of extra societal environmental influence. The intra-societal environment of the local level would include those characteristics found entirely within the community—such as the prevailing social structure, size of the community, density, age levels, or peculiar cultural norms—all of which help determine the volume and content of the inputs for the urban political system.

Even though the local political system is an open system involved in a continuing interaction with its environment, for purposes of analysis, these outside forces must be considered a constants or parameters which at any given time are unchanging. Thus the notion of a systems boundary, essentially represents an analytical construct determined largely by what the research desires to include or exclude as part of the system under investigation. In Easton's word, the boundary of a political system is "a symbol or spatial embodiment of the criteria of inclusion/exclusion a summary way of referring phenomenally to what we have included in or left out of a system."[3] For the purpose of political analysis, the environmental influences have been grouped into the following categories: Political structure, socio-economic characteristics and political culture. These parameters generate and condition the inputs (except those which arise within the system itself) which are intended to be processed by political system.

### Inputs

The inputs of a political system can best be summarized under two broad categories: demands and supports. The inputs furnish the raw material in which the political system processes. If people did not want or expect government to do certain things, there would be little need for a government at all. Thus demands can be considered the requests made by citizens individually or collectively for decisions or policies which require action on the part of some government agency or official. Various groups often find they are unable to resolve problems privately and therfore request, sometimes reluctantly, the involvement of those charged with making binding decisions for the whole society. The need for authoritative decisions does not always arise outside the system; some demands may be internally inspired. Demands must be expressed, explicitly or implictly, and should be distinguished from expectations concerning the "rules of the game" or norms of political behaviour, public opinion, ideology, and mere preferences. Thus every political system possesses certain mechanisms which serve to reduce, regulate, and channel demands made open it. The prevailing political ideology—belief, values, and myths—may serve as a potentially important barrier preventing certain demands from being seriously considered at local level.

Successful conversion of demands into outputs or decisions

makes it imparative for the political system to acquire certain degree of support for its functioning. This support is expressed in the forms of supporting actions (overt support) or supporting attitudes (covert supports) of its members. This however may be low or even negative. In such cases, the situation may be described as that of "output failure" which takes place when political authorities cannot or will not effectively cope with the demands of various aggrieved groups either in terms of quantity or quality.

Gabriel Almond has suggested an alternative scheme for grouping inputs into four functional categories. These are: political socialization and recruitment, interest articulation, interest aggregation and political communication. Political socialization is the process of induction into the political culture. Its end product is a set of attitudes-cognitions, values standards and feelings-toward the political system, its various roles and role incumbents. Although in Almond's scheme political socialization is treated as input function, some other political analysts treat it as both an input and an output of the systems. They are of the view that since political system itself through its decisions and policies generates so much reinforcement of prevailing political norms and values that the socialization process must be considered as a system output as well as an input.[4]

Political recruitment may be considered as a further extension of the political socialization process. Every modern government must devise ways of drawing persons from the larger society into positions of civic leaderhip. At the local level, knowledge of the recruitment process comes primarily from studies of the background characteristics of local decision makers. Similarly the interest articulation and interest aggregation functions are the crucial tasks performed by interest groups and political parties in modern political systems. These processes imply that the government in order to remain viable must in some way recognize those matters which are of concern to its citizens. For diffuse claims and demand of various individuals and groups to be effective, they must not be expressed but drawn together in such a manner as to present relatively few alternative policy proposals for government actions.

In fact interest groups assume the primary responsibility of articulating political demands while parties seek to form the largest possible interest, group coalitions, and, finally political communication involves a dynamic movement of demands and decisions from the parts of the political system to another as no operations of the political system can take place unless parts of the system can communicate with each other. Communication links together the parts of the system and also the present with past and the future, so that demands are followed by policies.[5] The term when used in the context of political cybernatics, consists of (i) a model drawn from the information theory and cybernatics, (ii) a theory of communication nets, and (iii) a set of propositions partially derived from other theoretical ideas, such as democratic theory, organization theory, and decision-theory, about the characteristics and effects of communications and their media on attitude change, public opinion formation, voting behaviour, maintenance and stability of a political system, consensus, coercion, political socialization, political development, perception and ideology.

## Outputs

Outputs of the political system are the decisions and actions taken by the official decision makers in response to the changing demands and supports generated by the environment and by the political system itself. At the community level, these outputs are the laws, administrative action or judicial decisions which tend to determine public policy. Perhaps, a distinction should technically be made between decisions, outputs, outcomes, and policies, although the terms are often used interchangeably. To Easton, binding decisions and implementing actions constitute outputs which he differentiates from their consequences or outcomes.[6] Outputs could be divided into two broad categories: rewards and deprivations. Rewards[7], consist of the goods and services which a person might review or be able to receive from his government. Deprivations, on the other hand, would include tax imposition as also such regulations and restrictions as are introduced from time to time for the maintenance of peace and order in the system.

## Feedback

Feedback is one of the most crucial concepts in systems analysis.

It is ordinarily used to indicate the capacity of the system to respond to stress by modifying or redirecting its own behaviour. The feedback process begins with the output of the system which have an affect on other systems or on the political system itself. Information about the impact of governmental decisions and policies must then return to the authorities (as inputs) so that the political system may adapt its behaviour to changing demands (through producing new outputs).

In fact, it is this process which gives political system its dynamic quality and it may be viewed as a series of succeeding steps: (i) production of outputs by the political system, (ii) response by members of the larger society (the environment), (iii) communication of information about responses to the decision makers, (iv) possible action (new outputs) by the political authrorities in response to the information received. Easton insists that the very persistence of the political system depends upon keeping this dynamic process functioning. Anything that delays, distorts, or served the flow of information to the authorities seriously interferes with their capacity to act and may result in a serious reduction of support for the system, Feedback, therefore, provides a key link in what Easton terms as 'goal-setting', self-transforming and creatively adaptive system.[8]

## Advantages and Limitations of System Analysis

A systems approach appears to offer, as we discussed earlier, several explicit advantages in the search for understanding political life. As Easton emphasized, the idea of political system compels the research to separate political activity from other forms of social behaviour-atleast for the purpose of analysis. In this sense the political system is regarded as a self contained set of political interactions embedded in, but analytically distinct from, the larger environment in which it is found.[9]

Aside from its capability to analytically separate interactions which involve authoritative allocation of values from a larger environment, system analysis focuss attention on the specific set of components or units making up a particular political system.

Identifying the distinct fundamental elements of a political system is actually an integral part of distinguishing that system from its larger environment. This process involves the crucial notion of a boundary which encompasses the political system indicating, atleast for the purpose of analysis, what we have included or excluded from the system.[10] Thus the approach requires from the observer to have a comprehensive look at all the dimensions and components of the authoritative allocation process. This generates a broad perspective to analyse relationship between system components and between the political system and its environments. Thus in systems analysis, it is essential to know how the political system is related to other system outside its boundary, since the outside environment furnishes the inputs for political activity.

Systems thinking is highly compatible with rigorous empirical research, providing a rich vein of concepts and working models to be used in a variety of substantive areas. Thus it may prove of significant value as heuristic device or as an aid to understanding in the search for empirically verifiable propositions. In this connection, system analysis has become increasingly associated with recent advances in mathematics and in the use of computer techniques. In general, system approach, stemming from interdisciplinary efforts to establish common forum of language and analysis across a variety of substantive applications, has infused new concepts into the language of political analysis, encouraged new ways of looking at potential phenomena in the context of all relevant variables, enabled comparative analysis through common knowledge of different system, facilitated the gathering of data and the empirical examination of politics, developed micro-analysis in conjunction with macro-analysis, and, most important, stimulated new queries, otherwise unasked, about basic political phenomena.

These advantages not withstanding, system perspective seems to have some serious limitations. One of them is that it cannot be treated as a theory in itself. A theory, strictly speaking, has explanatory power. And as the critics of their approach point out, systems analyses are not really explanatory they are essentially neuristic aids, or utmost guide in the search for testable generalizations. Besides, the approach has limited value in goal determination since it is basically concerned with systems persistence and not with the direction of its growth or evolution. It is of little use in dealing with matters of control power and influence. It is held that the concentration of persistence and survival detracts from an interest in "who gets what" and results in the charge that the approach harbors a status quo bias. Finally, it is generally felt that certain systems concepts are not easily operationalized, making it difficult to apply the approach to certain concrete problem of analysis. For example, the notion of a boundary separating the political system from its environment is particularly troublesome for many to visualize and would seem almost impossible to operationalize. However, despite these constraints, a growing body of system oriented research testifies to the usefulness of a systems on the framework for political analysis.

**References**


1. Anatol Rapport, "Systems Analysis: General Systems theory". *International Encyclopaedia of Social Science, op. cit.*
2. David R. Morgan and Samuel A. Kirkpatrick, *Urban Political Analysis: A System Approach,* (London: The Free Press, 1972) pp.67.
3. David Easton, *The Political System, op. cit.*
4. Irish and Prathro, *Politics of American Democracy,* pp. 15-17.
5. Jean Blondel: *An Introduction to Comparative Government,* (London: Weiderfold and Nicholson, 1969), p. 223.
6. David Easton, *Systems Analysis of Politics op. cit.* pp. 351-52.
7. Irish and Prothero, *Politics of American Democracy,* p. 72.
8. David Easton, *A Framework for Political Analysis* (Englewod Cliffs, Prentice Hall, 1965). 125-32.
9. D. Morgan and Kirkpatrick, *Urban Political Analysis,* p. 9.
10. Easton, A System Framework for Political Analysis, p. 38-39.

# Chapter - 7

# Social Structure and Polity

## Social Structure and its Components

Society can be viewed as an organized collectivity of human groups. Its individual components cannot behave independently of one another but are linked by bonds, the nature of which determines the types of social units. Kinship, sex, age, co-residence, matrimonial status, community of religious or social interests are among the unifying agencies, and in stratified societies, members of the same level form a definite class.[1] From this point of view, social structure implies an essemble of the patterned relations between human groups and individuals. It can be defined as the totality of patterns of collective phenomena that cannot be explained solely on the basis of human heredity and/or the non-human environment. This definition involves identification of the main components of a social system and inter-relations among them.[2] The components can be identified as (1) individual component involving a conception of personality or aggregated characteristics of individual personalities, (2) group component indicating a set of variables essentially referring to various aspects of the process of social stratification among people, (3) morphological component implying a set of variables pertaining to the spatial-temporal arrangement of individuals and the physical size of groups, (4) systemic component which focuss on the properties of inter-relationships among activities as such, independently of the people performing them, generally treating such activities as social roles, and (5) cultural component comprising ideas (norms, values, beliefs) which are learned and shared by people and are transmitted symbolically from person to person.

In fact, in social sciences there have been divergent views of social structure which basically refer to the questions of ordering and general relationships. Of these, we can refer to three view points which are cultural, interactionist, and morphological positions. The cultural point of view emphasizes the explanatory primacy of culture as a system of ideas that are learned, shared, and transmitted by people who in turn, are oriented to situations by virtue of the culture that they have learned. Situations thus evoke responses, culturally defined as role expectations, by virtue of which people find themselves interacting with one another, with the possibility of resultant morphological differentiation. The causal progression is from cultural-individual aspect of situation to the systematic aspects, to group characteristics, and finally, to the morphological aspects of structure. This approach thus stresses the inter-relationships of culture, personality, and social system, defining social structure as some combination of these elements with group and morphological considerations viewed as somewhat ancillary.

An essentially theoretical view of social structure emerges, wherein culturally defined systems of role expectations await the participation of people, and this participation either incidently yields group and morphological characteristics or implies as contextual constants.[3] In some respects, both the interactionist and the morphological positions represent a polar view of social structure which implies the people with highly generalized expectations about one anothers probable behaviour are taken as given and are morphologically presumed to interact with one another. From the ensuing reciprocal process of role taking and role playing, increasingly stable systems of role expectations emerge which in turn become generalized into subordinate systems of cultural norms. The causal progression, unlike cultural view, is from group phenomena to systemic aspects and finally to cultural pattern.

And finally, morphological conception of social structure is essentially similar to the interactionist version, but it is more macroscopically conceived. It assumes a disposition on the part of the people to engage in stable interactions relative to certain specified but highly generalized cultural expectations. Emergent systemic and cultural properties of situation therefore depended on morphological structure which, through variations in the members of people involved and their spatial and temporal relationships to one another, as well as to artifactual facilities, imposes limits on the possibilities of interaction capable of producing emergent characteristics. Those divergent viewpoints have produced, as we indicated earlier, opposing conceptions of social structure.

From the cultural standpoint, social structure emerges as an object of orientation comprising cultural and systemic elements in terms of which the actions of individuals, groups, and morphological entities occur or are directed. On the other hand, from the interactionist or morphological viewpoints, social structure, has, by and large, been thought of as the totality of group and morphological patterns, with individual elements contained in the group patterns and with or without systemic components, depending on the particular versions of theory. Cultural elements are viewed as orientially external, in either a contextual or an emergent sense, or they are for some purposes deemed irrelevant.

The theoretical controversies generalized by these divergent conceptualizations of social structure have been tried to be resolved, among other things by suggesting an eclectic view in which the five component elements are interrelated by a complex of dialectical tensions which, in principle can be concretely operationalized and explicated as a set of inter-related psychological and ecological causal chains cutting across the five aspects of social structure, with their operation resulting in more or less 'stability' and 'change'.

Keeping in view of the above broad perspective, we can discuss a few of the leading thinkers of one time in this context. Nadel[4] and Forte conceived of a structure through abstracting from the concrete population and its behaviour pattern or network of relationships obtaining between actors in their inter-personal roles. Further emphasizing the behavioural aspect, Warner and Lunt[5] have defined social structure as a system of formal and informal groupings by which the social behaviour of individuals is regulated. The essence of a social structure is this social relations and behaviour of members of a society. But it is important to point out here that it is not the ideals and expectations alone which have been constituting a social structure. Malionwiski had remarked that "one must not only consider the character of institutions and their traditional norms governing human conduct, it is equally important to study the real activities which may differ from the prescribed expectations owing to special pressures. The actual behaviour of individuals and the way in which the social standards, the ideal patterns, the sets of expectations change have also been considered an important constituents of social structure as the ideals and expectations themselves. Social structure thus has not been considered as something static, but something dynamic, rather both a process and a product.[6] In every community, the social relations, either between individuals or groups form the internal units of social structure. Linton has also pointed out that by studying the social relationships between individuals and observing the repetitive situations, it becomes possible to deduce the structural pattern of society.

Social life is described as the multitude of interactions and joint actions of human beings. During this interaction or relationship of which the social structure consists of a person conform to certain rules or pattern of conduct. Social structure therefore, has to be described by the institutions which define the proper and expected conduct of persons in their various relationships. Thus, social structure, as an arrangement of persons in institutionalized roles and relationships, symbolized the continuity of such arrangement.[7] According to Radcliffe Brown, the social structure, therefore, is to be defined as "the continuing arrangement of persons in relationships defined or controlled by institutions, i.e., socially established norms or patterns of behaviour.[8] In order to live together, every society has postulated certain laws which guide an individuals behaviour and maintain the uniformities and regularities in their social life. In other words, there is a set structure for every society which explains its existence. In accordance with this, Evans Pritchard explained that "a total social structure, that is to say the entire structure of a society is composed of a number of subsidiary structures or systems and we may speak of its social system, economic system, religious system, and political system. The social activities within these systems or structures are organized around institutions such as marriages, family, kinship, chieftainship and so forth, and when we speak of functions of these institutions, we mean the part they play in maintenance of the structure.

Thus Nadel observed that all the students of social structure agreed that in studying structure we study essentially the interrelation or arrangement of 'parts' in some total entity or 'whole'. We further agreed that the adjective 'social' specifies the character of that whole which is society or any of its divisions. It is however necessary to mention here that although social relations have been stressed in the study of social structure, yet the two concepts are not synonymous. In this context, Levy-Strauss make categorical distinction between the concepts of social structure and social relation. According to him, the social relations are the raw data of social experience of which the model or models comprising the social structure are built.

Thus the meaningful interpretation of social structure will necessarily involve our capacity not only to discuss the ensemble of social relations, but also to construct definite models or forms out of them. Parsons viewed social structures as systems of action which could be discussed at three levels, i.e., personality, culture, and society. Thus three levels represented distinct conceptual units of a society which was to be viewed as total system. What distinguishes one system or one unit from the other is not their content, but the way in which we were required to order our date about social relations.

Thus personality system could be distinguished from social systems by the difference in the foci around which they are organized. The personality of the individual is organized around the biological unity of organism. In contrast, 'the social system is organized around the unity of interacting group. Thus the analysis of personality is designed to show that which specific types of acts are related to the 'needs' of the individuals actors, while the analysis of social systems refers to the functional prerequisites and problem of group life. In addition to personality system and social systems, we have cultural systems—that is systems of meaningful symbols, which are represented by different cultural elements of society. Thus the most important aspect of social structures as system of actions were the institutionally defined goals and normative standards of society which tended to regulate the conduct of its members and provide a definite shape to the social texture. This is why Parsons emphasized the importance of role positions norms, values, institutions and collectivities in his analysis of complex systems.

### Social Structure and Social Stratification

Closely related to the concept of social structure is the system of social stratification which implies that both individuals and groups of individuals are conveived of as constituting higher and lower differential strata, or classes in terms of some specific or generalized characteristics or set of characteristics. In sociological usages the concept of stratification often includes, implicitly or explicitly, some evaluation of higher and lower layers, which are judged to be better or worse according to the scale of values. Such matter as relative moral wealth, relative equality or inequality, and degrees of justice and injustice are often involved in the concept of social stratification. The concept is therefore widely used in the political, ideological references in the social science analysis.

However, despite the difficulty of separating the contexts of moral and ideological controversy, on the one hand, and from that of social science analysis on the other, both theoretical and empirical tools have been developed for analysing social stratification. Mention may be made of the conceptual schemes suggested in the writings of Marx and Weber. Marx divided the society into two strata, or "classes" which represented the owners of the means of production and the workers whom they employed. The excessively simplified dichotomization of the social stratification in the Marxian picture of modern society seems to have exaggerated the amount of class conflict that has occurred and that is inevitable in such society. As a matter of fact conflict is endemic in the structure of every society, and the productive and occupational, aspect of modern society is certainly one source of structural source of conflict. But these are other sources, religious, ethnic and political which produce more conflict in modern world than even the more occupational difference. Max Weber, obviously unlike Marx suggested a trinitorian model of social stratification which is based on the concepts of class, status, and party, thereby introducing a systematic, explicit, and necessary differentiation in the available theory of social stratification. However Weber does not appear to have been much concerned with how to make a more precise ordering of social behaviour along the three dimensions of social stratification that he analysed.

The conceptual deficiencies observed in the writing of Marx and Max Weber in the context have been partially removed by a more sophisticated conceptual models suggested by Parsons and David and Moore, who have stressed the prestige dimension of social stratification and have treated what Weber called status as a generalized social phenomenon applying to all positions in the occupational structure of society. Prestige is resultant of two factors: a system of values, and the functional significance of roles as embodied in the occupational structure. Functional significance is determined by the relative capacity of a role for "producing" some service or good in society services and goals being constructed in the most comprehensive way possible, not in the limited economic way intended by Marx when he spoke of production. For, example, governmental, religious, artistic and ideological roles are functionally significant, as subject to evaluation, and as "productive" in some measure as are the roles of owing capital, managing a business, or tending a machine in factory.

Parsons, aside from his interest in the dimension of prestige, has also been interested in the power aspect of social stratification. In this context, he has stressed two general propositions-*first,* power is a positive social phenomenon i.e. the capacity for achieving goals in the systems and not just a negative phenomenon, i.e., the capacity to prevent others from acting as they wish; and *second,* power is not a zero-sum phenomenon, in which if A has more, then B necessarily has less. Rather power is a phenomenon that allows increments and their social consequences to be shared by both A and B, although not always in complete equality, of course. Thus a multi-dimensional conceptual model of social stratification provides an ample scope for its integral interpretation, especially in terms of such crucial elements as power, occupational prestige, income or wealth, education and knowledge, religious and ritual purity, family and ethnic group position and local community status enjoyed by the individuals and groups.[9] This is also clear by the following observation of Parsons in the context of social structure:

> "....The relation between personality and society, socially structured through what we have called service, provides the basic unit for the political aspect of societies. Political structures are concerned with organizing collective action for the attainment of collectively significant goals, whether on a society-wise basis or more narrow bases, either territorially or functionally defined. Advanced political development requires status differentiation within the adult population on some combination of two bases. The first involves levels of responsibility for coordinated collective action and the grounds of the institutions of leadership and authority. The second concerns levels of competence, based on knowledge, skill and the like, and assigns greater influence in collective deliberations to the more competent. A political systems differentiation form the matrix of the social community involves institutionalizing higher-order statuses in both these contexts, often in very complex combinations. The relation of such statuses to religious leadership, particularly the degree of differentiation between leadership in religious and in political contexts, may also present major complications. The imperative of legitimation, not only of the social order, but also of political authority in particular, indicates the main context of such complications...Lower in the cybernatic hierarchy is another basis of complication (i.e.) the maintenance of a normative order requires that it be implemented in a variety of respects; there must be very considerable-even often quite incomplete-compliance with the behavioural expectations established by values and norms. The most basic condition of such compliance is the internalization of a society's values and norms by its members, for such socialization underlines the consensual basis of a societal community.

> In turn, socialization to the grounds of consensus is reinforced at various points by interlocking interests, notably economic and political. However, no society can maintain stability in the face of varying exigencies and strains, unless the interest constellations of its members are grounded in solidarity and internalized loyalties and obligations."[10]

Parsons in his analysis of social structure and politics emphasized the application of four structural categories, i.e., values, norms, collectivities, and roles. These categories enable us to analyse structures in accordance with the functional paradigm which we have earlier discussed. Values take primacy in the pattern maintenance functioning of a social system. Norms are primarily integrative, as they arė supposed to regulate a number of processes which contribute to the implementation of patterened value commitments. The primary functioning of the collectivity concerns actual goal attainment on behalf of the social system. Where individuals perform societally important functions, it is in their capacity as collectivity members. And finally, according to him the primary function of the role in the social system is adaptive. This is particularly clear for the category of service, as the capacity to fulfil socially recognized role performances is the most basic generalized adaptive resource of any society, though it must be coordinated with cultural, organic, and physical resources.[11]

**Social Structure and Polity**

Polity represents a distinct and primary functional sub-system of society, which can be conceived of as theoretically parallel to economy and normative order of society as a total system. The adjective primary functional indicates that the polity should not be identified either with any specific activity structure with the society, such as government or with any concrete type of the collectivity of individuals. Analytically speaking, it can be conceived as the aspect of all action concerned with the function of the collective pursuit of collective goals. Thus the polity can be conceived of as a system involving the coordinated action of a plurality of individuals oriented to the attainment of a collective goal or a system of collective goals. Collectivity in this sense range from very small groups to the large politically organized groups and sometimes to inter-societal or transnational organization.[12]

Polity, like other social system, can be seen as comprising different component units and their inter-relationships. In that sense, polity as a distinct system involves a collectivity and its units are invariably 'members' who represent either individual persons in specific roles or sub-collectivities that themselves are ultimately reducible to individual persons in member roles. Its component units are characterized by four essential chracteristics:

1. Centralized commitments to the specific values of the collectivity, i.e.,their commitment to the collectivities effectiveness, which may be called their loyality;
2. Specified commitments consisting of rights and obligations to make certain types of decisions that integrate the commitments of collectivities with their own roles and status within it;
3. An integrative responsibility for implementing specific decisions and protecting certain interests of the collectivity, a responsibility which constitutes a normative context for particular roles or functions; and
4. A capacity to implement, through instrumental procedures decisions constituting obligations in particular roles. Capacity includes both competence in the personal sense and control of resources adequate for specific purposes.[13]

In fact, effective represents a value pattern for a collectivity. It is therefore required that all members should be equally committed to it as a value on the generalized level. Empirically however there are both variations of intensity of commitment, and alienation in the sense of conflicts over commitment, including complex ambivalences.

The operative functions of collective process tend to be structured primarily around the second and fourth of the above properties of membership roles. Specified commitment is very close to what is often called the operative members *sphere of responsibility*. Integrative responsibility, however, involves an additional component. It goes without responsibility in a clearly defined status to include a share of responsibility for defining the status.[14]

That there exists a close relationship between social structure and the polity involving specific action systems could be understood on the basis of the following diagram which demonstrates such relationship at the level of family or household.

| | | |
|---|---|---|
| | Labour Service | |
| | Wage Income | |
| Economy<br>A | Consumers Spending | Household<br>L |
| | Generalized Support | |
| | Effective Leadership | |
| Polity<br>G | Advocacy of Policies | Public |
| | Binding Decision | I |

*Source*: Talcott Parsons, Politics and Social structure (New York: Free Press, 1969). p. 209

The above diagram represents as Parsons observes "a parallel in the strict sense an analogy—and not an identity. Power as an output is not income in the economic sense, decisions are not commodities, support is not labour, and consumers' spending is not advocacy of politics. In an analytical sense, the "public", as the source of support and advocacy of politics, is altogether different from the household, as the source of labour and consumers spending, though members of households are at the same time parts of the public....(The) focus of political organization on the collectivity level is government. The boundary-interchange just outlined is that set of processes by which control of the government is decided, its major policies are worked out, and public attitudes toward them are influenced and brought to hear. The focus of mechanism by which the processes work out is what we call party system.

At the support level, the most important single process on the side of the public is voting because, under our constitutional system, this decides who is to assume the primary roles of responsible leadership.

The relationship between politics and social structure can be more explicitly understood in terms of the process of social differentiation and its implications on political power and political behaviour. The process can be observed in three broad areas: the economic-technological features which attend the creation of occupations and industrial and commercial organizations; the differences of status which affect inter-personal relations; and the institutional aspects which influence the manners in which differentiated roles are integrated into total or partial structures. In each of these cases the ways in which changes take place are partly influenced by historical / residual cultural features, partly by functional pre-requisities of situations and partly by specific contingency factors.[15] As Smelser has observed in his study of the Industrial Revolution in England, increased differentiation only becomes important when it seriously disrupts the life styles of large sections of the population.

The process of change causing disruption could be explained by identifying the economic, technological, demographic, and cultural features which causes this disruption. For, societies in early stages of industrialization three processes are simultaeneously affecting social stratification: the emergence of new upwardly mobile social groups, horizontal movement of manual workers from rural to urban and industrial occupations and the downward mobility or the displacement of elites. In some cases the first two shifts may be due to immigration. In most respects, the particular structural problems of an industrializing or 'developing' country can be initially plotted by the use of a typology which isolates these changes in stratification according to whether they proceed together or whether any one change is far in advance of the others.

In some cases, the social differentiation initiated by the process of industrialization may appear to be intensified while the others will appear to be affected less by those trend and, as such, may succeed in retaining the traditional structure. All this may be due to the kinds of land structure predating commercial and industrial development, and certainly the complexion of political structure accompanying industrialization would suggest strong evidence in the context. In any case, the development of more differentiated structures can be considered in two ways: one may look at the elements of cohesiveness, solidarity and integration accompanying differentiation, or look at those forms of social stratification preceding, and following from, differentiation. The two perspective, do, of course, interrelate but as much research has emphasized one perspective or the other. We briefly examine their merits and demerits.[16]

The emphasis on consensus and solidarity, characteristic of Durkheims sociology, is imporant in the beginning of differentiation. The major difficulty in Durkheim's theories relate partly to his biologistic conception of social change and to his simplified view of what society is. Mechanistic solidarity as defined by him does not represent all pre-industrial societies nor are the changes bound to lead to organic solidarity. What does happen is that the use of new production techniques, the vast changes in communication and the widening boundaries of social contact progressively weaken community, family and other forms of traditional solidarity. This in turn is bound to alter the basis of consensus and authority. In traditional societies of whatever nature, patterns of norms and values are closely interrelated. This may imply a mechanistic system, but it is certainly based on less/differentiated structures. As the productive technology and communication become more complex, so the norms governing particular areas of behaviour become more varied. People's actions in specific situations cease to imply normative consensus, because the situations themselves have become so diverse that a societal consensus on all these normative situations becomes virtually impossible. Consensus, such as exists, is found in general national value symbols and in the norms governing political behaviour.

The importance of Durkheim's conception of organic systems is that the idea of contract between different elements of society does replace status, but in most societies probably not for the whole system. It may, for example, affect economic relations, but not educational ones. Or, it may be found in national government but not local government. But such a discussion only makes sense if Durkheim's concept of solidarity is used for specific situations whose large collectivities act together for particular purposes, such as in times of disaster, way or major industrial unrest. In traditional societies, it is clearly exceptional because of the divisive consequences of differentiation for total structure, cultures, and norms. It may be possible to discuss mechanical solidarity with some meaning, but it is difficult to see organic systems having solidarity in this sense of cohesiveness. Organic systems are held together by contract, consensus, routinized conflict or by brute force, but rarely by solidarity in the face of danger or threat may produce consensus. This, however, is hardly what Durkheim meant.

The importance of power structure is therefore fundamental for explaining how societies, which are otherwise characterized by differences, instrumental relations and differentiation of normative situations, are held together. For Durkheim, in a mechanistic system, power accrues to those who hold the top of the status pyramid and they do this either by conquest or inheritance. In organic systems on the other hand, the power structure is produced by the 'needs' of the different levels of interaction system. The state reflects the moral consensus of the social system. 'Transitional' societies suffer because they have not found organic solidarity, therefore they tend to operate two types of social system simultaneously. The failure of politics is a measure of the failure of moral consensus. At all levels, this analysis is unsatisfactory, because it does not provide sufficient ground for analysing the effects of power on the social system. For Durkheim, power can only appear as a consequence of particular levels of interaction in society and he does not allow for interaction between political system and elements of the social system. Consequently, he does not help to define power as such.

These are, however, alternative ways of viewing the relationship between consensus and political power. Of course, it is true that cohesion and consensus may in some way 'represent' the moral basis of society and be the sum of the levels of interaction. Question emerges as to how does the power structure reflect this consensus and represent non-political interaction. One way of finding out may be to identify the values of consensus and attempt to establish whether they (a) reflect values of the particular elements in society and (b) are derived from historical or structural features inherent in the political system itself. Whether or not we can isolate values in a meaningful way, the problem of identifying elements in society returns us to the units used to analyse interaction. A simple functional model, as Durkheim and most of the structural-functional theorists imply, is based on functional autonomy: each unit in society is of equal importance. But this is not the case. The analysis of political power makes it clear that some elements in society have greater influence over political processes than other and thus the first exercise in isolating political power is to establish which these are. This is very close to Marxist analysis: the state is the landmaiden of the bourgeoisies. But, of course, this is insufficient logically. By the same series of arguments, it is possible to show that the political system can have greater power than the elements with which it interacts. This seems to be an expression of Wabers position also: as systems of bureaucratic rationality develop they may come to dominate all forms of political interaction.[17]

In order to get a logical view of this situation, we are required to classify political systems according to degrees of dominance from sub-sections of society and also according to degree of control by the system itself. Beyond this, the important question are, why one from persists rather than another, and whether there is any connection between forms of interaction and the kinds of ideology, values and symbols which dominate at different levels of the system. This is more satisfactory way of proceeding than classifying societies according to pattern variables and types of value orientation or by general social structures which are based on some form of moral solidarity or consensus. The form is the approach of Parsons and the latter of Durkheim. Thus, the most important issues in the analysis of relationship of politics to social structure is to explain values and changes in values and also norms and normative changes. Under this form of analysis, the consensus may seem to emerge from one sector of society which happens to dominate the whole or from political formulas which may draw heavily on tradition, or select elements of tradition, for purposes of legitimation it should not reflect the interests of one 'non-political' sector but the interpretation by the political elite itself of the values it considers necessary for maintaining order and power. This latter situation may arise in from exchange mechanism between different units in part also from the logic of political structure's own development. If we accept that this is possible, and the empirical evidence suggests that it is, then it may be easier to avoid the dichotomies presented by the functionalists, interactionists, and the conflict variations of political analysis. In the ideal type situations, it may be possible to find systems which approximate to a perfectly equiliberated society, where the interaction of different elements produces consensus without either political domination or terror. Alternatively, in many situations the opposition of competing sectors may at best be institutionalized, but it is not possible to talk about consensus and system integration.

But of course, no society is an ideal type and the elaboration of a simple typology which accommodates centrifugal and centripetal tendencies in relation to levels of political interaction allows both for societies in which consensus and integration exist and for those where dual or multiple conflicts permit no consensus. Although this approach implies a system, in the sense of these being inter-related parts, it is not a variation of Easton's model for the political system. In this model, the nature of the inputs to the system is of lesser importance than the system's own structure, in our case the 'inputs' are crucial in determining what that structure might be, though in some advanced societies, the dynamics of the political structure may override the inputs. This is another way of stating the centre-periphery thesis, though one which allows that the values of the centre may be derived directly from sectoral interests from an exchange between sectoral interests and those accruing from legitimation-mechanisms of the politicians; and those which seem to derive primarily from domination by a particular type of regime in creating its own client sector to give it a base of social power. There are transitional states where emerging sectors attempt to change the foundation of existing power, or where political elites may attempt to change their power base by appealing to sectors formally on the periphery, or, finally, where an old form of sector-political control collapses under new form of sectoral contest to allow the emergence of a new power structure.

In fact, from theoretical view point, each of these six varieties of political system may exist in any type of society. We can find that increased differentiation and specialization within sectors make the task of changing the basis of power more difficult, therefore to a large extent making exchange mechanisms between political control and sector control more likely. But it is possible that pre-industrial transformations will make the political control dominant even after increased differentiation.

**References**


1. Robert Lowie, *Social Organizations,* (London: Routledge & Kegan Paul, 1956).
2. Stanby H. Jr. Social structure Analysis' *International Encyclopaedia of Social Science, op. cit.* pp. 489-94
3. C. Kluckholar, Social structure.
4. Nadel S.F., *The Foundation of Social Anthropology,* (London: Cohen and West Ltd) 1958.
5. Warner, W. Lloyd & Lunt, Pauls, *The Social Life of a Modern Community,* (New Haven: Yale Univ. Press) 1965.
6. B. Malinowski, *A Scientific Theory of Culture and other Essays,* (Carolina: The Univ. of North Carolina Press) 1944.
7. R.S. Mann, Social structure, Social change and future Trends (Jaipur: Rawat Publication) 1979.
8. AR Radcliffe Brown, *Structure and Function in the Primitive Society,* (London-Cohen and West Limited) 1959.
9. Bernard Barber, IESS, *op, cit.,* p. 288-95.
10. Tolcott Parsons, *Politics and Social Structure* (New York: The Free Press 1969) pp. 15-16.
11. TC. Parsons, *op. cit,* p. 21.
12. TC. Parsons, *op. cit,* p. 317-18.
13. TC. Parsons, *op. cit,* p. 321.
14. TC. Parsons, *op. cit,* p. 322.
15. Joan Davies, *Social Mobility and Political Change* (London: Pall Mall; 1970) p. 97.
16. Joan Davies, *op. cit.* p. 98.
17. Joan Davies, *op. cit,* p. 100.

# Chapter - 8

# Political Modernization

## Development of Concept

Modernization is a peculiar form of societal development. It is not a new phenomenon, although the term was not used in the past as frequently as it is now. It was used more to discuss the introduction of new technology and new organization and less in regard to nations and social processes. The interest in new nations sparked the interest in the theory of modernization. Thus the concept was coined first. It provided a convenient vehicle by which sociologists and political scientists could return to problems and discussions on societal development which has been abandoned earlier, without at the same time creating a need to use the devaluated ideas connected with an earlier understanding of the process of development. In any case, modernization does not concern any organismic implications such as 'development' and growth' could have.

In sixties, a number of studies appeared propounding various retrospective and perspective theories on the process of modernization, announcing that modernization is actually ever present and everlasting, but that inspite of this fact, in some societies and under certain conditions, it does not proceed as fact as would be desirable. Conclusions from these works were meant to be instrumental in the formulation of prospective theories of development for new nations and more meant to generate politics which would accelerate the spread of modernization.

In conventional usage, "to modernize" means to "render" something old fashioned up-to-date or to reshape something out of date to suit the requirements of modern times. Thus people speak of modernization as characterizing all efforts to bring technology, ways of life, social organization, art, modes of production, and even fashion up-to-date. The scholarly understanding of the concept, however, does not necessarily correspond to this meaning. Thus, the problems of modernization are most often treated descriptively, and the concept is defined effectively and arbitrarily.

According to Marion Levy, Jr., modernization is a phenomenon that may appear in a more or less intensive form and that it is, therefore, graduable "A society will be considered more or less modernized, says Levy, "to the extent that its members are inanimate sources of power and/or use tools to multiply the effects of their efforts. Neither of these elements is either totally absent from or exclusively present in any society".[1] While he declares himself unable to suggest exact criteria by which to measure the continuum of modernization, Levy postulates that one can safely distinguish between the relatively modernized countries and those which have still a long way to go in this respect. He therefore, introduces a division of all societies into "relatively modernized" and the "relatively non-modernized".

It was only the last half century which witnessed the emergence of societies which (1) based their manufacturing technology to a greater extent on inanimate power than on animate power and where even the social organization is based on technical facilities, and which (2) in order to multiply the effects of their efforts apply such complex tools that considerable qualifications are required before working with them, and the slightest difference in a worker's skill may considerably lower or increase their productivity. Levy thus concludes that the existence of relatively modernized societies is a new phenomenon, especially characterstic of modern times.

Reinhard Bendix in his excellent essay entitled "Tradition and Modernity Reconsidered" give somewhat different set of assumptions. He points to the need for examining the development process, and the processes of modernization and industrialization as well, from the viewpoint of factors of timing and sequence. Because of these factors, he says, these processes are unique in every case; modernization cannot occur twice in the same way. We cannot expect the present processes of modernization to be analogous to the past ones, nor can we expect that the industrialization which usually accompanies modernization will have the same effects in the countries now being modernized as it had in the countries that were already industrialized sometime ago.

According to Bendix, a basic element in the definition of modernization is that it pertains to the kind of social changes which have occurred since the 18th century-changes which have led to political or economic "breakthroughs" in some pioneering societies and which have subsequently caused changes in follower societies. Thus, Bendix suggests that in the process of modernization there are always "advanced model countries" and "follower countries". In his opinion, when we speak of modernization, we usually mean the processes of social change similar to those which originated during the industrial revolution in England (1760-1830), and the political revolution in France (1789-1794). These processes transformed the two countries into "models" or "pace setter" countries, they were the most highly developed economically, socially, and politically. Other countries strove to catch up with these two; using every "short-cut" procedure they could think of. They were thus able to achieve the level of model country in much shorter time. Modernization has always consisted of internal changes in a country's economy and structure, but the internal changes have always been consequences of striving to attain the level of the model country. In all modernization processes, the government plays a particularly important role, since it initiates and stimulates modernization, obviously using different methods in different situations. Moreover, the greater the gap between the model and the follower country, the stronger the role played by the government in the process. Finally, the wide development of communications media puts a premium on education as a means of modernization, because it is more easily available than the capital required for modern technology.

In the opinion of other writers, modernization has to be viewed as essentially a process of sustained growth or development after the point of "take-off". At the same time, however, it was pointed out that a mere destruction of traditional cultures and structures does not automatically produce modernity, that new regimes which appeard sometimes with modern facades have to be embedded in societies which have retained many traditional qualities. Furthermore, although governments and regimes based upon such structures are unsuitable and shaky, there cannot be a return to the past. Finally, many writers recently pointed out that traditions continue to have a strong grip on societies, even after they have crossed the Rubicon to modernity. Especially they have the capacity to permeate the new culture and structure, and regenerate even after it seems that they have disappeared forever. In many Asian countries, tradition and modernity especially seem to be inseparable. Modernity embraces the cultural order, and the traditional culture permeates the new social and political structure, often exercising a strong impact on the function of the modern economy. Opinions, however, are divided on this point. Some experts think that even. though such societies are strongly rooted in the traditional order, they are non-the-less modern; others take the polar view, thereby arguing that modernity under such circumstances is only a facade.

David E. Apters' work contains a complex analysis of multitudious aspects and problems to both the theory and the practice of modernization. He has considered the topic on different levels of obstraction. Explorations of exemplary cases are built into the discussion. Thus he combines normative, behavioural, structural, and functional dimensions and allows one to look at the same issues simultaneously from diverse angles. Structure is treated dynamically as a process, and process as a permulation of one structure into another. Great importance is attributed to the impact of traditional culture on the attitude toward modernization, and diverse cases are examined which illustrate the problems. Finally, he introduced a typology of systems of political modernization as alternative instruments for inducing and promoting the transformation of modernizing societies. Thus he distinguishes the system of mobilization, reconciliation, theoretic and military oligarchy, and neo-merchantilism writing on the general nature of modernization, he observes:

> "Development, modernization, and industrialization, although related phenomena, can be placed in a decending order of generality. Development—the most general, results from the proliferation and integration of functional roles in a community. Modernization is a particular case of development. Modernization implies three conditions—a social system that can constantly innovate without falling apart (and that included among its essential beliefs the acceptability of change); differentiated, flexible social structures; and a social framework to provide the skills and knowledge necessary for living in a technologically advanced world. Industrialization, a special aspect of modernization, may be defined as the period in a society in which the strategic functional roles are related to manufacturing. It is possible to attempt the modernization of a given country without much industry, but it is not possible to industrialize without modernization.[2]

Thus the following instances of development can be distinguished: (a) Industrial modernization as development; (b) Non-industrial modernization, as development; (c) Premodernizational development. The application of these distinctions would allow us to treat modernization as a special, important instance of the development of societies, and instance where conscientious efforts are made to achieve higher chosen standards.[3]

When we speak of the modernization of new nations, it is to indicate those development processes or measures which are meant to transform these countries into up-to-date nations. Thus, modernization is not a self-sustaining evolutionary process progressing on its own. It is a striving to equalize one's own level of development with the most advanced and modern achievements of others. As Bendix has pointed out, there are always model and follower countries (or model and follower group) involved in this process. However, this is not a case of slavish copying, of the blind acceptance of achievements of somebody else, but an effort to achieve the desirable results in a way suited to ones own needs and conditions. What is even more important is that in the case of "following", the followers countries or groups often invent new, more efficient modes of action which allow them to out-run the previous pace-setter, as well as to establish new patterns of modernity, not necessarily in the same sphere as the previous leading country had established. This does not mean, however, that the process of modernization is sort of international race, or even an organized completion. Sometimes, it is a run for life, at other times, it is a mutual challenge. Yet in other cases, modernization is a striving for a better way to life.[4]

Thus modernization is a process, based upon the rational utilization of resources and aimes at the establishment of a "modern" society. A modern society is characterized, by the application of technology, which is reflected by wide-ranging control of the environment and the utilization of inanimate sources of energy, by extensive social interdependence, by urbanization, literacy, social and political mobilization, and a host of similar factors that are needed for development and growth. Popular identification with the history, territory, myths, and national identity of the state become reasonably effective. The old social units (tribe, caste, village) are subordinated to and not necessarily destroyed by the national community and lose many of their functions of social integration. In other words, the process of modernization undermines traditional society as inevitable part of change.[5] Dynamism, change, industrialization, independence, influence, power, internal unity; these are some of the attributes of modern societies sought by the political elites of the recently independent states. These elites seek to refashion old societies and to pattern the changes on the successful experience of a developed country.

## Political Modernization

We have seen that modernization, in the general social context, is a universal and complex phenomenon. Characterized by a core belief in rational and scientific control, it involves the systematic, sustained and purposeful application of human energies to the 'rational' control of man's physical and social environment for various human purposes. Benjawin Schwartz[6] describes it as the systematic, sustained, and powerful application of human energies to the rational control of man's physical and social environment for various human purposes.

Modernization stands for the transformation of the political culture in response to the changes in social and physical environments in view of this essential fact that political change "is intricately related to a wide spectrum of social and economic factors.[7] And to put it somewhat differently, modernization involves the diffusion of what one expert calls the "world culture" based on advanced technology and spirit of science, on a rational view of life, a secular approach to social relations, a feeling for justice in public affaris, and, above all else, on the acceptance in the political realm of the belief that the prime unit of the polity should be the nation-state. Whether introduced by external force, internal innovation, or conscious initiation, the world culture had made a strong impact on traditional ways of life.[8] Huntington thus describes it as "a multifaced process involving change in all areas of human thought and activity".[9]

Analytically speaking, modernization has been studied in three ways: (1) as a primarily economic phenomenon, bound up with the process of industrialization, (2) as a series of interconnected social and psychological changes that alter both traditional patterns of behaviour and individuals, perception; and (3) a variety of political changes, such as the differentiation of new political structures, induced political participation, the growth of nationalism, and so on. Of course, no sweeping revolution can be so readily compartmentalized; the economic, social, and political changes are intertwined, perhaps mutually reinforcing. These specific aspects of change and development, however, for the analytical purpose, are taken to represent specific forum of general modernization. Parallel to other forms of social change, political aspects of modernization involve the development of an institutional framework that its sufficiently flexible and powerful to meet the demands placed upon it. In short, the government must become fully capable of performing a wide variety of duties. Its capacities must increase, so that change can be accommodated within political channels. Political modernization is linked with economic growth and with social and psychological changes for the obvious reason that the capacity of a government to deal with demands is affected by economic and cultural factors. In fact, the process of political modernization involves three characteristics: (1) an increased centralization of power in the state, coupled with the weakening of traditional sources of authority, (2) the differentiation and specialization of political institution; and (3) increased popular participation in politics, and greater identification of individuals with the political system as a whole.[10]

A modernized political system is highly complicated. Political modernization multiplies the volume, range, and efficiency of official decisions. In order to meet the complex tasks placed upon them, the organs of government become "highly differentiated" and "functionally specific". Thus change is preceded by a gradual shift in the locus of power and authority. The traditional elite who included power on the besis of their hereditary position gradually lose their position and authority. Religious, traditional, familial and ethnic authorities are substituted by a single, secular, national political authority. The most important implications of political modernization can be explained in the context of political attitudes and behaviour. With a significant shift in political attitudes of individuals and groups, the nature and scale of political participation also alters. Widespread awareness of and participation in national politics characterizes a modern society. The participation comes in part through the growth of political parties and interest groups. Traditional social institutions, such as caste, are subtly transformed into vehicles of participation in political process. The result is that a society in which popular identification with the state as a whole—its history, territory, myths, and national identity-tends to supplant identification with traditional social units. The process of detachment from traditionalism does not imply that traditional social relations disappear. Particularism is not confined to the traditional societies of the Third World alone it is a universal phenomenon. But a fundamental distinction exists between systems in which local affiliations tend to define the most enduring political relationship for the bulk of the population, and the political systems in which individuals share a distinct loyalty to the system as a whole. As Edward Shils observes:

> "The constituent societies on which the new states rest are taken separately, not civil societies, and taken together, they certainly do not form a single society...Affirmative attitude towards rules, persons, and actions is necessary for consensus. They are the constellations of kinship groups, castes, tribes,

> feudalities-even smaller territorial societies-but they are not civil societies. The sense of identity is rudimentary, even where it exists. The sense of membership in a nation-wide society, and the disposition to accept the legitimacy of the government, its personnel, and its laws are not great. Society-wide institutions, other than the state are scant in (such) societies.[11]

Political implications of modernization is sometimes paradoxial. It has been observed that social change and participation may increase rather than diminish the scope and intensity of communal conflicts. It has been assumed that the erosion of traditional values through widened scope of social mobility, urbanization, literacy etc., entails a corresponding development of modern values. The process shows many more complexities, however. The inclusion of new values require two steps: (1) the weakening of long standing norms of social conduct through the uprooting of old social settings, values, norms, habits and commitment, and (2) the induction of individuals into relatively stable new patterns of group membership, organization, and commitment. But the result of social change may be revival and expansion of communal solidarity rather than an integration of diverse groups. Increased consciousness of group antagonism and cultural differences—not increased sentiments of national unity can be the initial result of modernization.

In Ceylone, for example, the replacement of ethnic by national loyalties was further away in 1961 than a decade earlier. Modernization increased the tensions between the Sinhalese speaking and Tamil-speaking ethinic groups, the unifying purpose of the independence struggle faded away, leaving behind a host of contradictions and cleavages. A somewhat similar trend has been observed in India when the big urban and industrial centres have exhibited the sign of growing communal tension among the major ethnic and linguistic groups. Political modernization, despite these inherent paradoxes of social change, tends to uproot old social settings, values, norms, and commitments. Although traditional values of solidarity may be weakened, they are likely to continue affecting political loyalties. Although social change does not directly or automatically lead to a deeply implanted sense of national identity, yet political modernization in the long run tends to promote, if accompanied by parallel conditions of social change, the process of national integration.

The reason for the persistence of primordial sentiments is relatively simple. An individual's perceptions and loyalties are shaped substantially during his childhood and adolescence through the process of socialization. Cultural change in new states has not yet brought a substantial change in long standing patterns of socialization for the majority of the populations. A child born in Western Nigeria, for example, will in all probability grow up speaking the Yoruba language; time bound folk tales and legends will inculcate in him a sense of Yoruba cultural identity; in a conflict pitting Yoruba against members of another tribe, he will be advised to support his ethnic 'brothers'. In short, this child will come to show the outlook, characteristic of his own ethnic group.

Lucian W. Pye bases much of his analysis of Burma's political oscillations upon family relationships that appear to produce an old combination of optimism and distrust, a combination which in varying degrees seems to be present in many transitional societies having difficulties in modernizing. These deeply expect a drastic change in social attitudes without transformations of the pattern of socialization. Hence, for the overwhelming proportion of the inhabitants of recently independent states, the attitudes implanted in childhood—the stress upon group solidarity in particular—continue to influence social and political action. Thus one of the pre-requiste conditions of political modernization is the transformation of cultural conditions, especially in the context of the normative mechanisms of early socialization, so as to create a framework of social solidarity coupled with national identity.

Obviously in African and Asian countries where conscious efforts for development have initiated the process of social and political change, the inadequate measures to replace the old mechanisms of socialization have tended to affect the nature and scale of political modernization. In this context, reply to two crucial questions is needed: *First* in what degrees the groups are receptive of social change and which are the groups posing obstacle to modernization; and *Second,* assuming that a hightened sense of national identity characterises that modernization might not an arouse a sense of communal identity within a particular region in resisting the efforts to arouse a global sense of national identity. As Welch observes: "The first question is relatively simple. Societies differ in their speed and care in adaptation; many of the distinctions among societies can be traced back to the nature of traditional beliefs, particularly the acceptance of change. But in almost all societies, the pains of transition can be eased by the proper utilization of tradition. The second question leads to the complex problem of social and political integration. Primordial sentiments do not appear overnight, but rather after a long and often acrimonious period of transition. The authoritarian and single party regimes in many new states draw their raison d'etre from persistent group loyalties. Until a sense of identity with the state as a whole—not merely with one's group—becomes widespread, ordered patterns of change are unlikely.[12]

We find, from the foregoing discussion that political modernization, as examined from the various angles is a comprehensive term which includes much with the ambit of politics, that is generally taken to cover the realms of economics, sociology, and even psychology. It refers to the change in political culture and political institutions as a result of the process of modernization-"that is everything like economic growth, increase of gross national product and per capita income, economic planning, greater industrialization accumulation of capital, increasing urbanization and a reduction in the proportion of those engaged in agriculture, scientific activity, improved transport and higher rate of literacy. The take off point for economic growth often occurs when agriculture claims less than five percent of the working population. From the economic point of view an implicit assumption is that economic and technological growth and increased consumption is inherently desirable.

Modernization is a mulifaceted process, and for this reason, political modernization is a concept having several dimensions as:

1. At the psychological level, it involves a change in the norms values attitudes, and orientations of people.

2. At the intellectual level, it involves a tremendous expansion of man's knowledge about his environment and the diffusion of this knowledge throughout the society.
3. At the demographic level, it implies improvement in the standards of living and progress towards the mobility of people and urbanization.
4. At the social level, it has tendency to replace the focus of individuals loyalty to family and other primary groups to voluntarily organized secondary associations.
5. At the economic level, it involves the growth of market agriculture, improvement in commerce at the expense of agriculture, development of industrialization and the wandering of economic activity, and
6. At the political level, a significant increase in the intensity and scale of the functioning of political structure and institutions as well as transformation of the bases of political attitudes, orientation and behaviour in terms of a system of new values that characterize the modern society.

Thus political modernization is to be treated as both a cause and a consequence of the genernal process of social modernization. It is to be regarded as a natural and inevitable culmination of the changes brought forth in the field of economic development mainly in the direction of industrialization and material advancement, changes in the nature and content of the political system, and also changes in the social and cultural spheres of life.

### Political Dimensions of Social Mobilization

Social mobilization refers, in the ultimate analysis, to a process of change, which happens to substantial parts of the population in the societies which show the sign of shifting from traditional to modern ways of living. It denotes a concept which brackets together a number of more specific processes of change, such as changes of residence, of occupation, of social setting of face to face association, of institutions, roles and ways of acting of experiences and expectations, and finally of personal memories, habits and needs, including the need for new patterns of group affiliation and new images of personal identity.[13] Needless to say that these changes through their cumulative impact tend to influence and sometimes transform political behaviour.

The term social mobilization does not merely imply a collection of changes which can be of different nature and occurring at different levels. It basically implies that these processes tend to go together in certain historical situations and stages of economic development, that these situations are identifiable and recurrent, in their essentials, from one century to another, and that they are relevant for political behaviour. It essentially implies that something is happening to large number of people in areas which undergo modernization, i.e. where advanced, non-traditional practices in culture, technology and economic life are introduced, and accepted on a considerable scale. It is however not identical to the process of modernization as a whole, but it deals with one of its major aspects, or better, with a recurrent cluster among its consequences. These consequences once they occur on a substantial scale, indulgence in turn the further process of modernization. Thus what can be treated for a short time span as a consequence of the modernization process, appears over a larger period as one of its continuing aspects and as a significant cause, in the well known pattern of feedback or circular causation. Thus viewed over a longer perspective, the concept of social mobilization suggests that several of the changes subsumed under it will tend to go together in terms of recurrent association. For example, any of the firms of social mobilization such as the entry into market relations and a money economy can be expected to be accompanied or followed by a significant rise in the frequency of impersonal contacts, or in the exposure to mass media of communication, or in changes of residence or in political or quasi-political participation. The implication of the concept is thus to assert an empirical fact—that of significantly frequent association which can be tested empirically.

In fact, social mobilization refers to a process by which major clusters of old social, economic, and psychological commitments are eroded or broken and people become available for new patterns of socialization and behaviour.[14] Thus the following points may be taken into consideration:

(i) Mobilization is taken to mean a process by which is induced not a mere state or level which can be worked out either from 'hard' objective indices, or simply abstracted from subjective notions like participation, levels of cognition, etc. These latter are treated as second order consequences here. Ideally the most fruitful way of measuring relative states of mobilization through time, or between different societies, would be by use of reference group theory within an action framework. Thus the whole concept of mobilization is related in its comparative or measurable aspects to the notion of substantial changes in defining new references for identifying different sections of population, as well as to the success of an elite in forcing acceptance of its new reference groups, both normative and comparative.

(ii) Social mobilization can also be analysed as a function in terms of the social system. In this context, it can be understood in its manifest and latest forms so as to fit the function of political mobilization into the broader political function of goal attainment.

(iii) The concept is neutral with regard to purpose. It is not always necessary to classify different experiences of mobilization at different times in accordance with any latent or declared purpose. Our main concern in defining it is more with the instrumental process in relation to the existential goals and values than with any overall assessment of the normative or ethical purposes of mobilization.

(iv) It is necessary, in any case, to define what is involved in the process of mobilization. It is essentially (1) attitudinal—a commitment to action, and (2) a means of translating this commitment into action or observed behaviour. This is a composite process involving different stages:

(a) the existence of values and goals requiring mobilization.
(b) action on the part of leaders, elites or insitutions seeking to mobilize individuals and groups.
(c) the institutional and collective means of achieving the mobilization.
(d) the symbols and references by which values, goals, and norms are communicated to, and understood and internalized by, the individuals involved in mobilization.
(e) the process by which mobilization takes place in terms of individual interaction, the creative and change of

collectivities and structures, the crystallization of roles, the effect on sub-systems and their boundaries.

(f) estimates of the numbers and people (or proportion of a population) mobilized and the degree of such mobilization for different sectors or strata of the population.

Edward Shils has pointed out that images of mobilization and of Mannheim's "fundamental democratization imply two distinct images of the process; (1) the stage of uprooting are breaking away from old settings, habits and commitments, and (2) the induction of mobilized persons into some relatively stable new patterns of group membership, organization and commitment. In this fashion soldiers are mobilized from their homes and families and integrated into the army which they serve. Similarly, Mannhiem suggests an image of large numbers of people moving away from a life of local isolation, traditionalism and political apathy, and moving into a different life or broader and deeper involvement in the vast complexities of modern life, including potential and actual involvement in mass politics.

Social mobilization as defined above, can be related to political theory. For this, it will be necessary to bring it into a form in which it can be verified by evidence, and to develop the problem to a point where the question "how" can be supplemented usefully by the question "how much". In its intrusive form, the concept of social mobilization already carried with it some images of growing numbers and rising curves. In so far as the constituent process of social mobilization can be measured and described quantitatively in terms of such curves, it may be interesting to learn how fast the curves rise, whether they show any turning points, or whether they cross any thresholds beyond which the process they depict have different side effects from those that went before. Notable among these side effects are any that bear on the performance of political systems and upon the stability and capacities of governments.[15]

The impact of social mobilization can be observed, among other things, on India's hierarchical social and political system. Weiner has observed that social changes accompanying modernization are facilitating the development and not the diminition of community interest in politics. The number of caste, religions, tribal, linguistic and ethnic associations is likely to continue to increase as the rate of social change increases, or even if it stays the same. These communty interests may not exist at precisely traditional level of fragmentation or cleavage. Social mobilization in India is not likely to lead to homogeneity, but it already seems to have aggregated some small groups of somewhat greater size. Social mobilization, therefore, does not necessarily freeze the traditional system at the pre-existing level of social cleavage. It may reinvigorate a social cleavage at a high level of interest aggregation.[16]

Jyotindra Das Gupta has observed that the language association of contemporary India have grown as a part of Indian political system. The associations have promoted social mobilization in their own language through literacy and linguistic modernization. Languages have provided for three associations, a way of binding people drawn from narrow occupational or local group loyalties into wider regional linguistic frameworks. These associations have also used modern organizational methods of political recruitment and socialization. The politics of language association in India, in short, illustrates the twin aspects of the effects of social mobilization on national integration. On the one hand, groups that shared cultural characteristics and language were able to put aside minor parochial differences and form a larger aggregate. But at this higher, albeit sub-nation state, level of aggregation and cleavage in the traditional system, social mobilization reinforced the divisions with other cultural and linguistic aggregations in India.[17]

We cannot, however, conclude, from the forgoing discussion that social mobilization invariably promotes national disintegration wherever there is differentiation by language or caste, or colour. In a hierarchical system of ethnic or linguistic stratification, with an agglomerative political culture, it is likely that social mobilization will not have disintegrating effects if the political culture of the system prior to the beginning of social mobilization did not legitimate ascriptive group political action. A hierarchical ethnic system includes the acquiscence by the social subordinates to the norm that more honour occurs rightfully to social superiors. An agglomerative political culture, moreover, has institutionalized patterns of social mobility over a long period of time. A long term pattern of individual mobility renders new ethnic group political behaviour by the social subordinated illegitimate and practically impossible. Social mobilization by itself does not automatically create ethnic group organizational capabilities. The social mobilization hypothesis done is insufficient to predict the probable political outcome. It is also necessary to specify the prior context and experiences of ethnic group political behaviour.

Morner and Pitt Rivers have emphasized in their study of the historical development of Latin America, a hierarchical ethnic system, an agglomerative political culture, and individual mobility. When social mobilization came, social sub-ordinates did not organize politically as groups. Social mobilization opened new channels for individual change and this reinforce, rather than changed, the pre-existing pattern. This can be examined in the following figure that illustrates Latin America position in comparative perspective.

| *Ascriptive Culture* | *Political Culture* | *Mobility Pattern* |
|---|---|---|
| Parallel (Belgium, Lebanon, Canada, Nigeria) | | |
| Hierarchical | Assimilative (United States, Liberia, Southern Africa) | |
| | | Group (India) |
| | Agglomerative | Individual (Latin America) |

*Source*: Samuel A. Huntington and Jorge I. Domingnez, *Political Development in Macro-political theory* by Fred I. Greenstein and N.W. Polsby, *op. cit.* p. 70.

It has been also found that individual mobility and social mobilization do not disrupt the traditional system. They reinforce it. The normative justification for the persistence of inequality has not been shaken, while new avenues for personal mobility have been opened. It does not follow, therefore, that the mere existence of social difference indicates the existence of drastically different cultures within a country or that social inequality leads automatically to violence. Brazil had a single shared culture for blacks and whites, which includes the recognition that blacks and whites are unequal and that individual upward mobility permissible and desirable—requires cultural 'whitening', while downward mobility leads to cultural blackening. This common egalitarian and normatively justified culture has been reinforced by social mobilization.[18]

It has been further empirically demonstrated that social mobilization, though closely associated with political variables, does not automatically lead to long-range implications for politics. A more automatic relationship appears in parallel ethnic systems or in those hierarchical ethnic systems with political culture that legitimize ethnic, caste, or religious group behaviour. But wherever these traditional legitimizing features have been lacking, the political effects of social mobilization on ethnicity are minor. And where the coercive power of the state is put at service of radical assimilation/exclusion policies, the dominant groups continue to rule. For example, in Latin America, dominant ascriptive social strata rule with little apparent cost, but also in the presence of considerable political, social, economic, and personal costs in order to freeze an ethnically immobile system with an uncertain long-term future.

In fact, there are only three processes of systematic long-term social mobilization en masse; military, religious, and political. Since all three fulfil broadly similar functions in creating community, they have much in common. For one thing, they all relate people tightly together in a distinct and often novel form, by evolving particular structures and by giving people common goals and references groups. In doing so, mobilization process either substitutes new priorities for previous ones, or creates conscious priorities on a general scale for the first time, where it did not exist previously.

Question arises as to how political mobilization differs from other form of mobilization and from the notion of social mobilization generally. One possibility is to analyse the problem in terms of sub-systems; politics is one normative integration, economic activity and kinship relations are others. We can measure their interaction in terms of changing range and density; thus we may often find in system predominant at any one time (dominant:

religion during the reformation, kinship in primitive societies, economic in communist societies)—the phase model. A second possibility is to introduce politics at an upper stage of the progression of value-addition in forms of collective behaviour. But norms and value-oriented movements have largely political reference, though they do not necessarily exhaust themselves exclusively in political action at the level they become past of societies goal-attainment function. The moment we are dealing with norms and beyond, we are also dealing with norm or decision-making machinery and are therefore in politics.

A third version-which can be treated as a logical extension of the latter alternative, is simply to define political context narrowly or broadly (change of policy, change of policy-making personnel or structures, change of value components of structure) and to take that part of any given social action, or any social situation for that matter. This really implies a completely different definition of politics-in terms of authority roles or actions concerned with the exercise of power. Such a definition approximates most closely to Lasswell and Kaplan definition of politics or Dahrendorff's model of society. The political process now becomes a component of social action all the way through the hierarchy from values down to individual roles. In one sense, it is probably the most satisfactory method since it avoids arbitrary and brittle classifications of process and action. However, it suffers from the grave disadvantage that it makes the political component of action or situations almost impossible to isolate. Comparison becomes very difficult and comparison in terms of change is the pre-requsite of the analysis of political and mobilization.

The second method of analysing political mobilization in accordance with the scale and level of its societal impact is most easily related to constitutional or elitist political cultures. In a strongly constitutional polity, norm oriented attack on, as well as defense of, the existing rules of the game will quickly reach the limits of the normatively possible if it carries sufficient impetus oscillation to value-orientation will be manifest and dramatic. This is because constitutional societies tend to incorporate their formal structures into their perspective ideology, and into the general definition of this given situation. Malfunctioning is therefore rapidly and closely identified with constitutions; any part is held to be functionally dependent on the whole and both antipathetic political action as well as sympathetic assertion oscillate easily to value orientation. We see this clearly in countries like France, German, and Italy, in new democracies like Nigeria and Turkey and in United States. In Apter's definition, all these are consummatory cultures as far as the dimension of their major political institutions is concerned.

In earliest societies, by contrast, conflict over norms encompasses a much larger but more self-contained areas. Escalation is more difficult, because the institutional structure of the polity is porous, flexible and in the last resort expendible we have this situation primarily in Britain and the Soviet Union, to a lesser extent in past war Germany and Japan; among the newer countries in Pakistan and Indonesia. On the constitutional dimension, these are thus relatively instrumental political cultures. Perhaps it should be emphasized that the issue here is the social possibility for antipathetic normative movements to escalate into value oriented ones, not the functional instrumentality or structural conduciveness for mobilization offered by elitist or constitutional politics.[19]

India, Switzerland, and Sweden, with composite cultures, represent a relatively difficult case. In India, it can hardly be indicated that this or that kind of cultural orientation will prevail in the polity. Is the structure independent of, or indifferent to, those presently managing it? Is congress a stable party or an unsufficiently differentiated womb for the Indian political universe? Can antipathetic political mobilization be contained in a struggle for norms, however acute (which might include the transformation of the political and institutional structure of, or will it escalate to engulf the very existence of the Indian Union? A substantial amount of the evidence regarding form oriented mobilization and counter mobilization in India has accumulated as a result of the issue of linguistic states. Between the decision of Bombay state into new linguistic states in 1956, and the similar decision of the Punjab in 1966, there has been regular and highly organized rioting of the traditional collective behaviour type. At times, it has escaped the control of the authorities, who in the whole have maintained that each new linguistic state must be the last. Yet these severe challenges have so far been contained at a norm-oriented level, often even at a collectively level; partly by concessions, partly by the ready collapse or deflation of the movements after a short while. The gloomier predictions for India have yet come to pass-though the resistence and authority of Mrs Gandhi's government seemed severely shaken by the end of 1966.[20]

It follows, from the foregoing discussion, that it would be useful to consider the nature of mobilization in the context of the four basic components of the social hierarchy-roles, collectivities, norms and values. To some extent, this is a simple progression, as we have observed herein before. Mobilizing people makes then either into a mode (if non-institutional but based on some general belief) or a collectivity by coercion (if institutional but not based on a general belief; press-gangs, enforced savings, etc.) Mobilizing people plus norms equals the minimum of political action. Mobilizing people plus values might be called a revolution or, if institutionally induced, a mobilized nation-at-arms. But in real life, things are not often as simple as this. No doubt social and political action increases in scope and intensity as issues move from the lowest level of roles of antipathy or support for norms or even values. But the effect we have already described as compression or short-circuiting prevents these components from being simple alternatives or even additives. The mobilization of collectivities (or conversely their identification as social and political obstacles to mobilization) need not end with escalation to the next highest category on our scale of norm-oriented action. In elitist societies, antipathy to individuals is often a sign and means of escalation from normative pre-occupations to value-oriented ones: individuals may become the symbol of norm-oriented change.

**References**

1. Marion Levy. Jr., *Modernization and Structure of Socieites,* (Princeton: Princeton University Press 1966) vol. I, p. 35.
2. David Apter, *The Politics of Modernization, op. cit.* p. 67-92.
3. Szymon Chodak, Sociental Development (New York: Oxford Univ. Press. 1973).
4. *Ibid,* p. 257.
5. Clawde E. Welch, Jr., *Political Modernization* (Belmont; Calif: Wadsworth Publishing company, 1971).

6. Benjawin Schwartz quoted in Maries B. Jansen, (ed), *Changing Japanese Attitudes towards, modernization* (Princeton: Princeton University. Press 1965) pp. 23-24.
7. Morton R. Davis and Vaughan Lewis: *Models of Political system* (Delhi, Vikas (1979) p. 93.
8. Welch, *op. cit.* p. 4.
9. S.P. Huntington, cited in S.P. Verma, Modern Political Theory (Delhi, Vikas: 1965; p. 303).
10. Welch, *op. cit.* p. 7.
11. Edward Shils, "On the comparative study of the New States" in Clifford Gleertz (ed). *Old Societies and New States: The quest for Modernity in Asia and Africa,* New York: Free Press of Glencoe, 1963) p. 22.
12. Welch. *op. cit.* p. 13.
13. Karl W. Deutch, "Social Mobilization and Political Development" in Jason L. Finkle and Richare W. Gable, *Political Development and Social Change,* (New York: John Wiley & Sons Inc., 1966) p.2-5-26.
14. Karl Deutch observes "Other things assumed equal, the stage of rapid social mobilization may be expected, therefore to promote the consolidation of states whose people already show the same language, culture, and major social institutions: whose population is already divided into several groups with different languages or cultures or basic ways of life," *Nationalism and National Development: An Inter-disciplinary Bibliography,* Cambridge, Mass: MIT Press, 1970; also see his Social Mobilization and Political Development in, *American Political Science Review,* 55: 453-514
15. Karl Dentch, *op. cit.*
16. Myron Weiner, *Politics of Scarcity: Public Pressure and Political Response in India,* (Chicago Univ. Press. 1962)
17. Jyotindra Das Gupta, *Language Conflict and National Development, Group Politics and National Lanugage Policy in India* (Berkely: University of California Press; 1970).
18. Samuel P. Huntington & Dominguex, *op.cit.* p. 70.
19. J.P. Nettls, *Political Mobilization: A Sociological Analysis of Methods and Concepts* (London: Faber Ltd, 1967)
20. Selig H. Marrison, *India; The Most Dangerous Decades,* (Princeton, 1960).

# Chapter - 9

# Social Dimensions of Nation-Building

## Nation-Growth

Nation-Building constitutes one of the most challenging areas of study in political sociology. Its importance can be understood in the light of the fact that nearly fifty percent of the countries of the world today have attained their independence and sovereignty only during last three decades and that they are supposed to be engaged in the crucial task of nation-building. These countries are engaged in a form of social change involving social mobilization for national growth as well as political development which together have offered a vast field of research and grist for the social scientists' mill. But before we proceed to analyse social dimensions of this crucial task of the new nation-states, we should be clear about the key-concepts, which will be frequently referred to our discussion.

For the purpose of distinguishing a nation, we can rely on the postulates developed by Karl Deutch who has defined a nation as any seizeable population or group of persons which can be called:

(i) Independent, in the sense that it is not ruled by outside;
(ii) Cohesive, by virtue of its markedly more effective habits of easy and varied social communication and cooperation, compared with their corresponding capabilities and motivations for communication and cooperation with outsiders;

(iii) Politically organized, in the sense that it provides a constituency for a government which exercises effective rule within it;

(iv) Autonomous, in the sense that it accords to this government such acclaim, consent, compliance, and support, as to make its rule effective; and

(v) Internally legitimate, in the sense that its habits of compliance with and support for the government or, atleast, toward mutual political cooperation and memberships in the nation, are connected with broader beliefs about the universe and about their own nature, personalities, and culture that their support for the nation, even in terms of adversity is likely and thus ensures its endurance.[1]

The concept of nation-growth is an organismic area used in order to refer to the historical process through which the present nation-state system evolved in the west. The image portrayed by the concept of "nation-growth" is often interpreted to suggest an organismic change, depicting the growth of a living thing that cannot be dissected without injuring or killing it and, moreover, a growth process that is expected to pass through certain fixed intervals of time and through certain fixed qualitative stages toward a maturity the form of which is unknown, and beyond which they are only decline and death or reproduction which starts a new, but essentially identical cycle. Usually this concept is used to describe the relevant historical process in retrospect.

**Nation-Building**

When many historians speak of the 'growth of nations" a good many of the present day statesmen and policy-oriented social scientists speak of "nation-building". As opposed to the organismic concept of "nation growth", the concept of "nation-building" is a voluntaristic and architectoric or mechanical one. The implication is that as a house can be built from timbers, bricks, and mortar, in different patterns, quickly or slowly, through different sequences of assembly, in partial independences from its setting, and according to the choices, will and power of its builders, so a nation can be built according to different places, from various materials, rapidly or gradually by different sequences of steps, and impartial independence from its environment. The most frequent use of this concept is in recent liberation dealing with the political process of the new nations of Asia, Africa, and Latin America.[2]

While dealing with the trends of nation-building in the newly independent states, one has to keep in mind that the scholars in the field have offered two types of perspectives: descriptive or analytic, and prescriptive and recommendary. Based upon several methodological assumptions, the descriptive approach has been presented to describe, and analyse and interpret the nation-building activity that is going on in new nations of Asia, Africa, and Latin America. And the prescriptive approach, based upon several normative assumptions, is meant to suggest, prescribe and recommend what the scholars consider as best to be done to make the nation-building activity in the new nations a success. The two approaches, notwithstanding their differences in terms of methodological emphasis, view nation-building as a process of socio-economic and political mobilization on the basis of a well-planned and well-coordinated set of voluntaristic activities.

## Focus on Activity

Nation-growth in the west, and nation-building in the *nonveau monde* has been viewed differently for obvious reasons. Karl Deutsch has observed:

> "Where in the past the formation and rise of nations were merely observed by scholars, today statesmen and voters increasingly want to do something about the process. They may want to establish or strengthen some national political entity of their own, or to emerge it with or separate it from other such entity. Or they may wish to strengthen, weaker, or otherwise change some other national political entity so as to promote values and interests of their own".[3]

Nation-building thus involves a set of important activity aimed at breaking up old empires, building new nations, and establishing new federations and communities. People and nations are not left as they were found by the statesmen and voters. The expansion of communication networks and trade transactions, cultural contacts, technological innovations, and the overall impact of modernization on moving people out of their villages and traditions into a new world of mobility, insecurity, shortage of commodities, and the need for more and more governmental services. Formal and informal political participation getting intensified day by day is the common experience all around. This approach of social mobilization makes the new states harder to govern by their own traditional elites in their own traditional says, and still harder to govern by foreigners from abroad.

Not only does this nation-building activity centre around insistence upon self-rule and resistence to foreign rule, but it also implies a quest for self discovery. Just as finding the size for any state at which it will be cohesive and stable, is in part a process of historical trial and error, so does the art of nation-building in the new states depend on the art of 'nation-limiting'. This is to say, if the nations-in creation are to be large enough to be economically viable, they should be small enough to be governed effectively by a government close to the people, responsible to popular needs, and sustained by popular support.[4]

Recent scholars in social science have to their credit discovered that the breaking and making of nations is a process, that is now occurring in most parts of the world, and that is a process that must be studied in its general and uniform aspects, specially if the unique features of each country and epoch are eventually to be understood better than they have so far. The key questions deemed to be asked in such an endeavour to understand the nations-building process are how and when do nations come into existence, how and when do they pass away, and how and when can men decide the outcome of their own actions? And much more pertinent are also the questions how and when do nations break away from larger political units, and how do they triumph over smaller units, such as tribes, castes, or local states, and more or less integrate them into the political body of nation?

**Descriptive Approach**

A number of studies on the nation-building process in the new states endeavour to produce model for describing, analysing and interpreting what is going on in those states. A general trend of all such studies is to focus upon aspects that are common to all the new nations. The two such common aspects focussed our attention into the common background and the common challenge of the new states.

Colonial subjugation, new sovereignity, and elite culture are often referred to as the elements constituting the common background of the new states. Occasionally cultural traditionality and technological backward ties are adduced to form this common background. It is held that it was only in a response to this common experience of being subjugated to and exploited by foreign rulers that nationalism started developing in these new states.

Rupert Emerson has observed that, the colonialist subjugation evoked three distinctive responses from the subjects state and that too in three successive phases. The first reaction of the peoples defence of the existing order, stirred, of course, by a drive for self survival. The next phase was a serving in the direction of an uncritical self-humiliation and acceptance of alien superiority. And the third phase, was, in the typical fashion of the Hegelian dialectics, a nationalist synthesis in which there was an assertion or re-assertion of a community with pride in itself and in its past, but still looking, atleast as far as its leaders were concerned, in the direction of modernization and westernization.[5] It was only a historical irony that imperialism forged the tools with which its victims could pry it loose. Thus again to quote Emerson himself "through global conquest the dominant western powers worked to reshape the world in their own image and this roused against themselves the forces of nationalism which are both the bitterest enemies of imperialism and, reversely, its finest fruit".[6] It was only after 1945 that new states could attain their sovereignty before the eyes of the world. As they have all been, until recently colonial territories were otherwise less than wholly governing, the very novelty of their sovereignty defines them all as new states. Thus, this novelty of sovereignty too is as common an experience for the states as colonial subjugation and imperial rule.

According to Shils, the above minimal unformity of situation and the common experience of being ruled by Western metropolitan powers and of seeking to free themselves of that rule, carry with them a number of attendent phenomena. For one thing, the constellation of common situation and common experience—and, to some extent, the awareness of this communality of situation and experience has generated a more or less common outlook too among the new states. To some extent, these together have defined the major tasks of the new states, and these tasks have far-reaching ramifications which are in many ways similar from state to state.[7]

### (a) Elite-Culture

The next element constituting the common background of the states is what can be called the elite-culture. In nearly all the new states, the governing elite has received a modern education and that too, often to a high level. More often than not, that education has been metropolitan in its source, and modern in its content, and the leaders would, in their turn, like to give a similar education to their people. But in contrast with leaders, the mass of the population has usually received no formal modern education whatsoever. Besides, majority of the masses continue to remain in a state of illiteracy and ignorance. As a result of this, the exposition of an elite educated in a tradition of exogenous inspiration and a mass rooted in a variety of indigenous cultures engenders problems that crop up throughout the world of the new states. For one thing, the elites are almost always nationalistic. In most of the new states, the ruling elites and their rivals still belong to the generation that conducted the agitation for independence from the foreign colonial powers. They are concerned not merely with self-rule, but also simultaneously to elevate the dignity of their traditional culture and their standing in the world. Further, it is also usual for them to wish to have, for the sake of attaining cultural modernity and economic progress, a modern culture diffused through the medium of a modern educational system running from the early years up to the university level.[8]

### (b) Cultural Traditionality

The culture of the new states is by and large, traditional, in the sense of having (i) a predominantly aggrarian society (ii) mostly village communities, (iii) highly stratified social life, (iv) static and passive attitudes, and (v) generally a tradition of autocratic government. Peter Merkl's characterization of the static nature of a traditional society is remarkable. He observes:

"Visible change form generation to generation is so small as to encourage the belief that given forms of social, economic or political relations are God—given and natural. A thick crust of custom builds up over many generations and provides a restrictive setting into which a person is born and which he will probably not transcend in his life time. Sons knew that they will never grow beyond the relation of their father. Women and inferior classes know their places in society and nourish no hopes of emancipation. An air of totalism pervades the whole culture, often sublimated in religions that place no value on material achievements and promise rewards only in a life after death.[9]

In the traditional society, people are born and brought up with a 'constructive self' never able to imagine to be or do anything other than what one is. Change is not only impossible, but is also an evil.[10]

**(c) Technological Backgroundness**

The new states are also in common marked by technological backwardness and the absence of large scale industrialization as compared to their older counterparts. Technology, in simple terms is the science of tool making. It is "a systematic, disciplined approach to objectives, using a calculus of precision and measurement and a concept of system.[11] Not only has recognition been given to the fact that human culture is dependent on its technological foundations, but it is also being accepted that man is a technical animal, and that technological change is the fundamental factor in human evolution.[12]

Due to several historical reasons, the Industrial Revolution and its rewards-growing supplies of land, labour, capital, organizing ability and big machine, all leading to sustained economic growth have remained the privileges of the west. The new states were-and still are greater deprived of industrialization and technological evolutions and this deprivation too constitutes an element to the common background of the new states. Thus colonial subjugation, new sovereignty, elite culture, cultural traditionality, and technological backwardness all gave an air of likeness and similarity to the new states.[13]

## Common Challenges

The new states, characterized by a common background, had to face a number of common or similar challenges. Atleast five such-challenges have been identified by scholars in the field. They concern the creation of (a) an effective government, (b) a modern economic system, (c) cultural modernity, (d) a national language, and (e) national integration. We can deal with these points separately as under:

### (a) Effective Government

The founding statesmen of the newly born countries, had to face, in varying degrees, the problem of establishing an effective government and staffing it with the indigeneous personnel. This problem has essentially two dimensions. On the one hand, the ruling elite have confronted the necessity of legitimizing themselves before the people. On the other hand, they all have also to accept the task of organizing and maintaining a political apparatus, that is, a rationally conducted administration, a cadre of leaders grouped in the public form of a party system, and a machinery of public order. Their task is made more difficult by the fact that the establishing of an effective government has to be done in the context of a traditional society or more frequently, in the context of a plurality of traditional societies.

### (b) Modern Economic System

The new states have all sprung up from traditional societies with an economy which is predominantly based on agricultural production. Such economy, employing traditional techniques of cultivation, is an impoverished one by contemporary standards of material well being. The elites in new states set their ambition on creating a new, modern, economic system to replace the inherited one. The task involved the development of the new economic institutions and techniques and persuading or coercing the ordinary members of the society into their acceptance. In fact, this way the imperative of building a modern economic system which could be possible and when (a) the basic economic structure has been established and remained relatively stable or steady, (b) the economics of scales were relatively well exploited so that there could be little increased efficiency from increasing the size of production units, (c) the existing industries proliferate within a national framework rather than stagnate on account of the unplanned growth of new industries, (d) demand is great for a wide variety of high quality products, and (e) large degree of dependence upon each other exists among various industries and among various geographical areas.[14]

In an attempt to identify when exactly an economy starts off to be modern, Rosto suggested a model of the stages of economic growth. He defined five stages: (a) tradition, (b) conditions necessary for take off, (c) take off, (d) effort to attain maturity, and (e) a high level of mass consumption. He identified the take off stage by the presence in a society of three factors:

(i) A rise in the rate of production investment from, for example, say, 5 percent and less to more than 10 percent of national income or net natioal product (NNP meaning income after deduction of expenses);
(ii) The development of one or more substantial manufacturing of sectors or areas with a high rate of growth;
(iii) The existence or quick emergence of a political, social and institutional framework which exploits the inpulses to expansion in the modern sector and the potential external economy effects he takes off, and gives to growth a continuing character.[15]

## (c) Cultural Modernity

Seen in the historical perspective, the developed or developing countries have emerged from a great variety of different traditional, pre-modern societies. While in Western Europe they developed from feudal or absolutist states with strong urban centres, in

Eastern Europe they emerged from more autocratic states and less urbanized societies. And in the United States and the first Dominions like Canada and Australia, they have developed through processes of colonization and migration, some of which were rooted in strong religious motivations and organized in groups of religious settlers, while others were based mostly on large scale immigration oriented, mostly to economic opportunity and greater equality of status. This, however, was the stay of the past. Today modernization and aspiration to modernity are probably the most overwhelming and the most permeating features of the contemporary scene. In other words, most nations are now-a-days caught in the web of modernized or continuing their own traditions of modernity. From these activities of the past and the present, a definition of modernization could be abstracted from the available literation in this connection.

"Modernization is the process of change towards these types of social, economic, and political system that have developed in Western Europe and North America from the seventeenth century to the nineteenth century and have then spread to other European countries and in the nineteenth and twentieth century to the South American, Asian and African countries.[16]

In fact, the concept of modernity involves, as we have seen earlier, socio-demographic aspects as well as several aspects of social organization. Denoting most of the socio-demographic aspects of modernization, Karl Deutch coined the word "social mobilization "which he treated as "the process in which major clusters of old social, economic and psychological commitments are eroded and broken and people become available for new patterns of socialization and behaviour".[17] Thus for Deutsch, the major indices of modernization are (i) exposure to the aspects of modern life through demonstrations of machinery, building, consumer goods, etc.; (ii) response to mass media, (iii) change of residence; (iv) urbanization; (v) change from agricultural occupations; (vi) increased literacy; and (vii) growth of per capita income. These indices refer mainly to physical aspects of modernization. As social aspects of modernization atleast seven indices have been pointed out, viz, role-differentiation, voluntarism; high level technology; democratic ethos; expansion of communication media; secularism; and humanism.[18]

The above mentioned characteristics of modernity refer to general modernization. In order to distinguish cultural modernity from general one, a number of scholars suggested specific indices. Rogers developed ten explanatory variables that describe a subculture of peasantry of the world of traditional attitudes and beliefs, largely incompatible, with modernity, indicated that even people in such sub-cultures did modernize and they changed their positions on a progressively expanding number of variables. These variables were mutual distrust in inter-personal relations; fatalism; empathy; limited view of the world; lack of an ability to differ personal gratification; limited aspiration; lack of innovativeness; familism; perceived limited good; and dependence on and hostility toward government authority.[19]

Alex Inkles in a similar study has asserted that modern man presents a general syndrome of variables that all hang together. Some of the important variables he indicated are: 1. openness to new experience, both with people and with new ways of doing things; 2. the assertion of increasing independence from the traditional authority and shift of allegiance to leaders of government, public affairs, trade unions, cooperatives, and the like; 3. belief in the efficacy of science and medicine and a general abandonment of passivity and fatalism in the face of life difficulties; and 4. ambition for oneself and ones children to achieve high occupational and educational goals.[20]

Similarly in political sphere, changes take place not only in the styles of political life but also in the existing structures and institutions. For instance, if exposure to modernizattion provokes in social groups an aspiration for increasing mobility, a striving for expansion of mobility is opportunity for each group toward the higher ends of stratification hierarchy, the resulting politics of mobility is cultured sound manoeuvres of the groups higher in the stratification to prevent change and maintain status quo, and of those lower in hierarchy to evolve a variety of patterns to smash this obstruction and status quo with a view to move upward. Thus politics caught in the vertex of the conflict of tradition and modernity becomes a politics geared to modify, accelerate or otherwise control the rate and direction of change, one way or the other. Thus, when the groups are highly charged politically, voting behaviour of individuals acting through these groups is not only a consequence of the rate of change as experienced by individuals, but in its turn directed to that rate so that there is an improvement in the value positions for the specific group of individuals. The shift in the pattern of alignment of groups and variability in the pattern are consequence which fallow from the behaviour of individuals seeking to modify the rate of change.[21] Such changes, both in intra group and inter-groups perspectives, hint at the emergence of a new 'political culture' at all levels of polity in the developing countries, which involves, among other things, remarkable shifts in value-preferences and changes in political behaviour of the people who are constantly exposed to the conditions of general modernization.[22]

### (d) National Language

In adaptation of traditional form of literacy and artistic as well as moral culture to the technique and content of modern education, and the development of modern studies of traditional culture is a major problem throughout the new states. From this confrontation of the exogenous and the indigenous of the foreign and the native, of the modern and the tradition, arises a major problem that frequently agitates many of the new states namely the language problem. In some of the new states, the language problem centres around the medium of instruction. Nearly all the new states face a situation in which the language of their modern culture is the metropolitan language that was the language of the former colonialist rulers. Then modern culture too is usually derived largely from their contact with the metropolis. Usually the language more frequently the languages of the natives, neither highly developed nor universally spoken or even understood throughout the territory. It consciousness of self respect and national dignity has made it imperative to adopt the indigenous language or one or the indigenous languages for all official and cultural uses: using a foreign language is regarded as an act of self derogation. In fact, the use of the indigenous language would reduce the gap, so painfully felt by so many of the highly educated ones in almost all the new states, between the masses and the intellectuals.[23]

## (e) National Integration

Invariably in all the new states, the societies consist of relatively discrete collectivities such as ethnic, communal, caste, religious, or linguistic ones that have little sense of identity with one another or with the nation as a whole. Practically none of the new states of Asia and Africa has reached a stage, where the people it rules have become a nation, more or less co-terminates with the state in the territorial boundaries, and possessing a sense of identity in which membership in the state ruling them is an important component.

Social Scientists, statesmen, and politicians alike have not been sparing in the use of phases like "dual" or "plural" or "multiple", societies, "mosaic" or "composite" social structures, "tribalism", "parochialism", "communalism", "pan-national" movement, "states" that are not nations, and "nations" that are not states. One is used to speaking of communalism in India, referring to religious contrasts; the same phrase is used to refer to social contrasts in Malya, and tribal contrasts in Congo. Regionalism, if the concept often employed to refer to disaffections in Indonesia and differences in the customs of Moracco. When the Tamil minority in Sri Lanka is set off from the Sinhalese majority by religion, language, race, region, and social custom, the Shiy minority in Iraq, is set off from the dominant Sunnis virtually by an intra-Islamic sectarious difference alone. Whole pan-national movements in Africa are largely based on race, and in Kurdistan on tribalism in Laos, it is based on the Shan States and in Thailand on language.[24]

Although, these sectarian movements appear to be different phenomena, at closer analysis they prove to be, in some sense, common. Hence the need for a theoretical framework to analyse and interpret those movements. Cliford Geertz has offered a very useful framework for the analysis of the problem. As observed by him, the people of new states are simultaneously estimated by two powerful, thoroughly inter-dependent, yet distinct and often actually opposed motive, namely, the desire to be recognized as responsible agents whose wishes, acts, hopes and opinions "matter" and the desire to build an efficient, dynamic, modern states. The first is the search for an identity, and a demand that identity be publicly acknowledged as being important: it is a quest for a social assertion of the self on being somebody in the world. The second is a more practical one. It is a demand for progress, for a rising standard of living, for a more effective political order, for greater area of world politics and for exercising influence among nations. The two motives are most intimately related, because citizenship in a truly modern state has more and more become the most broadly negotiable claim to personal significance, and become what Mazzini called the "demand to exist and have a name" is to such an extent fired by a humiliating sense of exclusion from the important centres of power in world today. Yet, the two are not the same thing: they stem from different sources and respond to different pressures. In fact, it is the tension between them that is one of the cenral driving forces in the national evolution of the new states, at the same time, it is one of the greatest obstacles to such evolution.[25]

The dichotomous, yet interdependent, situation needs to be further examined. The tension between the desire for self-assertion and state-building tend to take a peculiarly severe and chronic form in the new states for two reasons: first, because of the great extent to which their peoples sense of self remains bound up in the gross actualities of the blood, race, language, steadily accelerating importance in this country of the sovereign state as a positive instrument for the realization of collective aims. It is to be noted that the populations of the new states multi-ethnic, usually also multilinguistic, and sometimes multi-racial as they are tend to regard the immediate, concrete and to their inherently meaningful sorting implicit in such "natural" diversity as the substantial contents of their individuality. As they perceive it, to subordinate these specific and familiar identifications in favour of a generalized commitment to an overarching and somewhat alien civil order is to risk a loss of definition as an autonomous person, either through absorption into a culturally undifferentiated mass or what is even worse, through domination by some other rival ethnic, racial, or linguistic community that is able to imbue that order with the temper of its own personality. The need for a reasonably large, independent, powerful and well-coordinated polity as the only means of attaining social reform and material progress too is seen by them-clearly by the elite, and dimly by the rest. Much effort towards reconciling the two tendencies.[26]

### Prescriptive Approach

Dissatisfied with merely offering models for describing, analysing, and interpreting what they come across in this exploration of social processes some social scientists have gone a step further by attempting to prescribe what they considered best to the well being of the new states. Such prescriptions are of course, heavily loaded with the value preferences of this group of scholars. Notwithstanding this value dimension, most proponents of the prescriptive approach to nation-building have based their perceptions and prescriptions on one common foundation—the analysis of the implications of political development for the nation-building in the third world countries.

### The Process of Political Development

T.A. Mahan in his book *The Problems of Asia* had, as one of the pioneering theorists of the twentieth century American expansionism spoken of "growth" and the stages of political development which characterized civilized nations in comparison with other communities of the world.[27] Taking the clue from Mohan's ideas, a host of political scientists, especially in the American academic circles, have devoted their time and energy to operationalize the concept of political development. What prompted the modern political scientists and sociologists, particularly belonging to the United States, is the emergence of a large number of independent nations. States in Afro-Asian and Latin American regions that showed change from one position to another in a very rapid manner and thus informed them to refashion their tools of social and political investigation. Thus the new generations of political scientists came to realize that the non-western processes, could be successfully studied by them against the socio-economic cultural background they themselves had inherited throughout the centuries in the West and under the influence of which they had been operating now. The fact that these were different from the western political processes, being rooted to and drawing their sustenance from different cultural background induced them to widen their studies to the total context of the cultural and historical settings of the developing states.[28]

Luciaw Pye should be regarded as the leading light of the earlier batch of writers. "To analyse the concept of development in depth, and has kept on evolving his ideas on the subject, and has left an abiding impression on the entire literature of political development.[29] Pye virtually sets the pace in 1963 when he thought of political development in terms of cultural diffusion, and of adapting, fusing, and adjusting old patterns of life to new demands. He emphasized that the first step towards political development was the evolution of the nation-state system which he treated as a 'basic concept supporting the gradual diffusion throughout all societies of what we might call a World Culture. At this stage, he told us that the signs of political development could be traced at three different levels-with respect to the population as a whole, with respect to the level of governmental and general systemic performance, and with respect to the organization of the policy.[30]

The concept of political development as an academic fashination evolved in an interesting fashion. Feeling ill at case with the barren treatment of 'foreign governments' in the centres of political studies, European political scientists, especially their American counterparts, started looking for a more fertile way of studying" comparative politics.[31] Such an approach necessitated a focussing upon common political activities common to all political system, it was only a matter of time before the scholars who look for the indices to measure the degrees to which these activities had developed in various political systems. And in this quest, they struck upon the concept of political developments to be measured by the forms and degrees of political activity.[32]

It is interesting to note the way in which political scientists have shifted their attention from "foreign governments" to "comparative politics". In the introduction to comparative politics: A developmental Approach, Gabriel Almond and G. Bingham Powell, address to this question.[33] They point out that political science prior to World War Second sufferend from three major drawbacks, viz., parochialism, configurativism, and formalism.

(i) As a coherent discipline, the pre-World-War II studies of comparative government were largely confined to the

European area—Britian, France, Italy, Germany, and Russia. Studies of the political systems of Asia, Africa, and Latin Ame-rica were carried on by a small group of generally isolated individual scholars, or in the content of "area studies" rather than in the context of a general discipline of comparative government. As a result, the dominant core of the field consisted of the European "Great Powers" and whatever there was of general theorizing about form of government and pattern of politics was based upon this small though salient, sample of political systems.

(ii) Moreover, the dominant approach to the study of "foreign governments" was configurative, viz, concerned with illuminating the peculiar characteristic of individual political systems. There was little systematic comparative analysis aimed at lighting the political activities common to all political systems under consideration.

(iii) Finally, the whole approach was too formalistic: the focus tended to be on institutions and their legal norms, rules, and regulations, or on political ideas and idologies, rather than on performance, interaction and behaviour. Whatever behavioural studies were made, especially by such men as Merrian, Lasswell , Herring, Shattschneider, and Odegard in the 1920's were limited to the American sphere and had not made much headway; and in the case of these scholars, their "optimistic faith in the inevitability of democracy, especially strong in America, developed curiosity and interest in non-democratic forms of government. The same mood prevailed also during the period between the two wars. When even communism and fascism were viewed as temporary disorders of political pathologies; teaching in the field of comparative government was carried on under the fabric of "democracy and dictatorship", with dictatorship representing errors and political pathology, and democracy representing truth and political health.

But after the World War II, this state of affairs took a new turn. Soon the naive conception of democratic progress, and the intellectual structure of the discipline of comparative government which it had produced and maintained, became intenable. This sudden development was brought about mainly by three factors viz., nationalist explosion, power diffusion, and the communist challenge. Nationalist explosion involved sudden emergence of a number of new states in Middle East, Asia, Africa, with a bewildering variety of cultures, social insitutions, and political characteristics. Power diffusion implied that the nations of Atlantic community lost their dominance. International power and influence diffused into the former colonial and semi-colonial areas. And finally, communist challenge meant the emergence of communism as a powerful competitor in this struggle to shape the structure of national politics and of the international political system posing a new major threat to the prospects of democracy. Faced with this new situation, the Western, especially American, political scientists gave a new colour to their discipline: the change was marked by four characteristics-(i) the search for more comprehensive scope; (2) the search for realism; (3) the search for precision, and (4) the search for theoretical order. Out of this four-fold quest emerged the new comparative politics whose offspring is the concept of political development. As Stephen Wasby puts it:

"Political scientists were worried about the preservation of democracy as the dominant form of government in the world or simply about the best way of assuring that the fragile systems newly emerging would have best opportunity for stable development".[34]

It is clear that this fear of stability and war on the one hand, and zeal for the diffusion of democracy, on the other induced them to watch and measure political developments in other countries. Thus was fertilized the concept of "political development", and it developed in the womb of "comparative politics".

Although generated against the background of (a) a fear of political instability, wars, and revolutions, and (b) an over enthusiasm as to how to promote the democratic forms of government all over the world, the concept of political development means different political phenomena to different political scientists. Surveying these different interpretations, Lucian Pye has listed ten such meanings.[35]

(i) Political development as the pre-requisite typical of industrial societies.

(ii) Political development as the politics typical of industrial societies.
(iii) Political development as political modernization.
(iv) Political development as the operation of a nation-state.
(v) Political development as administrative and legal development.
(vi) Political development as mass mobilization and participation.
(vii) Political development as the building of democracy.
(viii) Political development as stability and orderly change.
(ix) Political development as mobilization of power.
(x) Political development as one aspect of multi-dimensional process of social change.

Abstracting from the various definitions Pye, postulates three characteristics of political development which seem to be most widely held and most fundamental in general thinking about the problems of development.

**(a) Equality**

A general spirit of attitude toward equality is the first broadly shared characteristic which is found among various approaches to political development. It implies aspects of participation, universal laws, and achievement criteria. Participation involves mass participation and popular involvement in political activities. However, participation may either be democratic or a form of totalitarian mobilization but the key consideration is argued out to be that subjects should become active citizens and atleast the pretence of popular rule are necessary. Universal laws for ensuring equality are meant to imply that the rules for governing the polity be of a universalistic nature, applicable to all and more or less impersonal in their operations. And finally, equality necessitates that the recruitment to political office should reflect achievement standards of performance and not the ascriptive considerations of a traditional social system.

**(b) Capacity**

The overall capacity of a political system is the second major theme found in most of the concept of political development.

The concept of capacity, which relates to the outputs of a political system and the extent to which the political system can affect the rest of the society and economy is supposed to imply three concepts, viz., governmental performance, effectiveness and efficiency, and rationality and secularism. Capacity entails the sheer magnitude, scope, and scale of political and governmental performance. The assumption, of course, is that the developed system should be able to do a lot of more and touch upon a wider variety of social life than the relatively less developed systems are expected to do. Capacity also means effectiveness and efficiency in the execution of public policy, the assumption being that the developed systems not only do more than others, but also perform faster and with much greater thoroughness. And finally, capacity also involves rationality in administration and a secular orientation towards policy.

**(c) Differentiation and Socialization**

A necessary pre-requisite of development is that the structures, institutions, and agencies must have their distinct and limited functions, leading to the emergence within the realm of government an equivalent of a division of labour. In other words, with the differentiation and specialization of structures, there should also come about an increased functional specificity of the various roles with the system. This should obviously be accompanied by a process of integration of the complex political structures and processes in a system: differentiation is not fragmentation and isolation of the different parts of the political system, but specialization based on an ultimate sense of integration. In addition to these elements, Pye has identified six types of crises that appear to be relevant for our discussion on nation-building.

According to Pye, those crises may be met in different sequence but all of which must be successfully dealt with for a society to become a modern nation state. These are: (1) The identity crisis, which has to be resolved in attainment of a common sense of national identity, (2) The legitimacy crisis, which has to lead to recognition of the authorities and their right to undertake binding decisions, (3) Penetration crisis, which means the building up of channels of downward communication, (4) The participation crisis, which refers to the emergence of interest groups and the resolution of the problems of mass participation in political process, (5) The integration crisis, which consists of problems and solutions-related to the organization of the entire polity into a system, and (6) The distribution crisis, which is a code for the variety of problems stemming from allocation of power, prestige, office, wealth and goods and services.

The problem which one has to encounter in attempting to view political development as a process of formation of nations are multitudinous indeed. The modern world is divided into nations occupying definite territories. Most people living in that world know approximately what the word "nation" means, but practically all attempts to define it seem to be unsatisfactory. In a lecture delivered at the Sorbonne in 1982, Earnest Renan had said:

> "I intend to analyse with you an idea which seems simple and clear but which tends itself to the most dangerous misunderstanding...In our day one commits a serious error, one confinds nation and race and one attributes to ethnographical or rather linguistic groups sovereignty analogous to that of real people".[36]

The position described by Renan could be observed even today becoming a member of a nation does not have exactly the same meaning in all languages. In the German and Slavic languages, for example, belonging to a nation and having citizenship is entirely different. Nations are differentiated on the basis of combinations of diverse criteria, in each case differently, on the basis of a common language, origin, distinctive national character, common religion, residence in a common territory, common culture and social organization, common interest manifest in national consciousness. A macro structure, a large group of people sometimes "numbering millions, exhibiting all the above characteristics and aspiring to a separate nationhood may still not be regarded as a separate nation by other. There are clearly nations which are not recognized as nations by the international community. Only if a group which is distinguished from other similar groups by its sharing of the above characteristics established itself under a separate independent government and obtains the full status of a separate and a recognized nation. Thus some nations do not have the recognized status of a nation, and many states encompass a number of nations.

Some scholars have attributed the appearance of European nations to the destruction of the political order of feudalism, the promotion of all or nearly all people within a society to the status of citizens, and with it the acquisition of rights to participation in the political life of the country.[37] Others have attributed birth of the European nations to the emergence of national economics. They believe that the links of all-embracing capitalist economic systems have commented the cultural and ethnic unities which had come to being in the European states earlier, bringing about the birth of modern nations. National consciousness emerged there on the basis of common interests of the society united by various integrative processes, among which the ecomonic one played the decisive role.[38]

Such views were especially promoted by Stalin and the Marxist writers employing his theory. The concept "nation" is defined in such literature too rigidly, and many of the new nations, especially in Africa and Asia, are not nations from the strict standpoint of such definition. Yet the idea seems to be valid that nation-wide economic systems coalesce, solidity and bring to maturity modern political entities. Reflecting on theories like the above, one can say that one aspect of political development is a still complex process of self-determination, establishment as a separate national political entity, enfranchisement, on going integration, especially as a result of economic development. Nationalism is the propellant force behind that kind of political development. And nationalisms, like nations exhibit diverse characteristics.[39]

Kenneth Minogue has said that nationalism begins as a Sleeping Beauty and ends as a Frankensteins monster. He distinguishes three stages in that process. The first, labelled stirring, is a period of awakening, of revulsion against foreign rule, culture and ideas. There comes the stage of the struggle for independence, followed by the third stage of consolidation. Beyond that lies the "integral nationalism" or totalitarianism. Yet, in reality not all nationalisms change into totalitarianism. Minogue's observation cannot be taken as a universal rule. Of course, in some cases nationalism bettressed colonialism and imperialism. In others, it just became the foundation of national existence alongside other nations. Indeed, especially in European history, nationalism has often had an ugly side. Yet, from this one cannot gauge that the ugliness was inherent, and that any nationalism will be transformed into a Frankenstein monster of totalitarian. Nationalism in Asia and Africa may not be a Sleeping Beauty, but it certainly is the driving power of modernization. There are also yet signs of change into a monstrous variety.

Thus it can be said that now-a-days, nations are built by mobilizing crucial sectors of society within a comprehensive framework of social change and, as such, nation-building, national integration, modernization, and political development are diverse sides of the same process of transformation of traditional into modern political entities. In any case, nation-building efforts in the newly born states has been explained in fragmentary perspective rather than a comprehensive historical framework of analysis. The theories of the late fifties and the early sixties tended to concentrate exclusively on the experience and the potentialities of the politics just emerging from colonial states and showed only minimal concern with the early histories of nation-building in Europe and European settled territories. The idea of the participant nation-state was indeed European in origin and had been exported to the developing world through colonization and ideological diffusion: yet there was a great deal of reluctance to draw directly on the rich European experience in developing models for the explanation of the processes of change inherent in the growth of national policies. There were many reasons for this reluctance: the great complexity of the European developments, the linguistic difficulties, the low level of communication between historians and generalizing social scientists. It was easier to deal in comparative terms with the less history-burdened, less documented and less scrutinized countries of the developing world: the working languages were fewer, because of the colonial inheritance, and there were fewer professional historians around to question the interpretations and classifications of the social scientists.[40] This gap in the analysis of nation-building has been in a certain measure bridged by a comparative study of political development with clearly defined priorities of investigation and the corresponding model, and hypothesis in this connection.

## References


1. Karl W. Deutch, "Nation-Building and National Development: Some locus for Political Research", in Karl W. Deutch and W.J. Foltz (eds) *Nation-Building* (New York: Aldine Atherton: 1971) pp. 11-12.
2. Pulparampil, *op.cit*, pp. 3-4.
3. Karl Deutsch, "The Study of Nation-Building, 1962-1966", in Karl W. Deutsch, and William J, Foltz (eds), *op. cit*, p. V.
4. Deutch, *op. cit*, pp. 1-4.
5. Rupert Emerson, *From Empire to Nation: The Rise of Self Assertion of Asia and African Peoples*, Calcutta: Scientific Book Agency, 1960.
6. Emerson, *Ibid*, p. 18.
7. Edward Shils "On the Comparative Study of New States", in Clifford Greetz (ed) *Old Socieities and New State*, (New Delhi: Amerind: 1971) pp. 1-2.
8. Ibid. *op. cit.*, pp. 1-2.
9. Peter Merkl, *Political Continuity and Change*, (New York: Harper and Row: 1967) p. 430.
10. Daniel Lerner, *The Passing of Traditional Society*, (New York: Free Press: 1958).
11. Daneil Bell "Towards the Year 2000: Work in Progress", *Daedlus Special Number*, 96 (Summn 1967) p. 643.
12. Victor C. Ferkiss, *Technological Man. The Myth and the Realities* (Calcutta: Scientific Book Agency, 1971) p. 27.
13. Pulparampil, *op. cit*, p. 24
14. Robert T. Holt and John E. Turner, *The Political Basis of Economic Development*, (Bombay: Vakils, Feller and Limams Ltd: 1966) p. 10.
15. W.W. Rostor, *Stages of Economic Growth*, (London: Cambridge University Press: 1960) p. 39.
16. S.N. Eisenstadt, *Modernization; Protest and Change*, (New Delhi, Prentice Hall of India: 1969) p. 1
17. Deutsch, *op. cit.* p. 494-95.
18. Eisenstadt, *Ibid.* p. 2-5
19. E.M. Rogers, *Modernization Among Peasants: The impact of communication*, New York: Halt Reinhard and Winston, 1969.
20. A. Inkles, "Participant Citizenship in Six Developing Countries:, *American Political Science Review*, 63, pp. 1120-41.
21. N.G.N. Kini. *Urban Voter in India: A Study of 1967 General Election in Nagpur*, New Delhi: Abbinav: 1974.
22. S. Akinchan, *Urban Growth and Political Socialization*, Delhi: Janaki Prakashan 1982.
23. Edward Shils, *op. cit.*, p. 3.
24. Clifford Geertz, "The Integrative Revolution: Primordial Sentiments and Civic Politics in the New States", in Clifford Geertz (ed) *Old Societies and New States* (New Delhi: Amerind: 1971) pp. 106-107.
25. C. Geertz, *op. cit.* pp. 108-9.
26. *Ibid*, pp. 108-9
27. T.A. Mahan, *Problems of Asia*, Berton, 1960, p. 3.
28. S.P. Verma, *op. cit.* p. 280.

29. Lucian Pye: *Aspects of Political Development,* (Borton Little Brown, 1966) p. 33.
30. S.P. Verma, *op. cit.* p. 275.
31. L. Wesley, *Political Science, The Discipline and its Dimensions,* Calcutta: Scientific Book: 1972, pp. 489.
32. Pulparampil, *op. cit.* p. 36
33. Gabriel A. Almond and G. Bingham Powell, Jr., *Comparative Politics : A Developmental Approach* (Borton: Little Brown 1966) p. 2.
34. Stephen Wasby, "The Concept of Political Developmental", *The Annals of the Amercial Academy of Political and Social Science* 358 (March, 1965), pp. 1-13.
35. Ibid., pp. 12-13.
36. Ernest Renan, "The Meaning of Nationality", in Hans Kohn, *Nationalism: Its Meaning and History,* Princeton N.J.: Van Notrand, (1955) p. 136.
37. Reinhard Bendix, *Nation Building and Citizenship.*
38. Walter sulz bach, *National Consciousness* (New York: American Council on Public Affairs: 1949)
39. Szyman Chodak, *Societal Development: Five Approaches with conclusions from comparative Analysis* (New York: Oxford University, Press, 1973) p. 233.
40. Stein Rokkam, "Models and methods in the Comparative Study of Nation-Building" in A.R. Desai (Ed.) *Essays on Modernization of Under-Developed Socieites,* Vol.I (Bombay Thackar & Co. Ltd. 1971) p. 226-27.

# Chapter - 10

# Social Contours of Modern Political Theory

## Politics of Modernization

It is worthwhile to discuss the views of Mitchell in this context. In his work on political system, he offered four requisite functions that are performed by a polity. These are: authoritative specification of the system goals; authoritative mobilization of resources to implement goals; integration of the system; and allocation of values and costs.[1] The deep influence of Talcott Parsons on this political scientist can be traced in this fact that polity is defined by him as a sub-system, primarily concerned with the mobilization of resources to meet the goals of the system. The treatment of the state as a 'sub-system' having its primary concern with mobilization of resources, as pointed out by Mitchell, takes him very near to Talcott Parsons, who described the factor of mobilization of resources as one of the four basic functions of the 'system'. What is of special importance about Mitchell is that he 'does not limit himself to a consideration of mobilization of resources to meet system goals, but rather ranges over all the functional requisites of the social system, pointing out way in which political processes contribute to the performance of all functions.[2]

Focus on the study of new political systems belonging to the developing countries of the third world has led to the inclusion of some interesting problems relating to the types and force that have played their part in causing rapid transformations in them.[3] Thus Apter gives us certain new directions in the spheres of systems analysis and structuralism functionalism that, apart from making a study of the political system in systemic terms, also deals with the classification and analysis of types of government. In his work on the "Politics of Modernization", we find that, in fact, the elements of the social system "are analysed mainly for the purpose of understanding the extent to which particular types of government or systems of authority operate best only in particular kinds of social environment; and how changes in elements, or relations, between the elements of the total system influence changes in governmental system.[4]

What strikes at the very outset in a study of Apter's political theory is that he tries to establish a sort of remarkable reconciliation between the normative and empirical dimensions of political theory. As he says: "I believe that the politics begins with models that are primarily normative and secondarily empirical".[5] By the very term 'modernization', he means a beginning whereby any societal culture allows individuals to develop a critical view of man in his relation to nature and society; then men begin to see life as involving different kinds of choices-personal, social, structural, and moral. The choices are made by the government that have implications and consequences for all members of society and the choices that are made by the government and accepted by the society over a period of time, can be said to constitute the morals aims of the society.[6]

A serious student of modern political theory may this finds in Apter what is known as answers to the questions familiar to the traditional theoriests. Though his attention is confined to certain political systems of Africa like Uganda and Ghana, he looks at the culture of people that should be described as "mixed" on account of being a crude hotch-potch of traditionalism and modernism-culture of the white people superimposed over the tribal culture of the black people. Since, the dependent countries adopted the political systems of their master countries and since these imported systems could not function well, there arose the basic problem of how the political institutional transfer could be effected in colonial countries. At the same time, it led to the creation of a more serious problem, that of ensuring that change in general is as orderly as possible, taking place in the manner that is in some degree predictable and that of ensuring that the holders of governmental authority succeed each other in a peaceful manner. These problems arise as a result of social and economic changes and, as a such, they require their proper solution in the context of social and economic system. The study of the third world countries naturally engaged our attention for the reason that this mixture of political, economic and other social problems" is perhaps most obvious there and so they present, as it were, a laboratory for extensive scientific analysis, if not experiment.[7]

Such type of study leads Apter to look into the politics of modernization from the standpoint of a structural-functionalist. First of all, he takes up the subject of modernization that he regards as a process that occurs predominantly in developing societies when it "may be described as the transportation of certain roles professional, technical, administrative—and the transposition of institutions supporting those roles-hospitals, schools, universities, bureaucracies".[8] As he adds: "Modernization is like hurtling through a tunnel at tightening speed without knowing what waits at the other end. Fear creates serious political problems". The structural-functional approach of Apter assumes the nature of a behavioural interpretation when we find him insisting that as roles' are no more than institutionalized forms of behaviour defined by functions, then there needs to be added to structural functionalism some other form of analysis which deals with the motives underlying behaviour.[9]

### Modernization of Political System

Apter's politics of modernization seeks to study political system in three respects-nature and purpose of the government, type and models of the government, and functions of the government.

(i) **Nature and purpose of the government:** According to Apter, the business of a political scientist is to see conditions under which a government can maintain itself during the period of transition from a traditional to modern form and without causing loss to its legitimacy. By legitimacy he means proper relationship between the authority of the rulers and the degree of support that the rulers are able to engender. Whether the government is democratic or of a secular-liberatarian model or of an opposite type called sacred collectivity, the emphasis should be laid on the institution of government entitled for using coercion and at the same time bound to flow the value system involving both moral preoccupations and those concerned with the performance of activities according to the criteria of efficiency.[10]

(ii) **Models of Government:** Instead of classifying government into the broad categories of liberal democratic and totalitarian, Apter suggests that the modernizing governments should be placed in the third category that should be designated as 'pre-democratic' and not 'anti-democratic'. He calls these political systems as 'accommodated' inasmuch as they can imbibe changes from one extreme to another and it is the function of the political scientist to know the direction in which society is headed in order to understand the basis on which its authority rests. He coins new terms like 'reconciliation system' and 'mobilization system' that may be identified with secular liberatarian and sacred collectivity models described above.[11]

(iii) **Functions of Government:** All political systems are characterized by a number of contingent functions. Thus, they must act as (1) the loci of sanctions in society, (2) the providers of symbols linking a people's past and future, (3) the responsible agents for the orderly arrangement and performance of roles in the system, and (4) the providers of criteria for deciding on membership and participation in the society.[12] Apart form performing these functions, all governments are characterized by a structure of authoritative decision-making' and a 'structure of accountability' that may be described as the main institutional requirements of government. Similarly, all governmental systems possess contingent structures which give an indication of the efficiency of the system. These are really 'sub-structures' of the

> structural requisites and include mechanisms for political recruitment, rule enforcement, and rule delimitation, the allocation and determination of resources and some mechanism through which, at some official level, government registers societal approval of its decisions and policies (a parliament or a central committee for example). In effect, contingent structures are mechanisms for carrying out policy.

It may, therefore, be visualized that Apters analysis, like any structural-functionalist, involves the search for the functional and structural prerequisties of the government.[13] However, the most representative contribution, in this direction is that of Gabid A. Almond who, though like Talcott Parsons and David Easton being in search of a functional theory of the polity, looks towards to the problems of how political systems change from a traditional to modern model and believes sincerely that he has succeeded in elaborating such a theory whereby it would ultimately make possible statistical and perhaps mathematical formulation.[14]

Almond proceeds ahead with certain considerations in his kind. First, he is for constructing a theory or an approach, that may explain how political systems change from one type to another particularly from the traditional to modern model. For this, he subscribes as well as contributes, to the theory of political development that hints on the point of explaining transition from the predominantly agricultural to the predominantly industrial society that affects a simultaneous change in the political system. Second, he is for presenting a classification of political system of what to present a classification of political systems is the factor of efficiency. While one political system can efficiently perform its functions under a set of given conditions and another political system cannot, it is clear that one is more efficient than the other. To put it in concrete words, we can say that modern political systems can perform their functions well and so they are efficient, while the traditional systems are not inasmuch as they prove incapable in this regard. It is this type of distinction that provides ample material for making comparisons in a cross-cultural perspective.

In order to develop a potential theory in this context, Almond has presented a set of important propositions. *First,* political change can be seen in terms of development alone. Thus, three degrees can be marked traditional, transitional, and modern. *Second,* since Almond is a structural functionalist and since he is for studying the traditional political systems of the Third World in comparison with the modern political systems of the advanced and developed countries, he seeks to identify the functions of the polity in modern western systems, and then to pursue his analysis of political modernization in non-western areas by investigating how these functions which are associated with distinctive political activities in Western system, are performed elsewhere. The basis for this view is Almond's own belief that anyone who wishes to understand the process of modernization in non-western societies must first be capable of understanding the process of developments, and current behaviour of the societies which, he claims, can be called 'modern' that is western societies. *Third,* a political system is a set of interactions that take place not between the individuals as such but the roles they adopt. *Finally,* political systems are like an 'open phenomena' and, as such, they are engaged in communicating with entities and systems beyond their own boundaries, and they are affected by and react to what happens beyond these boundaries in thier environment.

With these assumptions in mind, Almond presents his own definition of the political system. To him, political system 'is that system of interaction to be found in all independent societies which performs the functions of integration and adaptation (both internationally and vis-a-vis other societies) by means of the employment or threat of employment, of more or less legitimate, order maintaining or transforming system in the society...legitimate force is the threat that runs through the inputs and outputs of the political system, giving it is its special quality and salience and its coherence as a system".[15]

A political system is characterized by three elements-comprehensiveness, inter-dependence, and boundaries. Comprehensiveness means the set of interactions that affect the use of physical coercion; inter-dependence implies that the various sub-sets; 'boundaries' are indicative of the points where other systems end and the political system begins. It is well obvious that Almond offers systemic definition of the political system within the framework of structural-functionalism-an analysis which looks at political systems or coherent wholes which influence and, in turn, are influenced by their environment and for Almond it is the presence of 'legitimate force' throughout the system-in the last analysis holding it together-"that allows one to look at it in scientific terms; that is, as a whole.[16]

## Characteristics of Political System

According to Almond, a political system has four characteristics that may be called 'legitimate patterns of interaction'. They are:-

(i) Every political system has its structures, some of which may be more specialized performing more functions, while others may be less specialized performing less functions in it.
(ii) Whatever differences may be between the system and its structures, the same political functions are performed in all political systems.
(iii) Political structures perform a number of functions that may be termed multi-functional.
(iv) All political systems being parts of the society as a whole have a culture of their own that is always a mixture of the traditional and the modern.

It is on the basis of this study of the legitimate patterns of interaction that perform different functions in different political systems for the sake of their stability and maintenance. It "attempts to shift the locus of analysis from the observable institutional political mechanisms to any ones, where the actual performance of the functional requirements of the systems are located. This approach is inclined to emphasize the search for processes that maintain the stability of the system".[17]

If political system is made up of a set of roles, structures are sub-systems whose interactions are affected to a great extent by the weight of environmental factors, both internal and external, Almond comes to offer his system-functions analysis in terms of seven variables of input and output functions. He discuss four output functions-(i) Political socialization and recruitment, (ii) interest articulation, (iii) interest aggregation, and (iv) political communication. He discerns three output functions-(i) rule making (ii) rule application, and (iii) rule adjudication. According to him the input functions are performed by non-government system, by the society, and the general environment, while the output functions are performed by the three organs of the government known, in the traditional language, as executive, legislature, and judiciary. We shall discuss all these functional requisites in detail in the context of input-output analysis.

A deep study of Almond's political system and its structure and functions shows that it is a synthesis of Easton's conception of the authoritative allocation of values, Weber's definition of the state in terms of 'legitimacy' and Parson's view of the function of the political system as a sub-system of the total system. By way of explaining his definition of the political system, Almond "uses the expression more or less to qualify the state legitimacy in a particular study-in totalitarian systems legitimacy may be very much in doubt, in revolutionary systems it may be in the process of change, and in non-western systems there may be more than one legitimate system in operation. His justification for the use of the term 'physical compulsion is that this helps him in distinguishing political systems from other social systems. By using the adjective legitimate of the physical compulsion used which govern the inputs and outputs of the political system, he hints at its special quality and salience as well as its coherence as a system.[18]

Modern political analysis based on systems has established what is in fact an ideological order of priorities. It is perhaps significant that this applies especially to Easton and Almond as well as his followers, who tend to treat the political system as to some extent a unique system, and have attempted to integrate their analysis of the political system into the framework of a social system as a whole. By concentrating on an input-output notion of system, a priority for assessing effectiveness is established which focusses on the structure as more or less effective in processing input into output, and which tends to identify stability of structure with perceived effectiveness, and therefore legitimacy. Instead of viewing inputs and outputs as boundary exchanges between systems, an odd locational contradiction arises by which individual or groups are viewed as part of a system for some purposes (e.g. gate keeping), but as unattached or loose, part of no system, for others. This is both an ideological and methodological confusion; ideological because of the emphasis on stability, methodological because it compunds the concrete level of polity and the abstract level of system.

This narrow type of functionalism is thus not so much a general theory of politics but a conceptualization of a special case. Some of the limiting factors are:

1. The applicability of the model only to highly developed countries,
2. The applicability imposed by structural emphasis on stability, to evolutionary rather than revolutionary societies,
3. The emphasis on input and output which implies a pluralistic democracy of a special kind-one in which there is no tradition of any autonomous, self-conscious state, where the notion of 'neutral' institutions making up the structure of the political sub-system substitutes for the notion of a very unneutral or 'engage' state.[19]

**Structural-Functional Approach**

Seen in the development perspective, structural functional analysis postulates a model of perfection to which developing societies approximate to a greater or lesser extent, development becomes a stage in a pre-determined process. There are thus implicit prescriptive elements in the analysis, as well as explicit ones. As a matter of fact, developing countries themselves represent a unique model and, as such, the comparison between the developed and developing societies may throw as much light on the problems of the former as on any shortcomings of the latter, the type of inputs-outputs functionalism, as discussed earlier, cannot be of much help.

It is generally accepted fact that development in general and industrialization in particular involve some incrasing differentiations of structures and roles. Amorphous, diffues, multi-purpose structure and roles give way to more clearly articulated, single purpose, specific ones. The analogy, expressely or implicitly comes from economics; it is essentially the application to social activity of the empirically valid observation that a technologically modern economic system requires ever-increasing specialization within the general framework of division of labour. Yet in its social transplantation this economic concept creates several difficulties (i) the concept of differentiation is based on the assumption of a general diffusion of development or modernity; that differentiation across system boundaries will make the affected areas of or structures of both systems equally 'modern'. This assumption of system complementarity contained in the common assertion that routinized application of modern economic production techniques necessarily corresponds to a national equivalent of learning and personality adaptation by the practitioners is not always borne out by the eivdence.

The notion of differentiation is anchored in abstractions (roles, structures, groups) rather than in people. The same people and institutions play different roles consecutively (promotion, demotion, acting ranks). They play temporary roles (civil servants in administrative tribunals, rotating heads of the departments.) More often than not, functional differentiation is more a matter of role emphasis rather than genuine role differentiation. The Indian President is also the supreme commander of armed forces.

The perception of specificity and differentiation is sometimes more ideological than real. The increasing limitations of choices in elections and multiplication of elections themselves can simplify the electoral process into something like ringing the change up on a hill. The polity to function properly, might appear to call for such mechanistic efficiency (a by-product of a politic market ideology); all the elements of a ritualized mobilization which continue to affect the participants through time as well as makes them perform for a specific electoral occasion are pushed out of sight. The nation of orderly, efficient elections is very much an ideological property of 'democratic', pluralistic societies, and so this aspect is emphasized in considerable' excess of its real exclusivity or even saliency. There even exists an economic theory of democracy which purports to show not without reason and evidence-that, given a low level of knowledge, the acceptance of considerable over simplications of choice by political parties is in fact 'cheaper' than any attempt to reach higher levels of cognition which would enable a more sophisticated evaluation of choices to be made-but also result in a demand for multiple choice in the first place.

Analysis of social differentiation in structural-functional terms has been entirely defensive if not status quoist. Differentiation is frequently emphasized when one talks about strain and social actions to adjust to strain, either offensively (Smelser's notion of collective behaviour) or defensively (social control). Collective behaviour infact implies an antithesis to institutional action; it is by definition un-(and therefore anti.) institutional. The notion of the dynamic social strain or conflict is central to sociological analysis, and explains the whole problem of escalation or, to put it in sociological terms, value-addition. As the intensity and scope of social action need to increase in order to be effective, so the various differentiated structures, functions and beliefs are drawn into an increasingly generalized conflict either by aggregation or short circuiting (a better compression). Compression in trust mobilization or collective behaviour initially commits more resources and not less. But it also involves an efficiency factor in so far as it allocates resources in accordance with requirements through rapid structuring of action components, like a general who makes his heavily supported breakthrough on a narrow front. In developing societies, such fronts' are often socially narrow and symbols tends to be largely value-oriented.

Thus differentiation is not only a more efficient means of channelling upwards a growing complex of demands and downwards of decisions, but above social mechanism making for stability. It is defensive, like honey-comb of self-sealing compartments in a ships hull, which confirms the incoming rush of water (inward social action) to a number of spaces which are sealed of and 'sacrificed', but preserve the rest of the ship. The point of value oriented movements is that they are total, and aggregate of compress action through all compartments and therefore the entire social vessel. It wll readily be obvious that if this is so, then the idea of increasing pluralistic participation which in the most common usage is merely the active political principle of increasing differentiation-also becomes in past an ideological device to scatter and confine any desire or effort for radical social action. This is one way in which modern society is viewed. The differentiation of political functions, the increasing alienation of one function from another, and finally the prescriptive grading of one function against another-these are bastions of stability, or resistance to social change. Hence the paradox that organized, structured movements in most industrial societies tend to be maximally norm-oriented, while value-oriented movements are loosely structured, relatively unorganized-and, as a rule, lack in effectiveness.

**Limitations to this Approach**

We can indicate several shortcomings of the structural functional approach to the socio-political phenomena. As we have indicated earlier, it tends to focus primarily static relationships rather than dynamic that characterize human society and polity. Its main preoccupation is the problems of systemic survival, the requirements of the stable adaptation, and the operation of various functions and structures oriented towards systems maintenance.[20] The critics are not prepared to accept the interpretation of Merton who, while laying emphasis on the factor of dynamics says that the concept of dysfunction, which implies the concept of strain, stress and tension on the structural level, "provides an analytic approach to the study of dynamics and change."[21] As such this approach has the serious flow of being 'concerned with the present' and having no perspective of the future. What this approach really aims at is to look at the existing political system as a sub-system within the social system as a whole and then to study its structures and their functions not for the purpose of suggesting radical changes in them, but to devise ways and means to keep it like an ongoing concern. Thus not change but stability is the sheet anchor of the functionalists. It is for this reason that a critic like Gouldner accuses the functionalists of constituting the 'doviological conservation corps of industrial society'.[22]

The second limitation of the functionalists is that their approach defeats the very purpose of their own objectively misapplying their tools of empirical investigation while studying the political systems of the Third World. One may easily ask a question as to how the principles of empirical investigation devised in the sophisticated study rooms of the American University can be rigorously applied to the study of poor and backward countries of the Afro-Asian world and that too for the sake of knowing the social and political reality. Edward Shils was quite forthright in his assessment when he said that the basic problem of the 'new states' is that they do not form a single civil society; they are scarcely able thus far to produce a polity that can supply the personnel necessary to run modern society. They lack in the affirmative attitude towards, rules, persons, and actions that is necessary for consensus.[23]

The problem of religion caste, poverty tribalism, linguistic chauvinisms, sub-nationalism and the like, that are so much in force in various countries of the Third World, cannot be studied with the tools of empirical politics in a rigorous manner as hopefully devised by the sociologists and political scientists of the affluent countries of the Western world. As a critic says; "The masses of the third World countries are struggling to resolve their basic social contradictions and Almond and other functionalists are suggesting 'consensual model' for the study of such societies. The consensual model in politics emphasizes fundamental arguments in societies, while the Third World countries are confronting fundamental disagreements between the entrenched and the emerging classes. The empirical reality as it exists in these societies cannot be analysed with the functional framework. Hence, the functional theorists in politics, with their consensual moden and the view of the present which is devoid of any picture of the future, fail to provide empirically validated answers to what is happening in the Third World".[24]

The third limitation of the structural-functional approach What Marion Levy has termed as "fallacy of functional teleology". That is, it suffers from the tendency" to explain the origins of a condition or pattern of action in terms of its being a functional necessity for the survival of the system. The statement that a particular structural arrangement fulfils an important function is not an adequate explanation of its origin of existence. One may also find fault with the postulate of universal functionalism which suggests that all existing structures fulfil wholly or partially, a particular function.

It certainly overlooks the aspect of functional disintegration or breakdown. Likewise, one may put it as the fallacy of deductive functionalism that finds place in the tendency to develop deductivity a list of functional requisites and then to make sure to find structural patterns which fulfil these requirements. All this "lead, quite commonly to an unwarranted twisting and distorting of empirical realities in the interests of conceptual and theoretical neatness.[25]

Lastly, a critical examination of the structural functional approach from a strictly ideological point of view shows that it is all nothing else than an exercise to depend and justify status quo. The real pursuit of the functionalists is to save a political system from changing towards socialism. A serious endeavour to maintain a system or its change, by all means, peaceful and gradual, in the direction of 'modernization'signifies nothing else than an initiation or emulation of the 'western' model that presents an anti-thesis of a communist model. The functionalists are therefore, accused of being the dependers the bourgeoisie at home and of imperialism abroad.[26] It is for this reason that Marxists can never accept this approach who are guided by the maxim that philosophers have so far interpreting the world, the problem is how to change it.

It may be said that while Easton and Parsons presented on elaborate scheme of this system, Almond talks of functions without referring to a system in which functions have a meaning. That is, he is more concerned with his own sub-sets without first explaining and clarifying the premises of his main set. Moreover, whatever he says about his political system and its structural-functional mechanism is applicable to a western country inasmuch as he has certainly failed to offer as a workable formula whereby we may understand the social, economic and political reality of the poor and backward countries of the world. Likewise, his scheme of the classification of the political system cannot be applied to all countries of the world in a uniform or rigorous manner. Meehan has thus called it 'a very imperfect and loose model' that can be used to order political data and perhaps standardise observations of political phenomena. Again he "has not produced a theory, of course, not even a well-articulated classification scheme. The taxonomy is incomplete and ambiguous".

However, we can say that structural functional approach has its advantage in the study of selected affluent western democratic countries where alone it may look quite attractive for comparative analysis of political systems. It may also be added in its favour that it deals for the most part with a manageable collection of variables, and it provides a set of standardized categories that can be applied successfully to our widely disparate political systems.[27] The line of ideological criticism directed against it is not free from its own blame in view of the fact that Marxism has its own weaknesses. Both Marxism and systems analysis breakdown as full-fledged theories while dealing with the elements of social and political reality and its change in a proper manner. "In fact, however, conflicts are not as unilinear as Marx had suggested, nor, harmony as integral a factor in social and political life as it moves from one period of history to another.

Structural functional approach, notwithstanding its conceptual shortcoming offers a very meaningful perspectives in political sociology. It can help us to analyse such crucial elements as mechanism of integration, conflict avoidence, need-disposition and control, mangement gratification or social rewards, security against encroachment, response to outer world and adaptation, motivation and incentives, communication network, positive channelization of actions and negative minimization of disruptive tendencies, etc. It is because of this potentiality that the approach has found its application to systems analysis and the theories of development, the ideal typical index approach and social research in the Third World countries. However, we must strive to overcome its serious methodological limitations. Logical inter-relations of concepts carries its own dangers; it can be hardly claimed as a complete deductive system; systematic extension of action framework to complex social systems will itself be suspect; pattern variables as conceptual system are incomplete; and there may be the risk of exaggerating structural maintenance displayed by the social systems. In context of theories of development, and particularly in the context of its capability to treat political variables and their implications, it is particularly crippled by these weakness.

## Critical Approach

The views expressed by the critics of the structural functional approach are mainly on three points: they charge the protagonists of the approach (a) of being spiritualistic and metaphysical: (b) of having ignored the dimension of change, and (c) of prompting the future or being unable to deal what is yet to happen. We can deal with these points separately as under:

(i) The structuralist functionalist give the primary reponsibility for the integrative function to the cultural elements, the main unite of which are the family and the church (or religion). Although integration is said to be achieved by the coercive mechanism of the state, and the non-coercive mechanism of the family and religion, the dominant role in orientation is given to the latter. Such an approach has been criticised as being metaphysical and idealistic determining part of the system consists of "spiritual values" i.e. above all, religious as an element of the system discharging a necessary social function". Such a view is said to rule out the roles of conflicts and contradiction in society.

(ii) In the over-concern with stability the structural functionalist ignore the problem of change. They fail to give adequate attention to the fact that social "system" is never at rest, but always being subject to strains and conflicts. The little notice taken of change comes from their concern for order, stability, and survival of the system. Parsons, for instance speaks of 'ordered process of change', and admits that "a general theory of the process of change of social systems is not possible in the present state of knowledge".[28] This statement has earned for Parsons and his followers the change of conservatism and status-quoism. The charge is further made that the structural functionalists, viewing change on a gradual and adjustable process as against sudden and revolutionary, ruling out the irreconsilable antagonistic contradictions of a capatalist society. The sources of change are located in adjustment of the system to exogenous or extra-systemic changes, and not in mass revolutionary movements springing from within the system. The insistence is upon growth through structural functional differentiation, as well as invention innovation by members of groups within society is not considered as a relevant source of change.[29]

(iii) For the functionalists, the future seems to be a pre-empted reality: the 'higher' has already been achieved, i.e., the capitalist social system. It does not occur to them that the present contains its own seeds to destruction, as well as the seeds for the future order of things. Thus having an already realized state of affairs as the ideal, structural, functionalism is simply teleological, and it has no real perspective for the future. Since the protagonists do not accept that the present contains its seeds of destruction, they accept the 'master-installation of the present, and labour to preserve them from major change of fatal destruction.[30]

Thus structural functionalism appears to be utterly incapable of explaining, in a satisfactory manner, the complex political reality in its entirety: its concern with the present and stability is its strength and its weakness.While it can be same extent deal with the aspect of continuity in society, it is not able to do much about the changing aspect of reality, for which the Marxian perspective with its dialectical ethos is the strongest tool so far available. And yet a downright rejection of it as altogether useless in political analysis may be perhaps too premature, and too drastic a step. If it can given concreateness in analysing the continuity aspect of reality, it does prove to be useful to that extent.[31]

## References


1. Willian C. Mitchell; *The American Polity* (New York: Free Press, 1962).
2. Flanigan and Fougelman, *op. cit,* **p. 78.**
3. David Apter, *The Politics of Modernization* (Chicago: Chicago Univ. Press. 1965)
4. Davies and Lewis: *Models of Political systems* (Delhi: Vikas, 1971).
5. Apter, *op. cit,* **p. 10.**
6. Davies & Lewis, *Ibid.* p. 60.
7. Davies and Lawis, p. 62.
8. Apter, *op. cit,* p. 42.
9. Davies and Lewis, *op. cit.,* p. 64
10. Davies and Lewis, *op. cit.,* 65-66.
11. Ibid., p. 66-67.
12. Davies and Lewis, *op cit.* p. 69.

13. *Ibid.* p. 68.
14. Almond and Colman (ed.) *The Politics of the Developing Areas* (Princeton: Princeton Univ. Press, 1960) p. 59.
15. Almond, *op. cit.* p. 7.
16. Davies and Lewis, *op. cit.* p. 34.
17. Davies and Lewis, *op.cit.* pp. 36, 37.
18. S.P. Verma, *Modern Political Theory,* (Delhi: Vikas, 1975) p. 168-69.
19. Nettle, *op. cit,* p. 109-10.
20. Oran R. Young: *Systems of Political Science* (Englewood Cliffs, New Jersey, Prentice Hall, 1968). p. 29.
21. Merton. *op. cit.* p. 25, 37.
22. Gouldner, Reciprocity and Autonomy in Functional Theory "in Gross (ed) *op.cit,* p. 241.
23. Edward Shils, "On the Comparative Study of New States" in Geertz (ed) *op. cit.* p. 22.
24. Bhambri. *op. cit.* p. 467-68.
25. Young, *op. cit,* p. 35.
26. *Ibid.*
27. S.P. Verma, *Modern Political Theory* (Delhi: Vikas, 1975) p. 163.
28. Talcott Parsons, *The Social System,* New Delhi Amerind: 1972; p. 456.
29. Bhambri, *op. cit.* p. 461-63.
30. Ibid. pp. 462-63.
31. John K. Pulparampil, *Models of Nation-building: A Critical Appraisal* (New Delhi: New Publications, 1975) pp. 77-78.

# Chapter - 11

# Caste, Class and Politics

## Caste System

Caste as a traditional principle of social stratification involving ascriptive allocation of occupations, continues to characterize society and polity in India. Its extreme and 'classical' forms can still be observed in most of the villages of the state, where it continues to be a pervasive and all embracing phenomenon that control and defines social, economic, and political relations of the individual. It appears to be so much deep-rooted in cultural system that while the whole society has been undergoing a steady transformation, in the wake of urbanization and industrialization, its residual influences on social and political behaviour have tended to persist overtime. In fact, caste involving culturally defined patterns of institutionalized inequality, has itself been the greatest impediment to the efforts for social and economic modernization of the state. Even today caste system seems to have found its own way to survive the onslaughts of modern social forces, thanks to the ineffectiveness of social legislation and widespread prevalence of caste politics.

Discussion on caste system in India has recently gained impetus from the publication of Lauis Dumont's magnum opus, Homo Hierarchichus. His work is characterized by a significant departure from the conventional sociological approach to caste system in India. He clearly distinguished the caste system as a theoretical construct or, as he puts it, as 'ideology' from the actual reality of caste patterns and behaviour. It is this ideology that moulds the caste structure and conduct, even though existential conditions and counter forces limit and even reverse it in practice.

Caste is a group of endogenous people (a) living in most of the cases in a contigeous area; (b) supposed to be doing certain jobs in a hereditary way, (c) having a position in a hierarchy which is (i) purely local, (ii) spread over a wider region, (iii) spread all over India (d), at the top of this hierarchy were supposed to be Brahmins. At the bottom of this hierarchy were a group of castes whose touch was supposed to pollute the higher castes; (e) as a consequence of habitation area (villages and towns) in India were divided into an area in which all higher castes lived and another area in which the lowest or polluting castes lived.[1] In Indian social structure, caste plays a very important role, both as an elements of wider social structure and as a barrier or stimulant to the alien ideas and programmes. Caste norms, regulating functional or dysfunctional roles, and intra inter-caste relations are the favourite topics of social scientists in India and abroad. They then explain how various sections in the caste system are kept apart by complex observance, rules and regulations, inhibitions and prohibitions, restraints and restrictions for social interaction and intercourse in behaviour, in contact, in matters of commensality, exchange and ritual based relations.[2]

India is treated as an example of social stratification of its "ascriptive extreme" both in terms of degree and form. Discussing the amount of stratification, Tumin wrote; "No actual society has existed at either of these theoretical extremes, though a society as traditional India, with its more than 5,000 sub-castes, approaches the extreme of total inequality, and the agricultural communal cooperation in Israel, the Kibbutzim approach, the extreme of total equality.[3] Thus the caste model of stratification has been widely, if rather unquestionably, accepted by the sociologists not only in describing India, but sometimes, in studying other societies, as well.[4]

In recent years, ideal-typical view has been employed as theoretical construct representing an ideology in terms of which a number of empirical realities can be highlighted. It is with the help of this model that Dumont has tried to explain, in a dialectical purspective, certain areas of psychological, sociological or physical reality that characterize the caste system. We can discuss Dumont's views before embarking upon the general theme of this chapter.

In the relationship between the two power-holders, there is renounced-who can do without material possession, who can die voluntarily while still on this earth, cannot be defeated and cannot be killed. At one stroke, the priest solves the problem of death, which is the much feared and for this man of the world. The priest transcends death by voluntarily renouncing all which death deprives us of; he also goes frequently into death like trance, when he is lost to the world. The priest gives us all possessions. For a man of the world, this is very disconcerting, for the control over other humans, without which control over the forces of nature cannot be achieved, depends on the manipulations through fear and greed. The man who renounces the world and has already experienced "death" cannot be moved by either of their common motivations; he has escaped the means of worldly control (except propriation through offering of sacrifices).

The necessity which the worldly power holder, i.e., the Kshatriya must control all men in his realm, comes into conflict with the escape from worldliness which the Brahmin has effected. However the latter continued to live on this earth and, however minimal his needs does require offerings to survive. Furthermore, he needs protection and respect. Moreover, his removal from the entanglement in day-to-day-living gives him 'scientific' detachment and enables him to understand the affairs of the world, better in many respects than those who are continually involved in them. This advice in worldly matters is invaluable in economic, political and voluntary affairs.

The accommodation thus affected between Brahmins and Kshatriyas is illict arrangement from the ideological perspective of

Brahmins as well as Kshatriyas. Brahmins, if true to their ideology of purity and godlike other worldliness, cannot recognise the principle of power, but holders of power, and wealth cannot have in their ideology a place for purity and sanctity. The accommodation between them springs from the fact that power and purity pre-existed in mixed form before the evolution of the priesthood to the Brahmanical level. Indeed, we may argue that the priests once occupied a somewhat subordinate social position, for the simple reason that worldly activities-gathering of food and social organization of groups in hunting parties, etc, pre-existed the growth of rituals, sacrifice and priesthood. The rise of Brahmins therefore, is a 'revolutionary' development that occcurred at a later stage of social evolution. Thus Kshatriyas and Brahmins like two poles resting on the same base. This is one thing they have in common, the social base they rest upon is formed by the untouchables, who represent the negation of both sanctity and power and are deprived completely of religious merits of control of worldly resources. They get the worst of the two worlds. They are the bottom class as well as the lowest caste.

Here, it is worthwhile to take the note of what Demount considers the central principle of the ideology, namely the dichotomy of the pure and impure (or the pure and the polluting). The Brahmin, the ideal Brahmin, embodies purity. Everyone else is impure, though to different degrees. At the other extreme, stands the chandal, who embodies impurity. Similarly the parallel to this distinction between pure and impure, the typical and the ideal activity of the Brahmin, namely meditation (or purely spiritual activity) is completely pure: everything else and every other activity is impure in varying degrees. The complete material is completely impure. Mind is pure but body is impure; pure matter is completely impure and those whose activity is confined (whether by choice or polluting). The head seat of spiritual or mental activity is pure but feat, which tread material earth, are impure. The month which discharges mental or spiritual entities namely, thoughts and words which embody these are pure. Organs that discharge matter are impure. Thus, the dialetic of purity and generates the ideology of caste, which serves to polarise society, enabling it to fulfil certain goals and pursue certain activity.

The dialetic of pure and impure is itself but one pole in another dialetic, namely that of power (the territorial factor). Power generates the dialetic of domination and observance. In itself, caste is neutral as regards power relations; indeed, caste cannot relate to power, or to politics except in an alien metaphor. Purity and power are both exclusive. They come into conflict is so far as both demand the allegiance of the same individual, but they are not harmonic. Their necessary co-existence implies that neither is able to hold complete sway over the society. If the principle of purity were to hold complete sway, if all organization and activity were to be carried out in caste terms (if the society were to become completely caste traditional), there would be no place for power relations in it; it would be a political society. This is what Dumont means when he says that caste hierarchy does not imply inequality, for inequality implies a symmetric power relationship.[5] On the other hand, in so far power relations hold complete sway, i.e., if the society were to be thoroughly politicised, there would be no place for caste in it. Power dominance would drive out purity relationships. In this sense also, caste and class are exclusive categories. Only one of these can obtain at any place. But, in practice, both exist because neither prevails so widely and deeply as to become exclusive organising principle of society.

In India, however, caste is more inter-spread than class, and caste ideology more prevalent than the territorial principle or the power nexus. From this point of view, one can say that the fundamental social dichotomy in India society today is not between pure and impure; but between purity and power, between renunciation of wealth power and embracing them. Rejection of this world, or 'other worldliness' (ascetism) has been treated as peculiar characteristic of Hindu religiousity. Max Weber called Brahmins, the virtuous of renunciation, and, in developing this concept further, formulated his thesis of 'this worldly ascetism' of the Protestants (Particularly the Calvimists) to explain the motivating force of the rise of modern capitalism in Britain. It is clear however not the cult of renunciation in Brahminism is of different order than its European counterpart.

In Indian Society, two different factors seem to have been involved. In the first place, the ritual of making sacrifices to propitiate gods or forces of nation. Priests officiate at the sacrifices and act as intermediaries between their clients and the gods, for without their expert handling of the sacrifices it would be worthless and, indeed, might provoke the wrath of the gods rather than their beneficence. A sacrifice is, psychologically seen, as an act of self-denial, and thus contains the seeds of renunciation. But a qualitative transformation takes place when the priests begin to 'sacrifice' their own selves. In this way, they are symbolically or ritualistically lost to this world, but raise themselves above ordinary human being including those who command their services, namely, the men of power and wealth, thus assimilating themselves sipiritually to the supernatural reaches, becoming god-like. This situation give rise to two kinds of power: *first,* command over resources of this world and of this life, coupled with skill in using human and material force. The other is command over the resources of the ritual offerings, for it is clear that only politics of sacrifice, indeed supreme self-reliance , which is embedded in the caste system, can emancipate India from caste division and class exploitation.

We can infer, from the views presented by Dumount in his remarkable work that caste system as an analytical construct is an ideology in social behaviour, symbolizes an alignment between purity and power, for getting the best of the world. It is this illicit alliance between the pure and the powerful which has been responsible for pauperization of the unprivileged masses who have been systematically deprived of all their legitimate rights that they ought to exercise as bonafide members of society. Thus caste presupposes a demarcation line between those who by virtue of their traditionally dominant social position thrive on socio-economic resources and human labour in a parasitic way, so as to afford luxurious life conditions on the one hand, and those who, because of their inferiority of birth, area constrained to serve upper echelons of society, both morally and materially, on the other. Obviously, social segregation of the masses in the name of purity and sanctity, has been the root cause of their destitution. This lead us to the obvious conclusion that it has been first the social poverty: economic pauperisation has followed with the passage of time. Poverty of the teeming millions, therefore, has been an indirect consequence of social segregation. Unfortunately, most of the studies on caste, conducted in recent years, have been too conventional and status quoit to realize the necessity of analysing caste in terms of a political economy of social hierarchy in Indian society.

The protagonists of caste system in Indian society say that it gives a person an identity and a sphere of action and achievement. People identify themselves as belonging to a named family, a particular village and a particular caste. These are not only principles of identification but also of personal security to a certain extent. All the modern means of security like service pension, an old-age pension, a public medical service or insurance of some sort of other are not available in the India of today to a large majority of people. It is the family, extended or nuclear, which still cares for its sick or aged members who may have been working in a big urban centre. However, even there, protagonists have started realising the fact that caste today is proving to be tumbling block in the process of democratization of Indian polity. This is because it has tended to become the only effective way for securing effective political power and a command over the population of one's own caste. In this use of caste, all the old factors known to be possessed by the system play their role. The family with its network of blood and affinal relations is the nucleus of support. There the whole caste or a large part of it stands as supporter. To this may be added the factor of localization. If a caste is spread in large number over a certain small area which may be one or several election districts, that helps this leverage also. Another important factor especially in the present democratic election is the numerical strength of a caste vis-a-vis other castes. And last but not the least is the position a caste holds in a hierarchical system. A minority may be such a critical minority that its votes may decide who of the contending persons from the majority caste is going to win.[6]

It is clear that caste—both as an institution and as a system of social organization, continues to strongly influence—cultural, economic, and political aspects of Indian society. The vast majority of the population, observes Prof. M.N. Srinivas, not only want caste to disappear but they would probably find it impossible to envisage a social system without caste.[7] Even the social scientists with most militant turn of mind who condemn it is an obstacle to economic development and political modernization in the country have unwillingly admitted its pervasive character involving a state of mind which is among the most constraining facts of social and political life. Even recent empirical studies which have tried to explore the interaction between traditional social structure and modern democratic politics simply corroborate the fact that caste continues to be a predominant consideration for the average Indian voter, especially in rural areas, and, as such, it still appears to be the very basis of social and political mobilization. There is a happy trend today, however Electoral studies after 1962 point out the fact that caste, though it has tended to be reinforced as an ideology which forcefully resists the onslaught of the forces of modernization, has gradually, become less relevant for urban voter. There appears to be marked difference between rural and urban castes. Even in the case of rural voters who are under constant influence of urban mode of social life, purist or ritual category of caste has been loosened, though in a very slow manner. One of the major effects of adult franchise has been a shift in the locus of power from traditionally 'dominant castes' to mumerically stronger castes which involves political dominace of middle and lower middle castes. For, these castes, caste consciousness has been mixed with economic and political issues. Age, income, education, and communication seem to influence caste proneness of the voters of the castes, irrespective of their ecological and social background. Similar changes have been observed in the leadership positions of ritually high castes. There is a tendency on this part of seek support of the lower castes and even identify themselves at least functionally, as the leaders of these castes enjoy substantial numerical strength in a given area. Their leadership role being no longer characterized by dominance based on ritual status, they have been replaced by an emerging cadre of young and promising leaders from these castes. These significant changes are indicative of changing higher caste-low caste power relationship in a democratic framework of reference.

There is another important trend in this regard. The growing urge for participation in the framework for political democracy has given rise to various caste organizations. Most of these organizations with identical interests are marked with a tendency to combine as a class for obtaining, by way of suppressing, initially as an imperative of political expediency, inter-caste prejudices of the past legitimate shares in the gains of economic planning and modernization. This has greatly facilitated a shift to the locus of power from traditionally dominant forward castes to numerically stronger lower castes. Thus, the process of 'social emancipation' as well as 'political conscientisation' of the middle and the lower caste, seems to be facilitated by the growing exposure to mass media, awareness of the extended political institutions, and a growing urge to participate in the broad-based socio political process. This has been corroborated by two facts: the unprecedented increase in the number of young and educated leaders from these castes and the widespread emergence of intercaste organizations consisting of caste groups with identical economic and political interests.

## Politics of Modernization

The issue of reservation in government job and educational institutions, first to the ex-untouchables or scheduled castes and later to the backward classes, has become, in recent years, one of the most controversial issues with far reaching implications for social and political life. Opinions about the reservation issue have been sharply divided and as such it has generated a tendency of polarization in social relations and politics. We may discuss various dimensions of this issue in this chapter.

Needless to say that Mahatma Gandhi and Dr. B.R. Ambedkar were great champions of the scheduled castes. But not many of us know that they differed strongly on at least one issue, i.e., the issue of reservation for the ex-untouchables. It was at a stromy round-table conference in London, over a decade before India won freedom that Ambedkar sought reservations for the scheduled castes, on the lines of those for Muslims, in government jobs and educational institutions. Ambedkar felt that unless the harijans were delinked from the Hindus and separate provisions were made for them, they (the Harijans) would never be able to get out of the quagmire of poverty and ignorance. Mahatma Gandhi differed from Dr. Ambedkar on this point and instead chose to launch a nation-wide movement against untouchability. He gave these people the name of Harijan (meaning the sons of God) lived among them and tirelessly worked for their uplift. Uninfluenced by this,

Ambedkar alongwith his followers embraced Buddhism in order to cast away the unequal status suffered by them as Hindus. After independence, the Indian Government introduced the scheme of job reservation for the scheduled castes, however. Similarly the benefit of reservations was extended to other weaker sections of society. To begin with 15 percent of the government jobs were reserved for scheduled castes, 7.5 percent for the scheduled tribes, 10 to 20 percent for ex-servicemen and 3 percent for the physically handicapped. Thus our 35.5 percent of Government jobs were reserved. Apart from this an equal percentage of seats in medical, engineering and other colleges were reserved. Such reservations were permitted under Article 15 (4) and Article 46 for admissions to educational insitutions while Articles 16 (4) and 335 as well as Article 46 provide for the reservation of claims of the scheduled castes and scheduled tribes to services and posts. The scheduled castes and scheduled tribes apart, there are the other backward classes which have been clamouring for reservations. The first Backward Classes Panel of Kaka Sahab Kalelkar has suggested caste as a criterion for determining backwardness for reservation. The government, however, did not accept Kalelkar Commission's report and felt that the emphasis on caste was incorrect and the remedies suggested on the basis of caste would be more damaging than the evil of backwardness itself. With this kind of reasoning, the Government did not, find it necessary to draw a list of other backward classes. Instead, it left the entire matter to the discretion of states, advising them to adapt economic backwardness of criterion in place of caste.

In the year 1979, the secong Backward classes commission headed by B.P. Mandal was constituted. The criterion for Backwardness adopted by the Mandal Commission has been kept secret, as it has not so far been laid on the floor of the Indian Parliament. Mandal Commission, however, made it public that 50 per cent of the population would fall under the backward category and they it is said, too have emphasized the criterion of caste in determining backwardness.

Protest against reservation in recent years have been frequent. The anti-reservationists have stressed the danger to administrative efficiency and professional standards. They feel that reservation will have ill-consequences for every institution—the judiciary, the army, cabinet, administration, research establishments. This is because reservation, they say, will be forced in total disregard for competence, to reflect the demographic distributions and, as such, its consequences will be chaotic. Besides, such reservations violate ones right to equally before law as guaranteed by Article 14 of the constitution.

Sometime back, two court decisions-one by a High Court division bench and another by a three-member Supreme Court bench-brought the issue of reservations, both of job and admissions to educational institutions, into a sharp focus. The court gave its rulings in the light of the fact that the right to promote the educational and economic interests' of the scheduled castes, scheduled tribes, and other weaker sections of society was enshrined in the constitution by the founding fathers, and that this constitutional position itself pre-empted any debate as to whether or not we should have any reservation at all. Thus, for example, Justice V.R. Krishna Iyer, one of the three judges of the bench, felt that the issue of reservation was no matter of speculation or investigation, because the constitution itself has recognized the backward status of the scheduled castes and the scheduled tribes in socio-economic terms. According to him, there was nothing shady about the provision of allowing lesser marks as sufficient or adding extra marks to give the scheduled castes and scheduled tribes an advantage. This provision, he said, has been made under article 15 (4) and 16 (A). Justice Iyer had also reflected arguments about inefficiency as "Trifle Phoney", nothing that at the higher levels the Harijans constituted a microscopic percentage and even in the case of class II and class III posts, they are negligible. The court decisions, apart, it has been argued that the preponderant majority coming from the unreserved communities are presumably efficient. Therefore, dilution of efficiency caused by the minimal induction of a small percentage of 'reserved' candidates cannot affect the overall administrative efficiency significantly. Indeed, it would be gross exaggeration, according to pre-reservationists, to visualize a collapse of the administration; because 5 or 10 percent of the total number of officials in the various classes happen to be sub-standard.[8]

Let us examine the whole issue of reservation in a sociological perspective. The reservation principle, as we have earlier stated, was enjoined in the constitution due to a realization that without such arrangement, the spirit of democratic government would be instantly negated by the gross inequalities of the Hindu caste system. Yet, it was not a favour to Harijans, as most anti-reservationists presume, rather it was the smallest concession that could be desired without making a mockery of the objective of a just social order. Moreover, the post-independence political elite was not entirely unaware of the attractiveness of the egalitarian promise of communism. It must be remembered that at that time communism was the only challenge to the Gandhian ideology of gradualism in economic and social changes. Consequently the lowest stratum, the Harijans and the Adivasis, had to be protected against the corrupting lure of social justice held only by the leftist political parties in India. Hence the reservation principles. It called for the system the much needed efficacy and credibility with the masses, and Harijans and Advasis political defection from the system was deferred by a promise of crumbles at appropriate times, provided they played the game according to the rules.[9]

Widespread agitation against reservation indicate the fact that those rules are not being sought to be changed unilaterally. Caste Hindus seem to have determined that thirty years of the reservation arrangement have adequately compensated for centuries of oppression against the Harijans and that the latter have sufficiently overcome the psychological, educational and economic disadvantages occurring from that oppression to compete on an equal footing. Naturally, arguments against continuation of reservation is absurd. Yet, when examined closely, these arguments turn out to be claims of superiority due to being upper caste Hindus by virtue of birth. We can take the example of arguments of reverse discrimination. It is asked, in a somewhat reasonable vein, why should a brilliant student be denied admission to college simply— because he comes from an upper caste? The argument, at least, is a spurious one. Surely, isolated instances can be cited in its support. But it loses it punch when juxtaposed against the prevailing informal system of pervasive discrimination against Harijans. It would, for example, be a ludicrous for a Professor in Medical College to maintain that he repeatedly fails a Harijan medical student, because of the students' demonstrable lack of competence.

Has reservation created a vested interest in backwardness? It is a 'crutch' argument. That some Harijan leaders have capitalized on their community's poverty cannot mean that commitment to ameliorate the condition of the Harijan masses becomes either any less urgent or any less demanding. To say that the Harijans no longer need the 'crutch' of reservation system, is to say that our society and polity has become somehow so enlightened as to provide a genuine quality of opportunity for all. This is just not true. There are evidences to show that outside the governmental agencies, Harijans remain mostly where they always have been, i.e, at the lowest rungs of professional hierarchy. For example, a Harijan in the managerial ranks of an industry or in a leadership ranks of the trade unions, even of those unions purportedly looking after the Harijan's interests, is a rare find. Again, without the 'crutch' of quotas in housing, no Harijan doctor or educator, whatever his professional accomplishments, can move out of Harijans slums into a decent neighbourhood.

It has been said that the reservation has created class of elite among Harijans. No doubt an 'elite' can be identified among Harijans. But it is a natural sociological phenomena. An educated Harijan graduates into an elite group simply, because he has managed to acquire some skills that enable him to move beyond the poverty and deprivation in which the overwhelming majority of his brethren continue to live. His education and profession lend him a quality of separateness or, one may say, of elitism, but gives him little power in the wider social context that reamains unimpressed by his acheivements.

As for the question of efficiency, the arguments advanced are too queer to hold a substantial ground. Only a bigot can argue that the reservation has caused 'inefficiency in administration or elsewhere when the scheduled castes and scheduled tribes combine to boast of only 54 first class officers, out of a total of 2,848, of only 425 second class officers out of a total of 10,293, and of 37,490 third class officers out a total of 43,156. Or how can the quality of administration, educational institution, and medical care be compromised when who Harijans and the Adivasis have not managed more than two to five percent of seats or posts anywhere? Indeed, what the efficiency proponents really lament is that because of reservations, a certain portion of spoils and partonage goes out of control and manipulation of the already powerful in a widespread traditional social setting. Even the question as to how long the reservation will continue seem to be a desparate bid to thwart the process of democratization of administrative structure by removing age old social disparities through reservation. The answer to this question is simple, as long as the value system of Hindu society continues to render inoperative; any effective application of the equality of opportunity concept. The problem, the sceptic note, is that the Government cannot intervene unendingly to enforce legislative intent and constitutional obligations if the society at large remains untutored in the advisability of a particular social reform. The argument is a familiar one, and has been advanced and rejected in areas of untouchability, minimum wages, women's rights, land reforms, and other social issues, Moreover, only an unambiguous reaffirmation of the reservation philosophy can repdudiate the social outlook that demands for now only an end to reservations in medical care, educational institutions, and administration, but is intrinsically insatiable. A concession in one area is bound to be followed by demands in other area. The logical culmination of the anti-reservation argument would be an end to reserved constituencies in the Lok Sabha and in the Assemblies. But is the society and the polity in contemporary India, already so mature as to do away with these crucial policies of uplift of the weaker and oppressed sections? And will premature discontinuation of these policies be without for disastrous implications for the weaker sections in particular and the society as whole in general? These are some of the important questions which hint at the social and political dimensions of reservation policy in the country.

## Backward Classes : The Case of Bihar

Sometime back, Government of Bihar decided, on the pattern of other states like U.P., Haryana, Punjab and most of the South Indian States, a certain proportion of jobs for the Backward Classes of the State. The decision was part of a general policy to uplift some of the communities which have, on account of social disabilities suffered by them, languished behind in the process of development of the state as a whole. The basic concern behind such proposal thus was to ensure not only the extension of economic gains to these classes, but also providing them with adequate opportunities for participation in the political and administrative processes with a view to ushering in an era of development and distributive social justice. Such concern was obviously rooted in the understanding of Indian society in a historical perspective which involves 'institutionalized modes of perpetrating communication on the weaker sections of society. In fact, during the last thirty seven years little was done, except shedding a lot of crocodile tears on their sub-human condition to put an end to the usurious and sub-human life conditions of the people who belonged to socially and educationally disadvantaged sections of society and who deserved more official attention for their welfare than other sections of society.

It is this fact which had in fact prompted the setting up of Kaka Kalelkar commission during the Congress regime and B.P. Mandal Commission during that of Janata Party, with a clearly defined goal of going into the problems of the Backward Classes at India basis. While the recommendations of the Kaka Kalelkar Commission-25 percent reservation for Class I employees, 33 percent for Class II and 40 percent for Class III and IV employees remained unimplemented, those of the Mandal Commission has been shelved and there is mounting pressure on the Government to place it before the Parliament for enabling their implementation. Instead of formulating a national policy of reservation in the light of the recommendations of these Commissions, the various Governments, in a bid to prolong and subdue the matter, state governments were asked to set up their own commissions. While the southern states established their commissions as early as in fifties, no action was taken in the northern states. In Bihar, a commission was constituted only in 1971 at the instance of Karpoori Thakur, the then Chief Minister. This commission was chaired by Mongheri Lal who submitted his report in 1976, thereby suggesting a uniform 33 per cent reservation of government jobs for the socially and educationally backward classes, exclusive of the quota of jobs reserved for Harijans and Adivasis, which is in force ever since 1950. Although there have been no agreed national criteria for the identification of the socially and educationally backward classes, many states have, in order to avoid complications, relied on the Kalelkar formula which clearly accepted the caste as the main basis of backwardness.

The Mongheri Lal commission also brought out two lists-Annexure I made a note of the 94 most backward communities and Annexure II listed 35 relatively less backward communities. His report, however, was shelved by the then Congress Government which felt a little uncomfortable about it. Even Government inspite of its Party's manifesto to implement the Kalelkar Commission's recommendations, backed out on its promise. In Bihar, however, when the Janata Government decided to go ahead with polity of reserving twenty six per cent of the government job for backward classes, there was an uproar from the upper castes. As a result, the formula was slightly modified. Twelve per cent of jobs were to go to those listed in the Annexure I and eight per cent to those included in the Annexure II whose yearly income was less than Rs. 8,000. Of the remaining six per cent, three were to be reserved for women and another three for the economically poor among the upper castes, who were landless and whose income did not exceed Rs. 3,000 a year. The notification of the reservation policy by the Karpoori Thakur Government, however, was more a dangerous deception than clear enough to symbolize its real concern for the uplift of the backward classes. According to this notification, the process of reservation for backward classes was to remain the same as in the case of scheduled castes and scheduled tribes, i.e., twenty percent of reservation comprised even those who edged out general candidates on the basis of their merit. This meant that the candidates qualifying for the jobs on the basis of their proven eligibilities which outdistanced them even among the general candidates had to be clubbed within the twenty per cent ceiling, simply because they hailed from these social and educationally disadvantaged sections. Karpoori Thakur Government could hardly realize the mangitude of this malicious blunder which robbed the backward classes of their fundamental rights rather than providing them succour and solace even after centuries of social segregation and economic exploitation. As a matter of fact, this camouflaged mischief in the notification itself, was the glaring example of how anti-reservationist lobby succeeded in dominating and even distorting a government decision of crucial importance which was to embody the spirit of Indian constitution in this regard.

It is surprising that the job reservation which could easily be implemented in all the southern and most of the northern states, has met with stiff and organized resistance in Bihar. In Kerala and Kanataka forty percent jobs are reserved for the backward, in Tamil Nadu fifty eight percent, in Andhra Pradesh twenty five percent, in Maharashtra thirty three percent, and in all these states such reservations exclude eighteen percent job reserved for scheduled castes and scheduled tribes. The reason for the opposition to reservation in Bihar is more than unemployment and economic hardship which are used to shield the anti-reservationist stance, the age-old feudal characteristics of the social and political systems. In fact, the anti-reservation struggle itself has been responsible, in recent years, not only for the widespread awareness of rights among the backward sections, but also for turning the whole issue into what appears to be as a state-wide 'second-liberation-movement' in Bihar.

At this crucial juncture, it is worthwhile to highlight certain historical forces which have operated in most parts of the country and have tended to bring about a definite enlightenment among the weaker sections which now are asserting for their appropriate share in the gains of democratic planning and for their participation, at all levels, in the decisions and policies for their development. In fact the problem need to be examined in an integral perspective in order that a rational framework of public debate on the issue is carved out and the intellectuals who have faith in democratic values and norms of social justice may be cautioned against any conspiracy, connivance, and sabotage against the Governments concern for creating such administrative mechanisms which can allow equal footing to the backward classes who were desparately struggling against the traditional clutches of exploitation by the upper sections of society. Obviously, for examining the overt and covert dimensions of the problem, we shall divide the perspective into demographic, socio-economic, and constitutional contexts.

### Numerical Position

An idea about the position of backward classes in relation to the total population of the state will show genuineness of those upright and conscientious thinkers and politicians who have championed the cause of weaker sections of Indian society. According the census of 1931, the total populations of the state was 3,25,57,056 out of which the backward classes including scheduled castes and scheduled tribes numbered 2,95,22,730 which was approximately 91 percent of the total population. People belonging to the forward castes numbered only 30,34,326 which was not even 10 percent of the total population of the state. Caste wise break-up of the population of the forward castes is shown below:

**Population Data of Bihar**

| | *1931* | *1971 (projected)* |
|---|---|---|
| Brahmin | 10,95,054 | 18,95,429 |
| Rajput | 9,94,110 | 17,20,705 |
| Bhumihar | 7,22,561 | 12,50,647 |
| Kayastha | 2,22,666 | 3,85,231 |
| Total Population of the forward castes | 30,34,326 | 52,51,012 |
| Total Population of the backward castes and S.C. and S.T. | 2,95,22,730 | 5,11,01,988 |
| Total Population | 3,25,57,056 | 5,63,53,000 |

We can clearly see the numerical preponderance of the backward sections. It is this fact which has urged the pro-reservationists to claim as much as 90 percent share in administrative and economic opportunities. Obviously, this could be realized only when the people belonging to the backward classes are granted proportional representation in the political and administrative structures. Despite genuineness of their demand, very little has been done by the government in this direction because of the violent reaction of the vested interests which want, by hook or crook, to maintain thier monopoly and dominance on economic and political fronts. As a result little attention has been paid to their claim and even the official proposals for amelioration of the lot of backward sections has been jeered at by the anti-reservationist lobby among the bureaucrats and the politicians. However, in recent years, the demand of the backward sections has tended to acquire an unprecedented universal recognition and there has been clear indication of the beginning of an Era of Enlightenment among these people.

**Cultural-Roots of Exploitation**

It is strange that no sooner the erstwhile Janata Government in the state announced, under the pressing circumstances, their decision to reserve 96 per cent of jobs for the backward classes than the vested interests with connivance of the press and the political elite belonging to the forward sections started hatching up conspiracies to block the process of democratization of administrative structure in the state. Press started a systematic tirade against reservation with a view to misguide public opinion and providing propagandist protection to those who were worried about the undermining of their traditionally dominant caste position and about the future of their sons and daughters, who were to lose the undue privilege granted to them by the perpetuation of exploitative conditions. It is strange that even those holding the high rank in the government and the organization hierarchy of political party in power tried more than those who opposed the policy of reservation itself, to thwart the process by raising the bogey of economic criteria of backwardness. What is more, they succeeded, strangely enough, in obtaining, a similar declaration by late J.P. who, throughout his political Odyssey supported, in a true Gandhian tradition, the cause of the weaker sections of society. This was followed by undemocratic proclamations of many political leaders of high rank and office in clear violation of the spirit of their party's manifesto which has enabled them to obtain a massive political mandate in 1977 parliamentary elections. They were soon to be joined by the veteran leader JB Kripalani who to the extent of urging the government to make economic conditions as sole criterion for reservations. The unscrupulous utterances of the central leaders proved to be a shot in the arm of the anti-reservations who were determined to stall the government's decision by staging violent 'psycho-dramas' in the streets of Patna.

But why these psycho-dramas? The storm seemed to be virtually in a tea-cup. In Bihar, no more than 25,000 job opportunities are created every year. Of these 16,000 are in central Government undertakings and 9,000 in state government departments, state undertakings, and local bodies. Since 2,16024 percent of 9,000—are reserved for Harijans and Adivasis, only 6,840 remain for the rest. And if 26 per cent of these are allocated for the backward section, about 5,800 jobs will be available for the candidates of general categories. But the picutre is slightly different than it appears. Only about 2 per cent of the jobs have so far been filled by the Schedules Caste and Scheduled Tribe candidates. The rest of their quota has been grabbed by upper castes under the seemingly plausible plea of non-availability of 'suitable' candidates from these categories. This position was bound to continue even in the case of reservation for backwards as very few candidates, especially among the extremely backward castes were there to aspire for these jobs. It is true that a certain proportion of candidates who could benefit from the reservation hailed from relatively better-off middle castes, such as Yadavas, Kurmis, Koeires and Vaishyas. But it is absolutely mischievous to say that all of these candidates belonged to wealthy families of these castes and that majority of people of these castes were prosperous and powerful like feudal lords of upper castes. In fact, the proportion of land rich and economically well-off persons among these castes is almost the same as the proportion of land-poor and unpoverished among the castes. The case of even Vaishyas does not make an exception, because if we exclude Marwaris, Agarwals, and some effluent sections of Rauniyars and Kesarvanis, their position will be identical to other backward castes. Even the bulk of Koeires and Kurmis, with the exception of land-rich Dangis and Awadhiyas, respectively, constitutes the rural-poor in the villages. Likewise, excepting a slander proportion of land-rich and educated families, the majority of Yadavas live in extremely impoverished conditions in the villages. It is these people who have been constrained to sell or mortgage their small possessions of land and have become landless agricultural labourers over years. Conditions of these people are similar to those of the Harijans from the view point of segregation and exploitation. Those who have had a close look at the pattern off land-ownership, income and caste, can easily realize that the majority of even these middle castes still constitutes the wretched of the earth. However the anti-reservationists have tried to mislead the public opinion by portraying an image of these castes which has nothing to do with reality. Thus, the very fact that the press, the vested interests in administration, and malicious brand of politicians who invariably belong to the upper sections of society has succeeded in delaying and even distorting the reservation policy of the Government by creating nuisance in public life and giving the impression of having mobilized the whole society against it thereby rocking the governmental machinery, indicates the fact that how deep-rooted is the casteist attitude among the upper sections which are trying to stage a desparate fight or perpetuating the traditional dominance of 10 per cent people over 90 per cent of whole population.

Be that as it may, let us highlight some of the intricate elements of the problem, which have their root in the social structure itself. Indian society has been organized on the principles of heredity and ascription, i.e., the social status being determined by birth and in no case by economic status. The hereditory character of society is such as to allow the notion of purity and superiority to some of the castes which have been placed on the top of the social organization, best known as *Varna Vyawastha* that consists of the four categories of castes with polarity between Brahmins and Sudras. The purity and superiority of castes are based on two principles, viz., the birth and the hereditary right for subordinating others and getting immunity from physical labour for livelihood. This demarcates a line between those who thrive on the social resources and human labour in a parasitic way so as to afford luxurious life conditions, on the one hand, and those who are characterised by inferiority by birth and obligations to serve physically, morally, and materially the upper echelons of the society, on the other. This means that those who are immune from physical labour for livelihood have to preserve their dominant position in the society (presumably because leisure and luxury allows them to be more powerful mentally and materially), whereas a larger section of the society is subjugated, rather inhumanly to the interests of an obligation towards the upper castes. Here the concept of physical labour based on social segregation becomes a crucial factor which has nothing to do with economic position, as those who labour for others do so because it is socially required from them.

Therefore, it is first social poverty, economic pauperization followed with the passage of time. Economic poverty of the teeming millions, therefore, is a product of cultural segregation. The normative order of the society is so designed as to help the perpetuation of this segregation. Poverty of the millions is a cultural imperative which must be preserved at any cost. The whole situation warrants for an analysis on the lines which will sound like a critique of political economy of social hierarchy in Indian society. This can be contrasted with the Western society which is based upon entirely different principles. Social structure of the west is based not on birth and heredity (nobility is now a historical myth), but on income and material conditions.

In highly industrialized society, growing economic disparity between the social class is responsible for the tendency of political polarisation. Whatever the extent of class-conflict and competition, they are aimed at maintaining the growth of society as a whole in which the two classes, bourgeois and proletariat, struggle for ensuring even distribution of material income. Viewed in this perspective, proletarization of the industrial workers leading to class polarisation is confined to the economic scene, the social structure being extremely flexible without any institutionalized segregation in terms of rigid cultural elements like caste. Of course, one can be tempted to dismiss this theory by citing example of racial segregation and religious conflict, but these black spots of western democratic societies have nothing to do with social hierarchization with rigid and inflexible caste or class strata. Equality among men, therefore seems to be the basic foundations of Western society which is inspired by its biblical traditions. Thus the fact that the descendants of Adam and Eve were all cursed to earn their bread by the "sweat of their forehead" rules out any theory of segregation between man and man. Physical labour is must for all rather than a cultural factor for preserving luxury and leisure of a handful of people at the cost of blood and sweat of the teeming millions. Therefore, the intention that backwardness in Indian society should be determined by economic criteria is not tenable, as it ignores not only the historical facts but also involves a malafide intention in the name of democratization. We must remember that oppression and economic poverty are two independant categories. Former is rooted in the cultural order of society which encourages subjugation and exploitation whereas the latter is simply the outcome of institutional segregation in the social structure. It is the cultural parasitism which encourages pauperization and backwardness and not the vice-versa in any case.

## Politics of Deprivation

In fact, the framers of our Constitution under the Charimanship of Dr. B.R. Ambedkar had clearly envisaged such necessity and had stressed on the point of making necessary provisions in this regard. Thus the Government's proposed policy is directly related to the Article 16 of the Indian Constitution, which reads as under:—

> "Nothing in this Article shall prevent the State from making such provisions for the reservation of appointment of posts in favour of any backward class of citizens, which in the opinion of the State is not adequately represented in the service under the State".

Before the above provision was incorporated in the Constitution, the Constituent Assembly witnessed heated debate on the issue. One of the members of the Constituent Assembly Mr. Dharmaprakash expressed his preference of "Depressed Caste" to the word "Backward" but other members rejected his proposal for amendment. Likewise, Dr. Haridayanath Kunjru had objected to the use of the word "Backward" under the plea of ambiguity in the usage, which might lead to "many misinterpretations". Mr. Chandrika Ram, a M.P. from Bihar had asserted that the word "Backward" was amply defined in the Census Report, and as such, he pleaded for reservation of the job quota for the Backward classes which could be at par with that for the Scheduled Castes. Mr. K.M. Munshi, while intervening the debate, also contended before other members that "Backward Class" meant a class of people needing special protection in public services and so there was no reason for any kind of mis-apprehension. He also pleaded for the imperative of setting up a commission for examining the matter and suggesting as to which castes should be included in the list of Backward Classes. The dispute however, continued and a group of members led by Shri T.T. Krishnamachari wanted the deletion of the word "Backward" as it might render the Constitution as a "lawyers paradise". However, Late Dr. B.R. Ambedkar, while making replies to various questions of the members, observed that Constitution of any country might become "lawyers paradise" because of the fact of the country and the lot of its people. Thus while removing the doubts about validity of the usage of the term "Backward", he further observed that there were three points of view which needed to be reconciled. The *first* proposition was that there should be equality of opportunity open to all citizens, irrespective of class, creed, descent, sex etc.

*Secondly*, he felt that certain provisions must be made for the entry of classes who had been denied the privileges of being associated with the administration. *Thirdly*, he felt that unless certain reservations are made for the backward classes, adequate representation of this hitherto unpri-vileged section of the society, will not be made in public services. Hence the fact that no better formula could be introduced that one indicated in para 3 of Article 10 of the draft Constitution. Dr. Ambedkar's observations pacified the excitement of all the members regarding reservation in services for the backward castes. Later, after adopting constitution, the Government constituted the Kaka Kalelkar Commission, which after careful examination of every aspect of the problem, prepared a list of such castes, which were to be included in the long list of the Backward Classes for enabling them to be benefited from the protective provisions of the State in service policy. Thus it is amply clear that the question regarding the basis of backwardness has already been settled. To raise this question again and to make it an issue of further debate in order to nourish baseless controversies is nothing but a sign of dishonesty towards our Constitution. If we see the Schedule 4 of Article 16 of the Constitution regarding reservation of services for the Backward Classes, nothing will seem to be inappropriate. Still the largest proportion of the Government services in the State of the Central organizations are occupied by forward castes, who hold the key positions for virtually dictating the term in the Government. In such situation, the representation of the Backward Classes seems to be the foremost condition for their induction into administrative structure. Thus the plea for economic basis of backwardness is inconsistent with the Constitutional provisions which have been made after a long and careful examination of the issue. By providing reservation in Government jobs, we can ameliorate the lot of backward classes granting them freedom from social segregation and economic exploitation which alone can make them capable of marching hand-in-hand with forward sections of the society towards the national goal of social justice and economic prosperity.

**Castes Vs Income Controversy : A Rational view**

While one cannot gainsay the social necessity and constiutional validity of the policy of reservation of jobs to the Backward classes of social the educational grounds, there can be differences about the modalities of its implementation. Realizing the irreversibility of such policy, it has been suggested that while the importance of caste cannot be denied, income criteria should also be incorporated in this policy. Government's prompt acceptance of this suggestion has led to fixation of a ceiling of Rs. 12,000 annual income for allowing the benefits of a reservation to the members of backward communites. The gesture of the Government has still been rejected by those who give the plea that since 70 per cent of the total population of this State is below poverty line, the ceiling of income as such, has no meaning. It is strange that these people have suddenly awakened to realise the gravity of the situation which probably never existed for them earlier. Curiously enough, they are seemingly ignorant of the fact that the population of the State which continues to live in the conditions of stark poverty and starvation consists of mainly those belonging to the weaker sections of society, who have been denied freedom of initiative and social justice for centuries together. Of course, some castes among backward sections have become nouveauriche in the process of democratization of the economic structure, but one cannot afford to dismiss the whole idea of reservation while ignoring the impoverished lot of the backward classes at large. The ceiling of income, therefore, as proposed by the Government in any case, seems to be adequate safeguard against the possibility of some nouveauriche families belonging to particular castes, taking undue advantage of the situation. There should be clear difference between "backwardness" and "backwardism"—former implying the actual life conditions of the socially and educationally unprivileged sections and the latter not more than a political slogan for protecting vested interests among the backwards themselves. The hands of the Government deserved to be strengthened by an enlightened public opinion based on moral accountability of the forward castes, which can function as a watchdog on the administrative machinery responsible for ensuring percolation of the benefits to those who really deserve it. Short of this, the whole society may be carried to the brink of chaos and anarchy, nay a 'war of castes', everywhere in this country.

### References


1. Iravati Karve, "Caste and Modernization", in AR Desai (ed.) *op. cit.* pp. 115-18.
2. R.S. Mann, *Social Structures Social Change and Future trends,* Jaipur: Rawat Publications: 1979.
3. Melvin Tumin, *Social Stratification: The Forms and Functions of Inequality,* Englewood Cliffs. Prentice Hall, 1967 pp. 17-18.
4. Anil Bhatia, *Caste, Class and Politics, An Empirical Profile of Social Stratification in Modern India* (New Delhi: Manohar Book Service 1975) p. 5.
5. Surinder Suri, "New Perspective", *Seminar,* May 1974, pp. 34.
6. Karve, *op, cit.* p. 118.
7. Srinivas, *op. cit.*
8. Javed Faridi, "Job Reservation: How Much, For whom, and How Long? "*The Hindustan Times Magazine, New Delhi* Nov. 23, 1980 p. 1.
9. Harish Khanna, New Delhi "Why Reservations" *Hindustan Times.*

# Chapter - 12

# Sociology of Elite

The concept of elite refers to a fundamental feature of organized or semi-organized human groups and communities. Every society, simple or complex, agricultural or industrial, rural or urban-needs authorities or agents who can exercise power for the maintenance of social order. These authorities and agents of power are the symbols of common life and embodiment of the values that maintain it. Inequalities in performance and rewards support this arrangement, and constitute a basis for the coordination of authority, achievement and reward. The concept thus refers to those minority of individuals who are set apart from the rest of society by their pre-eminence in one or more of these various distributions.

In traditional societies, the pattern of distribution of authority and power is relatively simple as they invariably correspond to the traditional imperatives in this regard. In modern societies, however, they become complex as there is no single comprehensive elite but rather a complex system of specialized elites linked to the social order and to each other in a variety of ways. As society grows complex they become too numerous and varied to possess common features and affinities which characterize a traditional pattern of power structure. Such elites emerge in almost all spheres of social life-business, military, industry, commerce, culture, and politics. Elites in these areas differ in terms of their responsibility, sources of power and patterns of selections and reward. This plurality of elites tend to reflect and promote pluralism characteristic of modern societies[1] Thus in virtually every activity and in every corresponding sphere of social life, there is an elite. In fact, this is the sense in which Pareto had used this term. There is however, an important factor that differentiated these various elites, apart from their different skills and talents; some of them have more social weight than others because their activities have greater social significance. It is these elites-variously referred to ruling elite, the top influentials, or the power elite-which arouse particular interest because they are the prime movers and models for the entire society. Keller has classified different elites into two major categories—strategic and segmental. The strategic elites are those which have the largest, the most comprehensive scope and impact. The boundaries that separate strategic and segmental elites are not sharply defined because of the gradations of authority and the vagueness of the perceptions that assign positions to individuals. The more highly organized the elites are, the easier it is to estimate their boundaries and membership.

Social scientists' interest in the patterns of power structure have, in recent years brought into focus the importance of the study of elite in both developing and developed societies, especially in the context of the implications of social change for power. Contemporary studies on power thus differs a great deal from those of political thinkers like Plato, Aristotle, Machiavelli and Hobbes, who considered powers in relation to the state. They differ a great deal also from the psychologists view that power is an attribute of personality. Political-sociological view of power treats power as an attribute of social relationship. Max Weber had thus defined power as the chance of man or of a number of men to realize their own will in a communal action even against the resistence of others who are participating in the action.[2] Implicit in the definition of power by Max Weber is not the ego-orientation or the coercive right of the state but the conditions of pluralism which characterize present-day societies.

During the 16th century, the term elite was used simply to mean a choice. In the 17th century, it signified commodities of particular excellence. Later, it was used to describe the superior social groups.[3] It was used in England in non-political sense. Those with assured entries into 'high society' were designated as elite. In those days, although the aristocracy was very powerful and influencial force, yet that aspect was most covered by this word. The term was used to indicate the superiority and exclusiveness pertaining to personal relationships.[4] It came into vogue towards the close of the 19th century in the socio-political literature of Europe, Britain and America, and in 1930, through the sociological writings, especially those of Pareto, the Italian sociologist who is also one of the early precursors of modern sociological thinking. But what was precisely meant by the 'elite' is very difficult to discuss. It seems to have been used to mean different things. For instance, Pareto employed this term to designate a class which held a high status and commanded influence in the community.

From the writings of Pareto and Mosca, we conclude that the elite is a group of people who directly exercise strong influence on the government, and the 'governing elite' or political class is composed of distinct social groups. For Lasswell, the members of the elite are "the holders of high positions in a given society.[5] Cole refers to the elites as "groups which emerge to positions of leadership and influence at every social level.[6] Nadel has defined the elite as a "body of persons enjoying a position of pre-eminence over all others"[7], and to Mercier, the elites represent a "social category more or less enjoying prestige, status and exerting influences, by its example, over the whole or large sections of the population.[8] Humanists conceive the "elite not as a social level or category, but as a scatter of those individuals who attempt to transcend themselves, and accordingly, are more noble, more efficient, made out of better stuff.[9] By 'elite', Raymond Aron means the minority which in each of the enumerated professions, has succeeded best and occupied the high positions.[10] According to Kornhauser, the term elite is used in respect of "those positions in a social structure which are super-ordinate, such that the incumbent claimed and are granted social superiority. The term is also used to refer to the functions attached to social positions, especially the specific responsibilities to term and defend value-standards in a certain social sphere. Catlin employs it as the 'control groups', referring to members of cabinets and party chiefs, senior civil servants, Industrial bosses, senior executives and the 'influential people' who, for whatever reasons, can sway those who take decisions.[11]

Thus an analysis of the definitions brings out that such elements as superiority, power and organization are important in defining the term elite. Accordingly, we can treat the elite as those who are regarded as superior, influential and held in high esteem by the people. They may and may not, have formal positions in politics and government, but they are in a position to influence the decision-making process, set values and uphold them. Elites, therefore, are those influential persons who can get things done for the community. The assumption in analysing the elite has been that a relatively small number of persons, well organized, would hold power, whatever may be the nature of society. But the basis of some empirical studies of local communities, the view that an organized minority will rule the many all the time and in all the places has recently been challenged by thinkers like Dahl and others.[12] They maintain that the elite system may be possible in pre-industrial or recently industrialized societies where the social relationships, are comparatively stable and simple. They do not deny the existence of the elite but argue that the control of the society by the elite is not a permanent feature.[13] There are, according to Serene rulers but they are, according to Mosca, not packorganized. But the controversy regarding the rule by the elite persists in spite of several community power-structure studies.[14]

### Differentiation of Elites

Even the earliest known human societies had leading minorities of elders, priests, and warrior kings, who performed elite social functions. A chief in a primitive society, for example, enacted one complex social role in which were fused several major social functions, expressed through the following activities: organization of productive work, propitiation of, and communication with, super natural powers, judgement and punishment of law-breakers coordination of communal activities, defence of the community from enemy attack, discovery of new resources and new solutions to the problems of collective survival, and encouragement and inspiration of artistic expression. As societies expand in size and in the diversity of their activities, such activities also expand, and more elaborate, specialized leadership roles emerge such as, ruling caste, aristocracy, ruling class and finally strategic and segmental elites.[15]

In general it appears that where society as a whole is relatively undifferentiated, elites are few in number and comprehensive in their powers; where social differentiation is extensive, elites are many and specialized. The principal social forces underlying the change form societal leadership based on aristocracy or ruling class to that based on strategic elites are population growth, occupational differentiation, moral heterogeneity and increased bureaucratization. Strategic elites in such societies, who are specialized and differentiated, hold their status not because of blood and wealth but because of merit and skills which they possess. Thus in a large industrialized society which is marked by innumerable ethnic, regional and occupational differences and stratified as to work, wealth, prestige, style of life, and power, leadership cannot be trusted to a single ruler, be he chief, warrior, a priest, or to a single stratum marked by hereditary exclusiveness—and traditionalism. Instead, elites of this society are varied, specialized, and differentiated as to skill, style, background, and rewards. In this way characteristic attributes of the larger society are reflected by the stragetic elites through whom that society tries to realize its main goals and projects. The division of a society into many groups and strata is therefore paralleled by its ramification around a symbolic centre, or core, that signifies the common and enduring characteristics of the differentiated whole.[16]

In every differentiated society, there are patterns of belief and values, shared means of communication, major social institutions, and leading individuals or groups concerned with the maintenance and development of the society and its culture. These leading elements, by focusing attention and coordinating action, help keep the society in working order, so that it is able to manage recurrent crises in collective life. The varied and differentiated groups of elites can be classified in terms of their, four strategic functions. These are: goal attainment, adaptation, integration, and pattern maintenance. Goal attainment refers to the setting and realization of collective goals, adaptation refers to the use and the development of effective means of achieving these goals, integration involves the maintenance of appropriate moral consensus and social cohesion within the system, and, finally, pattern maintenance and tension management involve the moral of the system's units-individuals, groups, and organizations. Accordingly four types of strategic elites, which may include a large number of elites, may be identified: (1) the political elite (elite of goal attainment); (2) the economic, military, diplomatic and scientific elites (elites of adaptation); (3) elites exercising moral authority-religious leaders, philosophers, educators, and social workers (elites of integration); and (4) elites that keep the society knit together emotionally and psychologically, consisting of such celerities as outstanding artists, writers, theatre and film stars, and top figures in sports and recreation (pattern maintenance elites). Societies, however, differ in the way they corporate these functions into living institutions in some societies, usually at simpler stages of development one agent assumes responsibility for all four system functions; in other, several specialized agents emerge. In advanced industrial societies, the tendency is clearly toward several elites whose functional specialization is accompanied by a growing moral and organizational autonomy among them. At the same time, however, the overriding goals of these elites are, as they have always been, the preservation of the ideals and practices of the societies at whose apex they stand.[17]

## Recruitment of Strategic Elites

Elite replacement, which occurs in all societies, involves both the attraction of suitable candidates and their actual selection. What is considered suitable depends on the structure of the elite groups and on whether these elites assume comprehensive or specialized functional responsibilities. Recruitment mechanisms, however varied in practice, reflect only two fundamental principles: recruitment on the basis of biological and social inheritance and recruitment on the basis of personal achievement and talents. Although these two systems are not mutually exclusive, one or the other tends to prevail, depending on the system of social stratification, on the values placed on ascription and achievement, and on magnitude of demand for elite candidates in relation to the supply. These two principles reflect the general tendency within a social system toward expansion or toward consolidation. Under conditions of expansion, recruitment on the basis of personal achievement is likely to be the rule; under consolidation, recruitment based on inheritance of status. Each principle, moreover, has profound repercussions on social mobility, on the stimulation of individual ambitions and talents, and on levels of discontent among different strata. Each affects not only compositive of elites but also their social and moral outlook.[18]

## Rewards of the Elites

The process of selection or allocation is facilitated by the system of rewards offered to individuals assuming leadership positions in society. Some rewards are tangible material benefits such as land, money, cattle, or slaves, and others are intangible, such as social honour and influence. The specific rewards used to attract potential recruits to elite positions depend on the social definition of scarce and desirable values and the distribution of these values. Rewards may be a two fold role in the recruitment elites: they motivate individuals to assume responsibilities of elite positions, and they maintain the high value placed on these positions. They thus serve as inducements to individuals, as well as indicators of rank and position of influence.

In larger societies, not only the recruitment and selection patterns reflect the chances toward differentiation and autonomy among elites who are characterized by acquired skills, capabilities, and achievements, but rewards to them, too, have become specialized. Some elites enjoy large earnings; other popularity and fame, and still others, authority and power. Not all elites are equally wealthy, not all have equal prestige; only some have much more power than others and more have influence in all spheres of social life. The assumption of elite position thus also involves the acceptance of specific rewards associated with them. Responsibilities and rewards reflect two facts of the same coin and as such they can be analysed in an integral perspective only. The two are linked to recruitment, for rewards are the spur to the expenditure of effort that the duties of strategic positions demand.

The tendency toward pheralization of elites is likely to conflict with the other tendency toward the monolithic exercise of power and leadership. This is a problem in totalitarian as well as liberal societies. In totalitarian societies, the problem is how to persuit the desired flexibility and variety without corroding social stability. Conversely, in liberal pluralist systems the problem is how to achieve the necessary degree of social cohesion and moral consensus among partly autonomous, highly specialized, yet functionally interdependent elites. The cohesion and consensus are necessary if the society is to pursue common goals and is to be unifies in more than name only. In any case, there appears to a profound relationship between changes in social structures and the types of elites who get a major share in social influence and political power.

Thinkers like Pareto, Mosca, Michels, Burnham and C. Wright Mills have given specific theories about the formation and decay of elite as a group of individuals who influence the affairs of society. The core of classical thinking in the writings of these thinkers is the fact that there may exist in any society a minority of the population which takes the major decisions in the society. Because these decisions are of such wide scope, affecting the most general aspects of the society, they are usually regarded as political decisions even where the minority taking them are not 'politicians' in the usual sense of members of a government or legislative. Thus Mosca's political class includes the wider circle of those who influence government decisions as well as those who formally 'decide' policies. According to the classical elitist thesis the minority gets its dominant position by means beyond ordinary election. Thus the elite may be powerful as a result of the revolutionary overthrow of the preciously dominance group as in the case of the early Bolsheviks leadership in the Soviet Union. The elite may owe its position to conquest, it may be powerful becuase of its monopoly of the crucial productive resources of a society, or its influence may be due to its emboding in fact or in appearance certain social or religious values widely shared in a tradition-bound society, such as Brahmins in India as defined by Max Weber. But even where, as in modern societies, the dominant minority at the very least includes some who have been elected to positions of leadership, the elitists claim that electoral victory is not gained entirely by open democratic means. The appearance of democratic majority control over the minority is deceptive. The minority is in a position to manipulate the electoral process to its own ends by means of a range of measures from sheer coercion of voters, through bribery or the skilled use of propaganda to the selection of the candidates. The sovereign electorate will 'choose' its leaders from those acceptable to the elite. In such ways the dominant minority escapes the control of the majority. The elitist thesis does not merely assert that in a society the minority makes decisions and the majority obeys. This is an obvious truism with no power to explain political relationships.[19]

Because of their power, their organization, their political skills or their personal qualities, the members of the elite are always potentially capable of exploiting their positions so as to preserve the elites dominant position which enables them to impose their supremacy of the rest of the society. An implication of this is that the supposed elite constitutes a coherent, united and self conscious group—and these qualities appear in nearly all definitions - of the elite. Indeed, what James Meisel call the 'three Cs-group consciouness, coherence, and conspiracy are clearly necessary features of the concept of an elite. To be of any relevance to a study of political influence the group must act together as a group with some shared purposes. If the elite is the elite of the wealthy or of the product of private education they must act together as the defenders of the private sector in education in order to count as an elite in politics. The unity of the elite is sometimes seen as the outcome of the 'elites' social background and sometimes the product of the very organization of the elite itself—an esprit de corps arising from their common situation and interests, and joint action of the groups. Power breads conciousness of power. This is commonly alleged of bureaucracies. In every case, the cohesiveness of the elite is seen as one of its chief strengths.[20] This is however derived, in the ultimate analysis form wealth, economic influence, social status educational advantages which make the elite a distinct class or a class of many virtues. Hobbes in seventeenth century had also observed that both wealth and educational opportunities will tend to maintain the elites domination in subsequent generations, converting it into a hereditary caste. These advantages of *position* deja *prises,* as Mosca termed them, serve to increase the distance between the elite and other groups. They emphasize the exclusiveness of the elite and the difficulty of obtaining entry into it on any other than the elite's own terms. The strength of elite is in many respects indicated by its ability to lay down the terms for admission to the circle of the politically influential, terms which may include conformity to standards of wealth, social background, educational attainment and commitment to the elites interest and ideology. On the other hand, the elites survival may depend on its capacity to adjust to pressures from outside itself and even to admit element from other social interests into elite.

Although the 'classical elitists' had many common points in their writing, they displayed also crucial differences about the way a group needed to possess the qualities and social opportunities a group needed to possess if it were to gain an elite position. Four broad positions can be discerned. Firstly, there were those who, like Mosca and his disciple Michels, held that an elite owed its power predominantly to its organizational abilities. Pareto and his followers, by contrast, traced the elites position to the psychological make-up of both elite and non-elite, this being in turn explicable in terms of certain constancies in human nature. James Burham, attempting a marriage between elitism and Marxism, saw the power of the elite as a consequence of its control of economic resources, and finally C. Wright Mills similarly explained the elites dominance not as a product of the personal qualities of its members but of the positions they held in a number of key institutions within the society, we shall deal with these positions as organizational, psychological, economic, and institutional approaches to elite politics and society.

**Organizational Approach**

Writing on classical elitism, Mosca observed:

> "In all societies....two classes of people appear a class that rules and class that is ruled. The first class, always the less

> numerous, performes all political functions, monopolizes power and enjoys the advantages that the power brings, whereas the second, the more numerous class, is directed and controlled by the first, in a manner that is now more or less legal, now more or less arbitrary and violent and supplies the first, in appearance at least, with material means of subsistence and with the instrumentalities that are essential to the vitality of the political organism."[21]

For Mosca, the most crucial point in the explanation of elitism lay in a minorities capacity for organization. Elite position comes in as a result of its possessing, either in fact or in estimation of others in the society, some attribute which is valued in society. The attribute may be wealth, a concern for the public good, initiatory process, or status in a religious hierarchy. Elite control however, depends on the minority's capacity to weld itself into a cohesive force presenting a common front to the other forces in society. A minority, Mosca believes, has advantages simply because it is a minority. This is obviously because a small group is more readily organized than a large one. Its internal channels of communication and information are much simpler. Its members can be contacted more speedily. As a result, a small minority can formulate policies rapidly, can agree on the presentation of policies and give the appearance of complete solidarity in its public statements and actions. Changed circumstances can produce an immediate response from a group which is well organized, whilst its less well organized rivals or the largely inorganized bulk of the population flounder in search of the appropriate reaction. The ultimate in elite leadership will be that the majority looks to the elite for the right 'cue' when the majority finds itself in conditions unfamiliar to it. The consequence is that despite the apparent superiority of a majority over a minority, in any concrete situation, it will be the minority that will be the stronger. The unorganized majority will be merely a large aggregation of individuals without a common purpose or any generally acknowledged system of communicating information or coordinating policy. As Mosca puts it. 'The power of any university is irresistible as against each single individual in the majority, who stands alone before the totality of the organized minority.[22]

According to Mosca, although there is apparent superiority of a majority over minority in any concrete situation it will lead the minority that will be the stronger. The unorganized majority will be merely a large aggregation of individuals without a common purpose or any generally acknowledged system of communicating information or co-ordinating policy. As Mosca puts it, "The power of any minority is irresistible as against each single individual in the majority, who stands alone before the totality of the organized minority.[23]

Mosca divided the ruling class or 'political class' into a higher and a lower stratum. Influenced by the growing power in his day of the party machives, he regarded the innermost core of the elite as comprising the party 'bosses' who directed the party's electoral campaigns and thereby controlled the parliament. These grand electors as Mosca termed them, not only delivers the vote in the electoral area where their power is based but, most importantly, they pick the candidates. They determine the range from which the electorate must make its supposedly 'free choice'. A representation is them not chosen by the electorate. Instead his friends have him elected and hence—an excellent instance of Mosca's thesis—a candidacy is always the work of a group of people united for a common purpose, an organized minority which inevitably forces its will upon the disorganized majority.[24]

Although Mosca holds that every society will be dominated by a ruling class this does not imply that there are no substantial differences between political systems. They differ in two main respects—the direction of the flow of authority and the source of recruitment to the ruling class. These offer two axes along which political systems may be arranged for purposes of comparison. He discerned two 'principle' according to which authority flowed and two tendencies according to which elite membership was recruited. Authority in any political organization, either flows downward—the autocratic principle or upward—the liberal principle. In an autocracy officials are appointed and granted authority by some higher official. In any liberal system the rulers are authorized by those ruled—usually by means of election. 'Autocracy' and 'liberal' are 'ideal types' of systems of authority to which any given society will conform to any greater or lesser degree. Many will be mixture of these principles. In modern societies, this situation has given rise to what Raymond Aron has described a totalitarian tendency in a democracy.

Robert Michels, continued the central thesis of Mosca except the fact that he kept the ideological content firmly under control. He treated, in Political Parties, theories proposed but rather undeveloped by Mosca. Here again the central theme is that elite control depends upon organization. Michels extends this to mean not merely that organizational ability grants power but that the very structure of any organized society gives rise inevitably to an elite. In Michels celebrated formulation: "Who says organization, says oligarchy". Michels reference to oligarchy in an organization is clear. In a given organization of any size leadership becomes necessary to its success and survival. The nature of organization is such that it gives power and advantages to the group of leaders who cannot then be checked or held accountable by their followers. This is true despite the fact that where the leadership is elected the leaders are supposedly the agents of those electing them. There are two sets of factors which cause this result—organizational factors and psychological. Of these the organizational factors are by far the most significants. However, the organizational and structural forces pushing towards oligarchy are reinforced by certain psychological forces, largely by a negative kind.

Whlist socialist theorists have often assumed a high degree of political interest and spontaneity on the part of the bulk of population, he alleges that the majority is apathetic towards public matters. Most people are only concerned with politics when it affects their private interests. They have no knowledge of how the political system works. The same applies to the members of party organizations. There is a small inner group, who constitute the party action and are the truely influential below this group activity, interest and influence in the party may be represented by a pyramid—voluntary party officials a large stratum of these regularly attending meetings, a larger stratum still of enrolled members and, finally, large basis of non-membership who merely vote for the party. Thus Michels, though he has confined his analysis to political party felt that law of oligarchy was to have general application to all organizations including the organization of the state as such. The majority will never rule despite the formal apparatus of universal suffrages and the myths of majority will. Democracy in the sense of the rule of the whole people or the majority is impossible.

In any democracy, major decisions will continue to be taken by a powerful oligarchy. However, Michels gives a limited defence of democracy, instead of condemning it outright. It allows the emergence of number of rival parties—each led by an oligarchy—whose competition ensures a certain amount of indirect influence to the people who support they must cultivate. The democratic tendency restrains but cannot prevent the oligarchical. For Mosca elitism makes a compromise with pluralism when democracy is defined in terms of competition between oligarchies.

### Psychological Approach

The concept of elite in Pareto's work is much wider and more comprehensive than that of political bosses as described by Mosca and Michels, and it is sometimes wider even than Marx's ruling class. Paretos' elite theory is part of a much more general sociology in which social activity is explained by reference to certain fundamental psychological factors. Accordingly elites are seen by Pareto not as the product of economic forces not as building their dominance on their organizational activity but as the outcome of what he believed to be human attributes which are found constant through out human history.

In his most formal definition of elite, Pareto suggests that ability in every human activity—law, poetry, thieving—might, in theoretical terms be measured and each practitioner awarded marks according to his success. The lawyer would be awarded 10 and the one who cannot get a brief would be given 0. A 'great train robber' is again marked at 10 if he gets away with the money and the petty thief caught in the act gets no marks. The evaluation is not a moral one but is a measurement of displayed achievement, Pareto then proposes to identify a class of individuals with highest accomplishments in each branch of social activity and to treat this class as that of elite. This is then sub-divided into the governing elite consisting of the individuals who govern the affairs of the state directly, and the 'non-governing elite' comprising those whose activities are of little implication for politics. Pareto however considers this kind of definition of elite as of little meaning in sociological terms. According to him, perfect competition is true only in theoretical conditions; those with the highest ability reach the top of their activity. In practice however this does not appear to be a universal rule. Factors such as wealth, birth and corruption frequently give advantage to the less skilled to attain the leading positions, particularly in such less technical and rational activities as politics. Pareto therefore prefers to go far a distinction between the elite, both governing and non-governing, who occupy the leading position in society and the non-elite. Thus paralleling Marx account of history as that of class struggle, Pareto sees history of every hitherto existing society as the history of the relations between the elite and the non-elite and of the psychological make up of the persons in the leading positions. He believed that the vast majority of human activities were 'non-logical', i.e. were not rational in the sense of appearing to the actor and to an impartial observer both to be constantly undertaken to reach an attainable end to be appropriate to that end. What we usually observe, however is that men justify their conduct by giving it a 'veneer of logic'. If these theories of rationalization are analysed they will be found to be composed of two elements. One part is the justification itself which, however apparently logical, is nevertheless part of non-logical conduct. It varies from time to time and from country to country. It is termed by Pareto the 'derivation' and in the counterpart of Marx's ideology. The other part of the theory is more important. It is the direct reflection of the instincts or sentiments as state of mind of the actor, and are called by Pareto 'residues'. Human instincts and hence the residues which reflect them are, according to Pareto, constant throughout history.[25] He therefore discerns a number of important residues, to be later subsumed under two broad categories, which offer the key to the explanation of society including elite domination and elite replacement. These categories are, 1. residues reflecting the instinct of combinations—the impulse to put together ideas by the use of imagination, i.e., arts, ideology and political coalitions and manoevring would all stem from this class of residue which reflects active and inventive characteristics of individuals; 2. residues reflecting the instinct of the persistence of aggregates i.e. the tendency to consolidate positions once they are established; thereby reflecting the attributes of permanence, stability, and order which appear politically in appeals for solidarity, order, discipline and property. These residues however are not to be identified with traditionalism, as one may have, quite on the contrary, stable attachment to new or even revolutionary movements and a newly emerging social and cultural order. In fact, the first category of residues involves men of intelligence and cunning and are 'foxes' in Machiavell's language and the second category of residues involves men of strength, stability and integrity, who represent 'lions'. The two sets of qualities are mutually exclusive. Politics, however, requires both the lion and the fox—it is partly a matter of force and partly one of persuasion, meaning in Pareto's view gaining the consent of the governed by ruse. The style of governing any time will depend on whether the governing elite is composed predominantly of those characterized by either categories of the residues. The non-elite are over-whelmingly 'class II' in character—stolid, unimaginative but also with strong attachments to political ideals which satisfy their need for stable commitments.

According to Pareto, foxes govern by attempting to gain consent. They devise ideologies to attract the masses, conduct policies to meet immediate crises and satisfy the demand of the moment. Material interest is placed before the pursuit of the ideals. The ideal politician is the political fixer or 'wheeler-deeler'. 'Foxes' are not, however, prepared to use force to solve political problems. Misplaced humanitarianism leads to compromise and pacifism which totally weaken the regime when the ultimate manoeuvre has failed to deceive the elites more tough-minded apponents. The 'lions' manner of governing represents the opposite pole in political cycles. The pursuit of consensus is abandoned in favour of the use of force. Opposition may be ruthlessly suppressed Public order rather than private satisfaction becomes a chief end of government. Such elites are far from lacking in ideals, however, Vidence, including the forceful overthrow of a previous regime of 'pursuasive' elite may be used to defend values in religion and society against 'materialism', 'atheism', and 'corruption'. Many a revolutionary military regime makes such a claim. Pareto, contemptuous as he was of what he believed to be the corruption, sterile manoeuvrings and political cowardice of the continental democracies of his day, rejoiced in the use of violence by the men of action—the Caesars and Mussolinis. And he did not at all lament the victims who are merely indices of the courage and strength of men of decision who are ridding the country of a baneful animal pest. A balance of the qualities of lion and fox was Paretos ideal—as it had been for Machiavelli—but this was extremely rare in an elite. As a result the balance savings in history from one elite type to the other.

Pareto's elite is thus identified by the attitudes it shares and the conduct these give rise to Pareto, like Marx and for not very dissimilar reasons, is ambiguous as to agree of the cohesion an elite possesses. Three Cs—consciousness, cohesion, conspiracy—are less readily attributable to its particularly in modern democracies. Indeed, the objection might be made to Pareto's account that it is at times a description of a category 'top persons' rather than an elite as it has been explained herein before. Pareto rejects the 'conspiracy theory' of society. In modern democracies, for instance, any accord between the actions of the 'foxes' is a result of each of them taking independent decisions in pursuit of his own interest. But it is also possible that the aggregate of individual actions may not accord with the long term interests of the elite. Pareto saw, as Marx had done, that social actions can have unforeseen and unintended consequences. The lack of conspiracy and cohesion is evidenced by the ease with which an elite is displaced by another as a result of a host of individual actions which ultimately undermine the position of the elite. Foxes and lions fail to recognize the disastrous consequences to themselves of, respectively, their tender-mindedness and their stolid inflexibility.

**References**

1. Suzanne Keller, "Elites", *International Encyclopaedia of Social Science, op. cit.* pp. 26-29.
2. H.H. Gerth & C.W. Mills (eds), *From Max Weber: Essays in Sociology* (London: Routledge & Kegan Paul, 1967) p. 180.
3. Bertrand Russell, *Power; A New Social Analysis,* (London : Unwin Books, 1962) p. 25.

4. G.D.H. Cole, *Studies in Class Structure,* (London: Routledge and Kegan Paul, 1955) pp. 102-103.
5. Harold D. Lasswell, Daniel Lerner, and C. Easton Rothwell, *The Comparative Studies of Elites* (Stanford: Hoover Institute Studies, 1952) p. 6.
6. Cole, *op. cit.,* p. 6.
7. S. F. Nadel "The Concept of Social Elites", *International Social Science Bulletin,* VIII (3) 1956, p. 415.
8. P. Mercier, Evolution of Senegalese Elite, *Ibid.,* p. 441.
9. C. Wright Mills, *The Power Elite,* (New York: Oxford Univ. Press 1959) p. 13.
10. Raymond Aron, "Power and Status Relations", *European Journal of Sociology,* vol. 1 (2) 1960, pp. 260-61.
11. William Kornhauser, *The Politics of Mass Society* (London: Routledge Kagan Paul, 1965) p. 51.
12. George E. Gordon Catlin, *Systematic Politics,* (Toronto, Univ. of Toronto Press, 1962) p. 229.
13. Robert Dahl, *Who Governs,* (New Haven: Yale University Press) 1961.
14. S.K. Lal, *The Urban Elite* (Delhi: Thompson Press, 1974) pp. 3-5.
15. Keller, *op. cit,* p. 26.
16. Keller, *op cit,* p. 27.
17. *Ibid,* p. 27.
18. Keller, *op. cit.,* p. 28.
19. Geraint Parry, *Political Elites* (London; George Allen and Unwin Ltd., 1969) pp. 30-31.
20. Parry, *op. cit.,* pp. 31-32.
21. Mosca, *The Ruling Class* (New York: McGraw Hill, 1939) p. 50.
22. Mosca, *op. cit.,* p. 53.
23. *Ibid,* 53.
24. Party, *op. cit.,* p. 38.
25. Parry, *op. cit.,* p. 46.

# Chapter - 13

# Leadership

The subject of leadership has been a focal point of study in various disciplines, viz, psychology, social anthropology, sociology, political science and social work. Some researchers have usally tried to understand it through a process of mutual stimulation of leader—follower behaviour as a result social interaction. Others have tried to explain it with the help of individual characteristics, bases of authority and powers. R.T. Lapiere, and P.R. Fransworth treated leadership as the "behaviour that affects the behaviour of the people more than their behaviour affects that of the leader, whereas Krech and Crutchfield given thirteen and ten characteristics respecitvely of a leader. As a matter of fact, we cannot be sarosanct about the fixed charactertistics of a leader as the three factors time, place, and situation, play major roles in determining them. But it is true that a leader always has the authority and power of decision making which at times is held up when the community comes under the influence of outside world or when there is an irregular contact. In fact, the earlier theories of leadership may be classified into two categories, the first based on heredity and the other on traits. Of late, the modern theory is situational and an extension of it is known as situational-cum-personality theory.

Leadership is based on relationship between an individual and group which is built around some common interest and which behaves in a manner directed or determined by him. The superiority of leadership may be by free choice, i.e., presence of mutual understanding and interaction between the leader and the followers and the leader is accepted as a model because of his personal and social traits which come to light in a social situational field or dominance basis when the person compels others to follow his direction. He imposes his authority on others and the followers are driven by the emotions of fear. Thus we can conclude, from the various approaches to the genesis of leadership that: (1) a leader emerges in a group of individuals and hence group interaction is at the base of leadership, (2) a leader is motivated to satisfy certain personal needs and there is always a causal relationship between motivation and emergence of leadership; (3) leadership is associated with the requirements of the follower, and, as such the nature of leader follower relationship is basic to the emergence of leadership, and (4) whenever there is a hindrance or blockade against the group goal, the importance of leadership increases.

It has been observed that with the changing attitude and emergence of new elements of social organizations and values, some of these traditional leaders have to swim with the new current as there is fear of their being drowned in the ocean of the masses. Their fear is sometimes greatly accelerated due to emergence of new sets of leaders in response to the modern institutions and for the satisfaction of entirely emergent needs. The best leader however continues to be one who is in position to satisfy the traditional as well as the emergent needs of the villagers. He is a real leader in a sense that he functions as 'link' between the 'old and the new', institutions, values, needs, etc.[1]

Generally speaking, leadership has been seen as a group process through which individuals initiate activities for delivering the common objectives of the community by working together, stimulating each other, supplementing abilities and resources, and evolving an effective organizational or hierarchical pattern. The assumption here is that leadership is largely relative to situation and to group tasks and goals, group structure or organization, and to the population characteristics of the group including their culture. There are two essential aspects of leadership relation: the ability to influence others to cooperate, and the identification of common purpose or goal. Tead has observed, "Leadership is the activity of influencing people to cooperate toward some goal which they come to find desirable".[2] Pigors has emphasized the same idea in his definition. "Leadership is a process of mutual stimulation which, by the successful interplay of relevant individual differences, controls human energy in the persuit of a common cause."[3] Thus Pigors make a crucial distinction between leadership and domination. As he states: Domination is a process of control in which by the forceful assumption of authority and the accumulation of prestige a person regulates the activities of others for purpose of his own choosing. Leadership and domination may, therefore be described respectively as liberating and binding trends in social relationships. Leadership power is created through the integration of diverse purposes and the intelligent use of individual difference.

We can conclude that leadership is essentially an interactional phenomenon. The relationship between the leader and the follower is one of the several forms of interpersonal relationships which is intended to satisfy some of the defined needs of the leader and the followers belonging to the same social system. Thus the behaviour of one is generally influenced by the behaviour of the other, on the one hand, while the behaviour of both is determined by the nature and structure of social system in which they interact. Leadership is therefore, the function of triple situational phenomena (1) his personality traits, (2) his manner of communication with the followers, and (3) the perception of the leader by the followers as the satisfaction of their needs and goals. The leader-follower relationship varies along an authoritarian and democratic continuum, that either of the two goals to one pole or maintains an equilibrium between the two will depend upon the situation, i.e., the nature of the followers, and the ethos of the culture to which they belong. The leader according to this definition maintains and preserves the values of the system. In so far as he initiates innovation, he ensures that this may not distintegrate the pattern of interpersonal relationship, nor stand in the way of achieving the goals set forth by him and accepted by the followers.[4]

### Leadership: An Organizational Perspective

Leadership, in a general organizational perspective, can be

defined as interpersonal influence, exercised in situation and directed though the communication process, toward the attainment of a specified goal or goals of the organization. It invariably involves (a) the leader and his psychological attributes, (b) the followers with their problems, attitudes and needs, and (c) the group situation in which followers and leaders relate with one another. With this definition in mind, we shall now turn to specific components of leadership in an organizational perspective.

The components of leadership are four fold: interpersonal influence, exercised situation, the communication process, and attainment of a specified goal or goals we shall explain these components briefly.

**Interpersonal Influence**

The essence of leadership is interpersonal influence, involving the influences in an attempt to affect the behaviour of the follower through direct or indirect communication. In this context, it is necessary to draw a distinction between power and leadership. Power is a potential for influence. However, even though an individual may possess considerable power in relationship to another, he may for a number of reasons not use all of the power available to him. A leadership act reflects that position of the power available to an individual which he chooses to employ at the time. A concept of power frequently connotes a potential for coercion, based, for example upon physical force, informal social pressure, law and authority. In actuality a given leader typically has available not only these sources providing him with power, but also power derived from such inner resources as understanding and flexibility.

**Situation**

The concept situation has invariably been used to denote an activity or a particular set of activities engaged by a group; group characteristics, including interpersonal relationships; group goals.or need; and the cultural context. However, it seems appropriate to define a situation as including only those aspects of the objective contexts, which at any given moment, have an attitudinal or behavioural impact (consciously or unconsciously on the individuals in the influence relationship, and to recognize that the situation of the leader and that of the follower may differ from each other in many respects.

### The Communication Process

Influence relationship which characterizes leadership is possible only through communication. There are however many problems involved in differentiating conceptually between the communication and the leadership processes. We can view communication as the sole process through which a leader, as leader, can function. The process of communication involves five major aspects—source, receptor, message, interaction, and effect. The objective of a communication is to transmit a message from himself to an individual which the latter will interpret as the former desires. The communicators goal is to convey meanings, or ideas, without distortion. It is through this that the goals of leadership are realized. These goals are three-fold: group goals, personal goal of the follower, and personal goal of the leader. Group goals reflect what the group wants to do. A leader uses his influence to facilitate the groups attainment of its own goals. Personal goals of the follower imply such individual expectations which motivate the followers to interact with the leader. The leaders too try to realize their personal goals by mobilizing the individuals, groups or masses which show their values and commitments in social, economic, and political life.[5]

### Political Leadership : A Comparative Analysis

The study of leadership is as old as the study of politics for the one is inseparable from the other. Since time immemorial men have asked, debated, and sought to establish who governs are should govern, what are or ought to be the bases of political authority in a community, and how some individuals obtain and exercise exceptional influence over the making of public rules and policies when other do not. When we evaluate the fitness of the candidates for public offices, judge the performance of governmental decision-makers or compare our political leaders with those who aspire to displace them or rule other peoples, we compare and generalize. When we say here is an effective leader, a wise statesman, a just ruler, or on the other hand call a leader a tyrant, an opportunist, or a fraud, we make comparisons between what we see in a leader and what we expect of him.[6]

Professional observers and practitioners of political leadership, from time of Plato and Aristotle to our own, have made it their principal preoccupation to formulate such comparative generalizations—some of these have been ostensibly descriptive, others have been explicitly prescriptive and have sought to establish principles of proper political leadership on the basis of generalized assumptions about the nature of man, society and authority. In recent years, the scope and focus of comparative leadership analysis has been profoundly affected by a number of developments, however. Older theories and methods seem no longer adequate to explain similar types of leadership in very different cultures and societies and dissimilar patterns. The rise and fall of an unprecedented form of autocracy—'totalitarian' dictatorships—in industrialized as well as non-industrialized societies have posed the question whether fascist or communist dictatorships are cut off the same cloth along similar patterns, or only superficially similar manifestations of entirely different phenomena. Does authoritarianism a characteristic of developing societies or their industrialization, in fact, promote autocratic or oligarchic leadership in contemporary mass society? Hence the crucial question as to whether any specific type of leadership has anything to do with socio-economic and cultural factors in a given society.

New theories, new modes of analysis, and new research opportunities have tended to pave the way for development of comparative leadership analysis among the social scientists. New methods and facilities for collecting quantifiable data have provided them with an unprecedented amount of information about leadership patterns in past as well as contemporary societies. Recently developed sophisticated mode of quantitaive analysis has enabled them to explain and compare aggregate data and to test theoretical propositions about the behaviour of leaders and followers in various political systems. Interdisciplinary collaboration has promoted the search for new analytic models and concepts which can facilitate exact and logically consistent explanations and predictions.

## Political Leadership: The Related Concepts

The search for clear, precise, and generally applicable analytical terms has been major concern of contemporary efforts to study political leadership in various societies. As social scientists have learnt to probe beneath the manifest aspects of leaderships and have become correspondingly more sensitive to the relevance of numerous and complex latent factors, they have found it more difficult to agree on what leadership is and does. It is a great deal easier to distinguish between voters and candidates in electoral studies, or between superiors and inferiors in formal political organizations, than to establish clear, operational boundaries that discriminate between leaders and followers in all situations.[7]

Generally speaking, leadership has been variously defined in the contemporary social science literatures as influence, authority, power, and control over others. But how such concepts are to be defined and applied for comparative purposes remain a matter of considerable disagreement. Apparently identical or similar concepts - such as elite, authoritarianism and leadership role - may be defined in terms of very different operational criteria. On the other hand, various authors have given seemingly different conceptualization of power, influence, authority, and control - in quite similar operational terms. Or yet again, significantly different concepts and operational criteria may be employed to study similar subjects, such as decision and policy making.[8]

Some scholars have identified political leadership with formal positions, viz., officers, tasks, and functions along more or less traditional lines. Other emphasize performance. Leadership is seen as the ability to guide and structure they collected behaviour of a given group in a desired direction; so that the division of the leader are implemented by group action. The leader is followed because he is loved, admired, respected, or feared, because he can coerce, persuade, or manipulate group members, because he can offer psychic as well as material rewards and punishments, or because compliance with his wishes, sanctioned by habit, traditions or legal-rational behaviour norms. Still other definitions are couched primarily in both psychology and sociological terms. Here leadership is conceived as an attitudinal phenomenon in the mind of an actor who ascribes it to others, to himself or both and responds accordingly to stimuli from his social environment.[9] The following chart presents a comprehensive view of leadership and the related concepts, clarity about whom is a necessary condition for understanding the phenomenon of leadership itself.

## Leadership and Related Concepts

## (Derived from Leadership Literature)

| *Concept* | *Definition* | *Operation Criteria* | *Illustrative Data* |
|---|---|---|---|
| Leadership authority | A relationship of inequality sanctioned by the legitimacy of leaders to make and enforce policy. | The nature and extent of legitimating group norms. | Elite and/or mass consensus on rights and duties of formal positions, on means and ends of leadership behaviour. |
| Leadership control | The actual or perceived ability to provide or withhold benefits and apply sanctions. | Extent of leaders ability to extract conforforming group behaviour. | Comparing mean of control (for example, coercion, manipulation) with compliance on the part of group members. |
| Leadership autonomy | The extent of which leaders are independent of environmental factors. | Leaders ability to be their own referrent. | Intra-and extra systemic variables interacting with leadership views and actions. |
| Leadership skills | The nature, possession and application of methods designed to gain compliance. | Predisposition and capabilities of leaders and receptivity of group members to leadership ones. | Comparing goal orientation of leaders with success a failure to achieve group behaviour conforming with goals. |
| Statescraft | A measure of the successful or unsuccessful exercise of legitimate authority in sovereign entities and subcomponents thereof. | Determination of the efficacy of such authority in achieving stipulated goals. | Extent of achievements of stipulated objectives or subjective communal goals (for example, political stability, defence of the national interest). |
| Policy making | A process of choosing among alternative goals decision, makers, and course of action. | a. The ingredients which enter into the process. b. The interaction process between the relevant agents. | The extent of available information; perceived goals and capabilities anotives time pressure. b. Rules and Interpersonal relations in legislative |

| *Concept* | *Definition* | *Operation Criteria* | *Illustrative Data* |
|---|---|---|---|
| | | c. The relationship behaviour policy inputs and outputs. | judicial and administrative bodies. c. Comparing demands articulated by voters, interest associations, foreign governments with behavioural response of policy maker. |
| Leadership roles | Three definitions involving inequality between actual or aspiring group leaders and actual or potential followers. | | |
| | a. The position of leaders. | a. Offices occupied or sought rights and duties associated with position. | a. Prerogative attached to the leadership position. |
| | b. The behavioural "style" of leaders. | b. Nature of interaction with other relevant actors. | b. The extent to which the behavioural congruence is attained through coercion, manipulation, persuation etc. |
| | c. Orientations toward the incumbents of leadership positions. | c. Determination of reciprocal expectations associated with position. | c. Perception of representative or delegated functions degree of conformity with group norms in the view of followers. |
| The personality of a leader | Individual as distinguished from collective characteristic. Which influence attitudinal and behavioural patterns. | Determination of personality syndromes, their source, degree of adaptability and general impact on leader and or followers. | Instinctive needs requiring satisfaction,expression and want patterns degree of internalization of cultural norms. etc. |
| Leadership recruitment | The process of leadership selections. | a. The variables which promote or hinder the aquisition of leadership. b. The general process through which leaders are chosen and displaced. | a. Social background, ambition, skills, derivance respect, material values connections. b. Electoral process, coreer patterns, revolutions, etc. |

In fact, leadership represents a social institutions through which a given social group restores and maintains cohesion in its structure and organization. Social groups, irrespective of the differences in cultural attributes require leadership so as to function smoothly and effectively. No social unit or entity functions in an automatic manner. It can neither be described as resultant of association among individuals nor can they be attained in a situation of unco-ordinated assembly of individuals. The groups need a cohesive and disciplinary force for the maintenance of the structure as well as directing the individual members towards the attainment of groups goals. In the absence of these forces an anarchical situation may develop within the groups, except in those rare cases where ext-reme motivation of the members can maintain the morale of the group for some time. The leader is the source of the cohesive and disciplinary forces in a group. It is therefore sociologically believed that leadership is an essential attribute of a social group. Thus lea-dership as a universal phenomenon plays a significant role in all the different phases of the development of human activities.[10]

It can be said that leaders involves individuals who are con-sidered to be superior to the common people by way of posses-sing extra-ordinary attributes and abilities. A leader with the help of these attributes and abilities ensures cohesion in the social organ-ization and helps his followers to attain their common goals. Gen-erally, it is he who plays the role of a decision maker and retains his position of leader so long the people are convinced about his ability as a decision maker. The term leadership however is not synonymous to personal pre-eminence. In fact, there are two con-notations of the term. First, he is a person who is relatively more advanced and prominent and excels over other members of the group; and second, he is a person who provides guidance to others, act as the head of an organization, and holds command. There is again difference between leadership and authority. While author-ity is a sociological phenomenon located in the structure of asso-ciations, leadership is a socio-psychological phenomenon which tends to have its locus in personality traits of particular indivi-duals who can mobilize and coordinate group relations for the attainment of his personal as well as collective goals. Authority thus is a status relationship whereas leadership is a personal rela-tionship. Leaders in many cases does not enjoy the highest status in the hierarchy of the association to which they belong and those who actually enjoy high statuses and hold the authority are not necessarity leaders. The two terms, leadership and authority are therefore related but also conceptually different from each other. The competence of a leader to handle the interpersonal relationship within the group and other qualifications which he possesses pushes him to the position of authority and also influence over other members of the group increases considerably. Similarly authority and influence are not synonymous. Authority is power legitimatized by the norms of an associations and it is one of the factors which constitutes statuses that people hold. The leader in any social situation can function whereas the authority which he exercises must be legitimate. The terms influence is sometimes used synonymously with power but there is significant conceptual distinction between the two. "An application of power changes the actors situation and/or his conception of the situation—but not his preference. Resistence is overcome not because the actor subjected to the use of power changes his "will" but because resistence has become more expansive, prohibitive, or impossible. The exercise of influence entails an authentic change in the actors' preference, given the same situation, he would not choose the same course of action he favoured before the influence was exercised. A leader cannot exercise authority, whatever may the extent of his influence be on the people, till his status gets crystallized in an associational structure.[11] Leadership is also different from domination. "Leadership is a process of mutual stimulation, while domination is a process of control in which by assumption of superiority a person or group regulates the activities of others. We can also distinguish a leader from a ruler." "A leader is one who is in direct dynamic relationship with his following. He has little coercive power, his powers being a product of his ability to persuade his followers. A ruler is very much formal in exercises of power. This is due to the fact that in ruling their subjects, rulers exercise an organized and structured power".[12]

## A Rational View

Leadership, as a phenomenon of classic concern, compels attention from many vintage points and for several strategic considerations study of leadership has generally involved only one aspect of the problem: a mechanism devised by a given group for the efficient pursuit of collectively shared goals area for the efficient pursuit of collectively shared goals and for the satisfaction by members of those needs which may have been group invested.[13] In fact as every human group strives to utilize through the mechanisms of role differentiation the differential characteristics of the members to the advantage of all, leadership is linked to a role structure which essentially varies from one social situation to the other.[14] From this point of view, leadership is not only a combination of personal characteristics which distinguish an individual from others, but also an 'organizational-function which refers to patterns of power and authority for the fulfilment of the actual and aspirations of the group and for the perpetuation of desired values and norms in the cultural order. The leadership refers, on the one hand, end-oriented specific relations between a particular individual and other members of group, and to certain ideologies or values which pervade its social structure, on the other. As a matter of fact, every human group strives to achieve its desired objectives invariably through the instrumentality of its leaders. But the role of a leader goes for beyond this means and relationship. Acting as a living links between his tradition and modern social forces, operating at large, he strives to reorder or organize social life in a way which is conducive to universal acceptance of change and innovation.[15]

Leadership could be explained from various other angles. Apart from classical approach to the problem by authors like Pigors, Lapiere, Kretch and Crutchfield, Durkheim and Max Weber, a list of as many as 130 explanations of leadership has been suggested by V.S. Bentz.[16] After careful examination, it will appear that all of them could be grouped into five theoretical streams—trait, status, esteem influence, and situation—which tend to influence any definition of leadership. For our purpose, we shall be confined to the role of leader as change preceptor and cultural catalyst in changing social situations. Though essentially product of a given territorial and human situation, a leader has to be conceived of as a living convass where social elements of varying colours find their expression for making total image of society. This is only in a social setting which may be marked with democratic ethos, that elements like sobriety, rationality, empiricism adaptability and comprehensiveness are considered to be the main attributes of a leader. Sobriety includes comparison which could be harnessed to fulfil creative purposes that are needed to uphold the cause of the collectivity. Rationality implies an awareness of the likely consequences of the course of action that may be required in varying contexts. Empiricism ensures that ones reasoning derives from a comprehensive knowledge and profound understanding of the facts in a wider perspective. Adaptability, involves change perception and a capacity to adjust ones behaviour in terms of new cultural initiatives. And finally comprehensiveness involves a critical constructive spirit which could hear upon the problems facing the community at various levels.

Acquisition of those attributes enables a leader to mould public opinion in a desirable way and thus create the bases for the emergence of a consensual society. In doing so, he takes into consideration a number of factors deriving from varying contexts and, as such, its quality of representation coupled with an motional appeal, itself becomes a 'standardized conformity'. A leader therefore, has to accommodate cultural traits of various groups and make a coordination of the methods that are usually adopted by their members for resolving intra-group disputes. He has again to assess the facilities available to them for forming and articulating a balanced judgement about various issues, the degree to which the interests affected are mutually compatible and the depths of motion at which they are felt as vital by the groups concerned, and above all, the measure of confidence people show in his responsiveness to public opinion expressed in a variety of ways. A true leadership therefore is an unfailing conciliation and compromise between conflicting interests of the people of his political entourage and the unprejudiced understanding of his social and moral obligations.

A leader represents socially defined aggregate of people who are to be represented at the higher levels of social organization. In fact, these levels determine the nature and dimension of the political system. Within a given system a small community, in order to safeguard its existence, aspires for an effective participation in the political processes, which could be possible only through the extension of its institutional spheres in the collective framework. It is at this stage that leaders' coordinating role starts. Conscious of the identity as well as interests of his group, he strives to ensure permeation of values of wider system in the cultural order of the local community. Thus, caught in the vortex of an all encompassing politics, he is constantly faced with the dual task of maintaining the emotional link with his community by showing unfailing responsiveness to its traditional urges and expectations, and, at the same time, of promoting functional efficacy of the system at local level through social mobilization of the people in a larger framework. In fact the dual nature of leadership roles is more pronounced in communities which may find themselves at the threshold of a cultural crisis than in those which may relatively be isolated and unaffected, mainly due to 'communicational inaccessibility', by the increasing role of society. In the former communities, leadership will be prone to the acquisition of such attributes as honesty, ambition, courage, farsightedness humidity, impartiality, dynamism and universalismic predisposition, and in the letter, it will tend to be adhesive, autocratic, selfish, particularistic, opportunistic and ascriptive in character. As a matter of fact, any systematic study of the bases of status, esteem, and influence of leaders, in varied social solution, will entail a dichotomy of these attributes, which refer to two polar types, rural - urban, traditional - modern, stereotype progressive of the leaders when social conditions change, promoted by internal dynamics or extraneous factors, a reorganization of leadership is required alongwith reordering of cultural and economic order. In such situation, traditional pattern of leadership may gradually be replaced by a transitional character which may symbolize the intitial phases of political modernization. As the changes in political life become institutionalized, the existing or emerging set of leaders are culturally constrained to imbide the desired values or traits of the society in order to keep pace with time.[17] A shift in political attributes is them a shift in cultural, economic and political order of the society itself. It is in this context that, despite an increasing criticism, trait or situational approach to leadership has to be treated as of immense value for a sociological venture, particularly in the context of developing societies. Furthermore, analysis of leadership traits, in a dichotomous perspective, can alone help us to find organic linkages between the micro-political system and the macro political systems and, thus, to explain modernizing impact of such linkages on the political life of local communities.

Changes in leadership attributes essentially reflect certain shifts in personality structures. The shifts are necessitated by a constant interaction between the effects of early socialization and the actual constraints of change. Effects of early socialization determine the basic character structure of a person that abounds in his 'psychosomatic' condition or the sum total of his biological and psychological characteristics. It is through this process that the individual internalizes fundamental social norms, forms specific attitudes towards cultural, economic and political objects and recognizes his status and roles to the system. Situational factors imply behavioural imperatives of changing environment which affect peripheral as well as core elements of personality system, in a progressive manner.

As a matter of fact, the whole concept of personality growth relates to the premise that development of individual's personality entails forms of behaviour which will be advantageous under the conditions imposed by the environment, as also to the premise that the function of personality is effectively performed when the advantageous behaviour is produced with the least effort and delay. Interaction between the three factors—the childhood influences, the psychosomatic conditions, and the existing situational factors—leads to significant changes in the 'psychodynamic' structure of the personality. It is through these changes that the individual forms specific attitudes towards new elements of a given cultural situation and makes necessary adjustments in his behaviour in accordance with them. In the context of leadership, the changes entailed by psychodynamic structure hint at the overwidening range of functional effectiveness of the personality of leaders in a given system. These changes have also been designated as 'latent attitude structure' for pointing out those personality features that have the greatest influence on the leaders manifest political attitudes. The term consists of attitudinal predispositions which represent a propensity to adopt certain types of attitudes in response to the stimuli presented by particular political objects.

All possible combinations of attitudes towards political objects could be arranged on a continuum from traditionalism to modernism. Traditionalism implies attachment to parochial community and its traditional norms and values, which will be reflected even in political behaviour. Modernism implies conscious acquisition of those attributes which symbolize increased capacity for adaptation in terms of changing social environments and gradual secularization of political outlook and behaviour. In between the traditional and modern polar types, there lies numerous combinations of attitudes towards political objects reflecting a blend of traditionalism and modernism. The gap between two polarities could be designated as transitional phase. In fact, as people become less traditional, they tend to become more favourably disposed toward continuity in decision making and enforcement. Change has to be mediated between the socio-political structure, and through the attitudes that sustain the structure. Attitudes that cluster toward the 'modern' end of the continuum also tend toward acceptance of the 'supra-national community', and an adaptive mobilization of self-imposed societal adjustments. Modernity encourages introspection or self-criticism as a necessary corrective to those in authority and traditionality the dogmatic, or coercive devices of political mobilization. Thus, keeping in view the varying attributes of the leaders, which correspond to different stages of the continuum three major patterns of leadership can be suggested. There are: 1. traditional or dogmatic, 2. situational or transitional, and 3. modern or democratic. Even in a system which is highly exposed to the forces of change such as urbanization or modernization, the presence of three sets of leaders, though in varying degrees, cannot be ruled out. In any case, political modernization will be reflected by the increasing number of transitional or modern types of leaders and gradual dwindling of those with traditional or dogmatic attributes. This trend can be witnessed not only in the urban centres but even in the areas which may be located around them. However, the number of these leaders will fluctuate according to the intensity of change or modernization which will vary from one area to the other.

The study of leadership is crucial in understanding of political behaviour. The political researches have so far been confined to the study of governmental organizations and the political behaviour of the people, particularly voting behaviour, the two important ends of the policy making continuum. Gradually, in recent years, there has been an inclination to shift the focus from these elements to the intermediate processes, such as leadership, group structure and communication patterns. It has been observe that politics by leadership is one the distinguishing features of the twentieth century. If the eighteenth century enunciated popular sovereignty and direct democracy as a major theme of democratic thought and the eighteenth century was connected with the challenge of stratification and group conflict, the twentieth century trend have made us sensitive to the role of leadership. The search for the values of security and equality have led to changes in character of politics. If one were to delineate this newer pattern of politics by leadership, it would include the following: (1) the shift in the centre of conflict resolution and initiative from parliamentary bodies and economic institutions to executive leadership; (2) the proliferation of the immediate office of the chief executive from its cabinet restricted status to a collectivity of coadjusting instrumentalities; (3) the tendency toward increased centralization of political parties with the subordination of the various parties as instrument for chief executive; (4) the calculated manipulation irrationalities by political leadership through the vast power potential of mass communication; (5) the displacement of the amateur by professional politician and civil servant; (6) the growth of bureaucracy not only as a source and technique to executive power but also as a fulcrum which all constentants for power attempt to employ; (7) the growth of interest group in size, number and influence, with the tendency toward bureaucratization of their internal structure; and (8) the changing role of the public that finds its effective voice in direct and an interactive relation with the chief executive.

The type and pattern of leadership vary with the social and political structure and institutions of societies; and, as such, the attributes and characteristic of leadership are generally contingent upon the economic and cultural features of the society which are characterized, by it. Therefore, leadership is a reflection of society itself. A leader is supposed to be endowed with those characteristics which makes him capable of mobilizing the masses for the fulfilment of the well defined objectives of the collective life. It is because of his distinguishing qualities that he is expected to take decisions which are conform to established norms of the system. Connotations of leadership emphasize innate and scare qualities which enable an individual to command the respect and loyalties of others while intuitiuely making the correct decision. Pfilfner and Presthus[18] observe that leaders have been found to excel the average members of the group in intelligence, scholarship, dependability, social participation and socio-economic status. Bertrand Russell, the famous philosopher, also felt that leaders must excel in those quantities which confer authority, viz, self confidence, skill and quick response in selecting among alternatives. Others have indicated qualities like strength of conviction, relatively wide knowledge and forceful will. However, recent researches in the context of traditional modern dichotomy of leadership have indicated both positive and negative attributes. The positive attributes are independent thinking and ability to take appropriate decisions in the larger interest,[19] outspokenness, regard for national interest, intelligence and foresight, kind and sacrificing nature, primemovers collective action. And the negative attributes are: attachment with particular caste and religion, tendency to please all with false promise self-interest influence among political bosses, and expert in factional politics.

It has commonly been agreed that the command of symbolism and facility in organization are the two important requirements of modern leadership. None of these factors are entirely new for our contemporary period but they are highly developed in modern time. Symbolism during our time is more mobile in its forms in comparison to the primitive symbolism. Leaders in modern societies are to devote their energies not only for manufacture of effective symbols but also to prepare the atmosphere for their acceptance which involves modification of attitudes, intensification of hatred and adoration and making appeals to the emotional and intellectual life of the people. The leader in the modern world should also possess the skill in mass organization which has become so essential for modern, social and political control.

The observations in this context by various thinkers lead us to list the following attributes of leaders in contemporary societies.

(i) The leader must be able to sense about what is going on around him. In other words, he must feel the trends of events or the undercurrent in the social and political spheres of the society and also be able to assess their potentialities and magnitudes.

(ii) The leader should have personal contact with different varieties of people in the society. In many cases, the people approach the leader for seeking guidance which they feel the leader is capable of giving instead of personal gains. A bold, aggressive, or sympathetic, or idealistic type of leader is expected to have such type of following.

(iii) He should also be capable of dealing with the various interest groups with conflicting interests in a manner that is conducive to getting their sympatheitc predisposition. He is required to behave like a shrewd diplomat. The leader should be able to bring unity among the various races, religions, classes, regions, and cultural groups. In the case of conflict between two different groups, is expected to act as a concilliator not only for bringing them closer but also paving the way for a 'workable' consensus.

(iv) He must possess enough potentiality and vision to put forth formulas, policies, ideologies, plans or strategies required both during the time of war and peace. In some cases the leader may not be actual inventor and might borrow the ideas from some other men with more intelligence and understanding. But even in that case he will be appreciated for his readiness to accept valuable suggestions and incorporating them in his political programme.

(v) He should be characterized by a high degree of risk taking behaviour. He should be a brave man prepared to take risk in certain combats with the groups hostile to him and trying to overthrow him, both within and outside the party. In many cases, his reputation as a brave man will save him from such hostilities.[20]

## Types of Leadership

Leadership is the most crucial element in the political system. It would be rather impossible to conceive of a system and its process without knowing the types of leader which may be available at a given point of time. A leader plays active part in a political organization and emerges on the basis of his active, contributions, and offices which he might have held, as a public figure at various levels of the polity. An effective and successful leader is a person who represents the temper of the age and minds of the people and also a supporter of the values held by the nation and the party he represents. In this context, it would be worthwhile to identify the various types of leadership, these are:

(1) Informal and Formal Leadership
(2) Manifest and Latent Leadership
(3) Non-strategic and Strategic Leaders
(4) Bureaucratic and Charismatic Leaders
(5) Positional and Personal Leadership

(1) Much of the internal capability of a political system depends on the leaders and their commitment to the cause of the nation. The formally constituted leadership has three alternative ways of functioning. It can either function in an impersonal manner or in a self styled and formal manner. The former type represents a highly institutionalized form of leadership whereas the latter a leadership which is basically a product of circumstances and is foisted on the people. Then there are cases of despots like Hitler, Mussolini and Stalin who exercise the functions of formally constituted leadership on the basis of their personal will power and the ability to dominate over others. Such leaders do not care much for the existing laws and institutions of the society. Another specific type of leadership refers to leaders with extra-ordinary eminence and a charismatic appeal, like, Abraham Lincoln, Jawahar Lal Nehru, Churchil and Julius Nyerere, who may become very much personal while remaining within the institutional bounds. An Amitai Etzioni observes the power of an organization to control its members rests either in the specific positions (departmental chief), an individual a persuasive person or a combination of both. Personal power is always normative power; it is based on the manipulation of symbols and it serves to generate commitment to the person also commands it. Positional power, on the other hand, may be normative, coercive, or utilitarian. An individual whose power is chiefly derived from his organizational position is referred to as an official. An individual whose ability to control others is chiefly personal is referred to as an informal leader. One who commands positional and personal power is a formal leader.[21]

(2) We can observe, invariably in every community, those persons who are supposed to actively and significantly participate in the political decision making. Such persons can be differentiated on the basis of not only their status and esteem but also the degree of influence and intensity of participation in actual decision-making Manifest leaders are those whom presumably well informed official of the communities voluntary organizations considered to be the most obvious leaders.[22] There is another group of people involved in the process of political decision making, who do not participate in the decision-making very frequently in comparison to the manifest leaders. These people are less manifestly powerful than others but many of them are still part of political leadership. The initial distinction between the manifest and the latent leaders is a difference in reputation, renown, or visibility to presumably informed citizens.[23]

(3) If we analyse leadership in terms of its effectiveness for social and political mobilization, the patterns of leadership behaviour could be characterized as stragetic and non-stragetic. The stragetic leaders aim at bringing as much improvement as possible in everything related to organization which includes strengthening the defensive and offensive frontiers and also their advancement. This type of leadership can, therefore, be described as restless which crosses the limits of the day of day task of organizational life. "The essence of strategic leadership is adaptability and creativity. In other words, it is able to draw upon its own experience and knowledge and that of others, and to synthesize these into a new plan of action. It is productive of new ideas and innovations; it is unsatisfied and curious, constantly seeking further opportunities to exploit.[24] The non-strategic leadership, as contrasted with the strategic one, is usually preoccupied with the routine and habitual. It is also unchanging in nature. It cannot however be inferred from this that the non-strategic leaders are unefficient as far as the routine administration of an organization is concerned. Quite on the contrary, their efficiency lies in the effective handling of the problems which they may confront in routine administration. The non strategic leaders differ from the strategic ones in the matter of their vision about the future and the degree of sensitiveness toward the problems of long term implications.

(4) Bureaucracy involving large scale formal and informal organizations prominently found in economic, political and religious, is generally composed of those important persons who work for the government and upon whom the administration depends. The characteristics of bureaucrats depends on the purposes of the state, the manners in which they are selected, and the traditions associated with public service. Their characteristics therefore may vary from one country to the others. In some countries, for instance the bureaucrats consider themselves as a separate class distinct from the general mass. Internally, bureaucracy's principal characteristics as ideal type consists in an adequate balance between competence and responsibilities on the part of its various units. The requisite standards of competence vary with the nature of the task, and are connected with the related evolution of culture in the instrumental fields, the various technologies, etc. It is only very late that full fledged science becomes an important component of competence. Responsibility is associated especially with the nature of the authority and leadership operating within organization. The fundamental problem is balancing the two essentially independent elements of competence and authority.[25]

The primary function of bureaucracy, as Weber has pointed out, is the gradual elimination of the personal, intensive and value factors which form the basis of leadership of stereotype.[26] From this view point bureaucratic leader is a contradictory term. In the opinion of Pfiffner and presthus an analysis of the bureaucratic leader as a deviation from the ideal type as suggested by Max Weber and Harold D. Lasswell provides suggestive generalizations. They have seen that the modern organization requires huge executive branch, a development correlated with the expansion of private enterprise and the increasing demand for services by the "customers" of government. A similar pressure toward the bureaucratization of leadership followed. The charismatic or natural leader who possesses a personal and revolutionary appeal, opposed to tradition and above institutional rountine, is soon brought under control of existing organizations as his dogmas are modified to meet the reach of his followers. Friedrich similarly studies the development of administration in Western Europe and the United States and found a recurrent pattern of growth, including centralization of control and supervision, division of labour, qualifications for office objectivity, provision, continuity and discretion in policy determination. The trend in modern organization towards bureaucracy in turn provides a certain structural and psychological framework which requires the executive leader to develop certain attitudes in order to succeed.

The charismatic nature of leadership has drawn the attention of a large number of social scientists who have tried to analyse it from their specific professional angles. It is generally agreed that a leader who possesses, atleast in the eyes of his followers, some virtue which is more than normal human instinct or the grace of God and by dint of that he is supposed to take right action, has been treated as a charismatic leader. The word charisma denotes. Those attributes of a person who is capable of instantaneous mobilization of masses because of his irresistible and almost hypnotic personal appeals and influence. Generally speaking, the term charisma can be attributed to any one with stormy qualities of leadership, but by usage it is reserved for the dynamic, irresistible type of leader, i.e., a person who has an area of magic and magnetism about him and who has an emotional sway ever his people who can be pushed into a state of delerium by his mere presence or an effect of his speech. In view of this they have been called the coast shaker and the mover of mountains. The leader who extends his control over the followers by means of the force of his personality may be called as a typical charismatic leader. The followers consider him as a person endowed with supernatural or superhuman qualities which represent their aspirations. Sometimes the political agitators can be accepted as saints having the quality of charisma. The legitimate leaders like the legally appointed president or headman of an organization are different from the charismatic leaders. The legitimate leaders in some cases, may be charismatic in nature. In every case the charismatic leaders possess or come in possession of some legitimate standing. Moreover, the charismatic leaders, during the period of crisis or political unrest, exercise more influence. In other wors, they have a wider appeal in comparison to the traditional or legal leaders who are associated with those institutions which are judged as dysfunctional with the spread of crisis. As Allyndeous the charismatic leader is more than a man among men. He is able to excite the deepest emotions of his followers and to generate an acceptance that is based on faith and belief in him and on irrational rather than rational assessment. He has a strong personal magnetism, and an implacable faith in himself and his destiny.[27]

Origin of leadership is based on certain emotional qualities found in a person. Such a leader makes his follower believe that his role as a leader is pre ordained and in a special way he draws inspiration and enlightenment. The followers believe that charismatic leader is divine God and develop a sense of devotion to him.[28] "Weber argued that the charismatic leader was often the personification of a revolutionary movement. He would emerge in time of crisis, as if sent by God, with a solution to problems that others have been unable to solve. In this century, Gandhi, Nehru and Shastri in India, Nyerre and Lumumba in Africa, Nasser and Khomeini in the Middle East, Castro and Allende in Latin America, represent excellent examples of charismatic personalities. According to William H. Riker, "Maxwebber secularized the word charisma to describe the feature of a leader's personality which seems to his followers to be the grace of God or atleast a more than human instinct for right action.[29] Similarly, many others have also described such a leader as charismatic who extends his power over the follower by virtue of the force of his personality. The followers believe that the leader possesses some supernatural or super human qualities which symbolize their aspirations. Such qualities are showed by saints and demogogues. The leaders functioning within the framework of law such as an elected president or a traditional ruler differ from charismatic leader. Of course some among them may also be regarded possessing charismatic qualities. The charismatic leaders in most cases try to achieve some legitimate standing. During the period of transition or unrest the people do not readily accept the traditional leaders because the institutions with which they are identified are defined a dysfunctional, and in such a situation the appeal for charismatic leaders increase.[30]

Such leaders must invariably possess certain personal qualities. The qualities are manifested in their action and recognized by the followers. The leader who is successful decision maker is often regarded as possessing the quality of charisma. The charisma of success was implicitly recognized in traditionalistic ideology of Chinese empire. If the emperor was disastrously unsuccessful in war, or even in his realm suffered from a great famine, he was said to have lost "the mandate of Heaven". On the other hand, if he was successful, his success confirmed his hereditary charisma. A successful Latin American dictator is more often considered as charismatic. Moreover, is his case, his success is merely his demonstrated ability to gain and keep power against whatever opposition offers itself.[31] Marion J. Levy has described charismatic leadership as special phenomenon in social history. The followers of such a leader never question any of the actions of the leader and simply carry out his dictates. In other words, the followers have blind faith in their leader. Charismatic leadership is a characteristic phenomenon of either relatively 'non-modernized' or 'relatively modernized' societies. The governments headed by such leaders have been found relatively unstable. Although they have generally brought about rapid and volumnous changes in governmental policies, it has also been observed that a disastrous situation has ensued from their failure to produce desired results within stipulated time. The source of veriability for charismatic leaders emanates from the problem of finding out thier suitable successors. The problem becomes more acute when the leader is supposed to possess greater charismatic power and believed more blindly by his followers. Because in such cases, the gap becomes wider between the leader and his successor. Moreover, the status of a charismatic leader is an achieved one and as such he does not appreciate the idea of any other individual fielding himself up to his successes. He rather considers it as a threat to his stability. Another important characteristic of charismatic leader is that they are identified with military exploits. "There have been many charismatic leaders in history who are not governmental leaders, but there have been virutally no charismatic governmental leaders who have not substantially identified with military exploits, both at home and abroad.[32] Johnson has however, pointed out that all the supporters of a charismatic leaders are not genuine worshippers. Many are opportunists and careerists. Many have allowed themselves to be 'bought off'. Many are simply afraid not to hail the leader as they are told. Even the genuine worship is to a large extent produced by propaganda.

**Political Leadership and Personal Leadership**

Leadership of positional type involves a dominant position

which a person holds within his society or group. This leadership or the dominant position is ascribed on the person by virture of his family background, for example, if a person is born in a royal or other influential family, holding a high position in occupation, hierarchy etc. "People who are asked to 'lend their names' to programmes and causes have this kind of leadership; it is abstracted from any particular skill or competence they may personally possess.[33] The personal leadership is in most cases an achieved status. The achievement depends on the attributes of leadership which the individual possesses. A person who can successfully pursue his social role and also can influence the behaviour, directly or indirectly or, other person achieves the status of a leader. The personal leaders can be divided into three categories: expert leadership or the leadership enjoyed by the specialists in a particular area of technical competence; charismatic leadership; and managerial leadership. Elsewhere leadership has been divided into three categories: (a) crowd compeller type with agressive attributes able to compel its followers to obey the orders by using coercive measures and dominance (b) Crowd Exponent type of leaders involving able and learned persons. In other words they are considered as experts by their followers and because of their abilities emerge as leaders. Thus leaders make sincere efforts for the amelioration of the grievances of their followers and prepare plans by exercising their minds and crafts; and finally, crowd representative type of leaders who can voice ideas and aspirations of thier followers at different levels of polity. Obviously, the behaviour of such leader is determined by the desires and dictates of the people who it is supposed to represent.

Many scholars working in the area of leadership have suggested operationally useful typology. Bartlett has suggested these categories in this regard: (1) Institutional leadership involving persons of widespread appeal in the religious, educational, and cultural fields; (2) Dominant leadership referring to those who do not believe in persuasion and try to force their dictates on their followers; and (3) Persuasive leadership indicating those who try to keep their followers in good humour by all available means of persuasion. Sergent has given an exhaustive list of seven categories of leaders. These are (1) Persons of eminence in their groups, such as headman chiefs and other institutional leaders (2) Symbolic leaders whose legitimacy depends upon the legal structure of their groups, involving respect but not real authority and rights to take decisions independently; (3) experts whose special abilities or extraordinary qualities are accepted as leaders by the common people; (4) executive leaders possessing ability to run an organization with efficiency, such a secretaries in government department managers, directors etc; (5) coercive leaders characterized by authoritarian dealing with their subordinates and power to punish those who decry their authority; (6) the reformist leaders who are found in the different spheres of public life, especially in religious and political spheres; and finally; (7) the charismatic leader with a casting impact of their personality or their followers. R.W. Naje has given a simple dichotomy of leadership, with two extremes of attributes—the one static and the other dynamic. Wolf has classified them as (a) radical, (b) conservative, and (c) scientific. Bogardús, however, has suggested six types: (a) mental (b) executive (c) social (d) paternal (e) autocratic, and (f) democratic. Similarly, Kimbal young has classified leaders into six types: These are: (a) The political Boss. This type of leaders is the product of modern democracy. Not necessarily a leader of the whole nation, he may operate at the levels of a province or state or city or may be associated with a distinguished organization. The stability or continuance of the political boss depends on his success in selection and for that purpose requires expert skill in manipulation of the situation and things. In other words, the political boss is an expert manipulator. His association with politics is mechanical and in order to preserve his political power he has to face tensions and conflicts frequently. Such type of leaders possess wide knowledge of the techniques required for organizing their followers and they also act as the purveyor of reward and punishment among their followers. (b) The Bureaucrat—The main function of a bureacrat is to supervise the works of those working as his subordinates. A bureaucrat generally has a number of people working as his assistants and they are on the pay rolls. The bureaucrat functions within the framework of the rules framed by the government and also helps to reinforce these rules on others. This type of leader is institutional, functional, intelligent and disciplined in nature. The bureaucrat loves privileges and is also capable of running the administration. (c) The Diplomat—The role of a diplomat is different from other type of leaders. He is not concerned only with matters related to international understanding but also with the matters internal to the nation or government. The diplomat carefully observes the ideal of the nation or government which he represents. The diplomat is generally appointed as an envoy to a foreign country where his functions are guided by the norms set up by his government. He also endeavours to explain the policies and ideals of his government to the people of the country where he is supposed to discharge his ambassadorial functions. Diplomat is skilful in the use of the words although they are frequently a cover for his aims. As one famous commentator puts it, if a diplomat says yes he means perhaps, if he syas perhaps, he means no, if he says no, he is no diplomat. (c). The Democratic leader—The democratic leader too is the product of modern democracy. He is different from the political boss because unlike the latter he is more disposed towards the service to the society and people. He is more tolerant and nearer to the people. He does not impose his ideas like the political boss, over others. He is not coercive in his approach and does not believe in either murderous plots or war and conflicts. He is sympathetic, considerate, and persuasive and also committed to the cause of betterment of his people. (d) The Agitator—The agitator is revolutionary in his approach. He is staunch believer in the ideology which he follows and takes recourse to revolutionary measures in order to bring changes in social order. He stands for the eradication of corruption in the society and does not like to listen to the arguments of his opponents. (e) The Reformer—This type of leaders are found in a greater number in democratic societies. The reformers are idealists and preach their ideals among the people with untiring zeal. They are generally prudent and make use of emotional words to bring changes or reformation in the society. They are rigid in their approaches and do not compromise with their opponents for the solution of any, problem which is contrary to their ideals. (f) The theorist - A theorist leader is an inventor of new concepts with the help of logical arguments. These who are convinced with those arguments become his followers. A theorist is more a philosopher and scientist and lacks enough skill for handling the complicated governmental affairs. In modern literature on leadership, generally two types of leaders—authoritative and democratic—have been used for the sake of analytical facility. The two types of leaders vary from each other in terms of status, influence, esteem, attitudinal desposition, operative techniques etc. The authoritarian leader does not care much for the opinion and suggestions of other members of the group but in a democracy the people are free to express their opinions. The democratic leader does not only invites such opinions from the people but also gives them high priority. Popularity of a democratic leader depends upon his skill of group welfare and intelligence to carry the people with him. The authoritarian leader, on the other hand, places his own decisions above all other opinions expressed by the people and also tries to impose the same over the people. The authoritarian leader wields more absolute power than the democratic leader: he alone determines policies of the group; he alone makes major plans; he alone is cognizant of the succession of future steps in the groups activities, he alone dictates the activities of members and the pattern of interrelations among members; he alone serves as the ultimate agent and judge of rewards and punishments, for the individual members and hence the fate of each individual within the group structure. He behaves like the dictator of the group. The democratic leader does not differ from the authoritarian in the amount of power but in the nature of his role in the group structures. The democratic leader encourages maximum involvement and participation of individual members in group activities and also the determination of its objectives. Unlike the authoritarian leader, the democratic leader acts as the agent of the group and tries to avoid the growth of hierarchical group structure characterized by status differentials and special privileges. The democratic leader also attempts to strengthen the group structure by encouraging interpersonal contacts and reducing intra-group tension and conflict. A group headed by an authoritarian leader may collapse in his absence because without his support the group cannot continue its existence. The democratic leader does not make him so indispensable for group activities and the success of a democratic leader, in fact, is judged in terms of the extent to which the group can function when the leader is temporarily absent from the group structure.[34]

## Leaders and Followers: Conceptual Distinction

There exists a clear conceptual distinction between the leaders and the followers. In every group, irrespective of size purpose or nature, the difference between the leader and the follower can be clearly observed. In the study of leadership the knowledge of interaction between leaders and the followers is required for arriving at the most valid generalizations. In any group where the distinction can be made between leaders and followers the relationship of dominance and submission is also marked. The leader and the followers both possess power impluse but in the case of leaders it is explicit and in the case of the followers it is implicit. The followers are jubilants at the victory of the group and consider the success of the leader of the group in the race for power as their success. Not in all cases the followers are reluctantly following their leaders. In most of the cases they do it willingly. The leader is taken as captain possessing necessary skill and courage to lead the group to the position of supremacy. Most of the people among the followers lack self confidence and also feel themselves incompetent to lead their group to victory. Among human beings love for power is a universal phenomenon but the limit for the craving for power is not equal in all cases and person with absolute love for power are rarely found. So long a man is confident of his competence to handle the problems of the group he likes to be in power but in the absence of such confidence he likes to follow a leader. Inequality in the distribution of power is also a universal phenomenon in human societies. This can be claimed on the basis of our knowledge about the most primitive to modern societies and can be explained on the basis of functional necessity and human nature. The working, human communities often involves collective enterprises and such enterprises for their successful completion require a person or group of persons who provide necessary guidance. Construction of a building, for instance requires a plan and similarly a time table is required to run the public transport system efficiently. This is true in the case of even the most democratically constituted groups. The human nature, as pointed out by Adler, is of two different types: Submissive and imperious. The former, almost essentially, occupies a servile position and the latter is always anxious to be superior to other and desires to rise at the top. Such persons are found at the forefront at the time of revolution and also in a situation which needs a dictator. It can, therefore, be said that desire for submission and desire to command are common and real. Some people by nature like to be follower and other by virtue of their qualities command over others. In between these two extremes, the third group consists of the average person who prefer to follow a leader in some situation and like to act as the leader is other situations. The impulse of submission, in most of the cases, is rooted in fear. In an alarming or uncertain situation the people resolve their differences and prefer to work according to the orders of a competent leader. When the situation demands full cooperation of the different sections of people in a group or community, it is necessary that they should be loyal to a leader who is accepted by all the parties concenred.[35] "Most people feel that politics is difficult, and that they had better follow a leader—they feel this instinctively and unconsciously as dogs do with their masters. If this were not the case, collective political action would scarcely be possible.[36] The social psychologists of group behaviour have also pointed out that the morale of group may improve in a fearful situation. It is well understood, for example, that unity may develop in face of a common threat or damages to a group.

It will however, be wrong to treat the role of leader as mere domination and that of the followers as mere submission. In fact, the leadership and followership can be viewed as "interrelated role specialization" prevailing in all stages of political system from Panchayat to Parliament. Leaders and followers have reciprocal expectations of each as to the behaviour of the other(s) in carrying out the complementary tasks. Leaders by virtue of their position explain and communicate the task to be performed by the followers and the extent to which the latter comply with those tasks reveals the leaders influence over followers.

As for the reasons of obedience and acceptance of leaders in political behaviour, one comes across various explanations. Most of these explanations relate to the observance of established rules and procedures of formal organizations or government bodies and hence they are very inadequte for the purpose of analysis. As a matter of fact the degree of obedience to leaders is always contingent upon the degree of acceptance of the leaders by the followers and their willingness to act according to suggestions given by the leaders. This again is related to clear understanding on the part of the followers about what they are expected to do and also they should have the proper means to carry out the expectations.

Questions may, however, be asked about the reason for acceptance by some people of suggestions, instructions, or proposals given by others. There are several reasons. First, the habit or inertia on the part of the followers as a reason for accepting the advices of the leader who has already been recognized by the people. Compliance of leaders suggestions in such cases is automatic and the followers simply cannot think of doing otherwise. In other words, it is a conditioned response created by training or experience. Second, the suggestions made by leaders are accepted when the followers find merit in them and also consider them as most appropriate to the situation. This generally happens when goals and values are commonly shared by the people and the situation is defined in the same manner. Third, the identification of the individuals with the aspirations of the group or the feeling or loyalty to a group, organization, or individual may also be one of the reasons for accepting the suggestions coming from the group or the individuals. Fourth, confidence in the ability of the leader to take correct decision because of his special knowledge as skill makes a man to accept the suggestions made by leaders. Fifth, when the person making a proposal or suggestion is considered as possessing legitimate right to do so his suggestions are accepted. And, finally, a person obeys the orders of the leader because he expects that he will be rewarded in some way if he does and punished if he does not?

**Recruitment of Leaders**

Every society has in built mechanisms and a set of criteria for selecting right brand of leaders. Explanation so far offered mostly refer to the question of recruiting efficient persons who had from the central focus of the bureaucratic organizations. Very little light has been shed on the social significance of recruiting political leaders, for the task of selecting right type of leaders atleast in modern societies, can be left neither on the goodwill of people nor on the caprice of the supernatural being as this may have disastrous consequences for the collective life. Even in democracies working strictly within the framework of law accepted by the people there are some safeguards in the task of selecting the right type of executive leader.[37] The governmental leadership mainly related, according to contemporary social scientists, to the executive aspect of the government and such leaders as the persons forming the central foci of the government are recruited in three different ways: (1) recruitment on predominantly patricularistic criteria, (2) recruitment on the basis of charismatic qualities, (3) recruitment on the basis of predominantly universalistic criteria. The parti-cularistic criteria of recruitment can be found in underdeveloped and traditional societies where the kinship plays decisive roles in the selection of personnel in this form. Hereditary monarches, chiefs, mobles etc. are recruited on particularistic ground and this form of selection gives maximum stability to the government. Further, the use of this form is not strictly limited to the non-modernized societies. In the most highly modernized societies particularistic criteria enter into the recruitment of even the most important leadership roles. In so far as particularistic elements enter into leadership choices in relatively modernized societies they tend increasingly to do so by way of non germane criteria rather than social barring.[38] Leading implies a shared direction, and this, in turn often implies that all parties to the leadership relation have a common goal atleast similar or compatible golas; and as Hollander and Julian. [39] observe a leader's influences suggest a positive contribution towards the attainment of these goals. Thus, any act of leading implies interactional relationship and leading is one form of interactional influence. Definition of the simplest unit of analysis in leadership has led to the identification of four basic elements in the relationship: (1) the leader, who has characteristics of ability and personality and resource relevant to goal attainment (2) the followers, who also have relevant abilities, personality characteristics, and resources; (3) the situation within which the relationship occurs, and (4) the task with which the interacting individuals are confronted. The nature of leader-follower relationship and the characterization of the act of leading are to be understood in terms of interaction between these sets of variables. Here it is necessary to emphasize the point that while identifying the attributes of leadership which form the basis of their acceptance and followers' obedience, we should not treat the followers as group of passive, callous and intelligent individuals. They are not to be treated as an aggregation minus leaders, for they too fulfil active roles. As Gibb says: "It is part of the selection of the group concepts to imply that all members actively interarct in the course of movement in a common direction. Leaders and followers should be seen as collaborators. The concepts of leading and following define each other. There can be no leading without following and, of course no following without leading. Not all members of any given group will, at any particular time, and with a particular leadership, be followers, but all members will at some times, under some conditions, be followers, or they will forfeit their membership. Neither are followers exclusively confined to this role, any more than leaders are exclusively and always engaged in acts of leading".[40] In fact, leaders and followers frequently exchange roles and observation has shown that the most active followers often initiate the act of leading. In fact, the leader-followers relationship is always contingent upon the characteristics of a situation implying values and attitudes with which the individual or the group has to deal in a porcess of activity and with regard to which this activity is planned and its results are appreciated. These characteristics are: (1) the structure of inter personal relations within a group; (2) the characteristics of a group taken as a unit; (3) the characteristics of the culture in which the group exists and from which group members have been drawn; (4) the physical conditions within which the group finds constrained to act; and (5) the perpetual representation, either the group and among its members, of these elements and the attitudes and values engendered by them. Research, have shown that a person does not become a leader by virtue of any particular pattern of personality traits but rather by possession of any attribute that, by virtue of its relevance to the situation and its situationally determined evaluation by other group members, establishes a relation of leading-following.

From sociological angle, leadership is the exercise of power or influence in social collectivity, such as groups, organizations, collectivities and nations. This power may be addressed to any or all three very general and related functions: establishing the goals purposes, or objectives of the collectivity; creatiing the structures through which the purposes of the collectivity are fulfilled; and maintaining or enhancing these structures. All of these functions are amenable to empirical investigation, particularly in bureaucratic settings, where much of the research on leadership is conducted. A leaders exercise of power and influence implies "making things happen" through other, leaders may engage in a number of activities in furthering this purpose. They may coordinate, control, direct, guide, and mobilize the efforts of others. A recent focus on the leaders' role in motivating members implies that they may counsel, support, help, persuate, or illicit the participation of others in some degree of goal setting. Leaders may also manipulate, entice, reward, coerce, or harass, although some scholars exclude these from the definition of leadership. The commonly accepted sociological position is that the relation of leadership arises only where a group follows an individual from free choice and not under common or coercion, and secondly not in response to blind drives but on positive and more or less rational grounds.

**Leadership and Democracy**

Although leadership has been considered as an indispensible phenomenon in democratic societies, there are scholars who feel that leadership and democracy are in the ultimate analysis, incompatible with each other. Leadership inevitably becomes eligarchic, even in political organization that start democratically and one committed to a democratic ideology. Leaders themselves are incapable of deflecting this historical process; democratic and idealistic leaders succumb eventually to the corruption inherent the power. Michels, for example, has given a number of arguments in this connection. First, the masses through incompetence and apathy cannot and do not want to participate actively in the political process; they prefer to be led. Second, democracy is structurally impossible in large and complex social systems, as there is no way of arranging the systems so that the views of the many individual members can be heard and taken into account. The unpracticability of democracy is especially apparent in organizations or nations undergoing conflict with others. Finally, the tendency toward stigarchy result from the character of leaders themselves and of the roles they must play. Because of their cultural and educational superiority over the masses, leaders form a distinct elite. The status, prerequisites, and privileges, associated with the leadership role serve further to separate the leaders from the masses. In the long run, they develop vested interest in thier positions, which they must protest. Furthermore, a personal lust for power, which is characteristic of leaders, intensifies their efforts to enhance their power, and leaders will resort to ulterior devices toward this end. In "democratic parties leader will employ emotional and demologic appeals to manipulate the gullible masses. They will control the party press, using it to describe themselves in the most favourable light while deriding their opposition within the party. They will exploit their special information and knowledge of the organization to out manoeuvre opponents. And if, despite these tactics, the leaders should be overthrown, the new office holders in their turn will undergo the inevitable transformation which renders them in every respect similar to the dethroned tyrants. It has been rightly observed that the revolutionaries of today become the reactionaries of tomorrow.[41]

**References**

1. B.N. Sahay, *Dynamics of Leadership,* (New Delhi: Bookhive, 1969) pp. 1-2.
2. Ordway Tead, *The Art of Leadership,* (New York: McGraw Hill, 1935) p. 20.
3. Paul Pigores. *Leadership of Domination,* (Boston: Houghton Mifflin, 1935) p. 16.
4. K.D. Gaugrade, *Emerging Pattern of Leadership; Comparative study of Leadership and Social Structure* (Delhi: Rachna, 1974) pp. 5-7.
5. Irving R. Weschler and Fred Massarik, *Leadership and Organization.* A Behavioural Science Approach.
6. Lewis J. Edinger (Ed.) *Political Leadership in Industrial Societies: Studies in Comparative Analysis* (New York) Robert E. Kriger Publishing Company, 1976).
7. Edinger, *op. cit.* pp. 4-5.
8. Ibid. 5.
9. Ibid. pp. 7-9.
10. D.K. Biswas, *Political Sociology Calcutta:* Firmer KLM Private Ltd. 1978 pp. 49-50.
11. Ibid, pp. 98-99.
12. C.J. Friedrich, *An Introduction to Political Theory,* (New York: Harpur and Row, 1967) p. 125.
13. E.A. Fleishman, *Leader Behaviour: Its Description and Measurement* (Ohio: Ohio State University, 1957).
14. E.S. Bogardus, *"Leadership and Social Situations", Sociological Research,* 16, pp. 164-170.
15. D. Zeleny, *"Characteristics of Group Leaders", Sociology and Social Research,* 24, pp. 140-49.
16. V.J. Bentz "Leadership: *A study of social interaction",* quoted in Berrnard M. Bass, *Leadership, Psychology, and organizational Behaviour,* (New York: Harpur & Row)
17. Brij B. Khare, *India: Political Attributes and Social Change.* (New Delhi: Light and life publishers)
18. Pfiffner J.M. & W.R. Presthus, *Public Administration* New York.

19. Russell Betrand, *Power: A New Social Analysis*, New York, 1953. *London: Aden and Unxwin: 1938.
20. Merrium, C.F. *Systematic, Politics*, Univ. of Chicago Press (Chicago: 1945).
21. Ezioni, A., *Modern Organizations.* (New Delhi: Parentice Hall of India: 1965).
22. Agger, RE, Goldrich D and Swason BE, *Rulers and Ruled: Political Power and Importance in American communities* (New York: John Miley, 1964).
23. Agger, *op. cit.*, p. 329.
24. Hardwlck, CT and Landuyt, *Administrative strategy* (New York: Simons Broadman Publishing Corporation, 1961) p. 33-34.
25. Parsons, Talcott, Political Systems and Bureaucracy, in Pizzarno A Political Sociology (Harmond, Worth, Midllsex:1977), p. 58-59.
26. Weber, Max, Protestant Ethique and Rise of Capitalism.
27. Allyn, Charles, *Sociology: An Introduction* (New Jersey: Parentice Head, 1972).
28. Allyn, *op. cit.*
29. Riker, W.H. *The Theory of Political Coalition* (New Haven: Yale University Press, 1962).
30. Biesanz, J. and Bieszanz, M., *Modern Society* (New Jersey: Parentice Hall), 1968.
31. Johnson, H.M., *Sociology: A systematic Introduction* (Bunhar: Allied Publication 1960).
32. Levy, M.J. (Jr) *Modernization and Structure of Societies* (New Jersey; Princeton University Press) 1966.
33. Johnson, Harry, M: *A Systematic Introductions* (Bombay: Allied, 1970).
34. Krech, D. and Cructchfeiled.
35. Biswas, D.K., *Political Sociology*, (Calcutta-Firms KLM Pvt Ltd.) p. 131.
36. Russell B, *op. cit.*
37. Gladden, E.N.-*Approach to Public Administration*, (London: Staples Press, 1966).
38. Marior J. Levey, *op. cit*, p. 453.
39. Cecil A Gibb, *Leadership: Psychological Aspects, International Encyclopaedia of Social Science, op. cit.* p. 91.
40. Gibb, C.A., *op. cit*, p. 93.
41. Michels Robert, *Political Parties: A Sociological Study of the Oligarchical Tendencies of Modern Democracy* (New York: Callier 1962).

## Chapter - 14

# Political Dimensions of Social Mobilization

Social mobilization refers, in the ultimate analysis, to a process of change, which happens to substantial parts of the population in the societies which show the sign of shifting from traditional to modern ways of living. It denotes a concept which brackets together a number of more specific processes of change, such as changes of residence, of occupation, of social setting of face to face association, of institutions, roles and ways of acting of experiences and expectations, and finally of personal memories, habits and needs, including the need for new patterns of group affiliation and new images of personal identity.[1] Needless to say that these changes through their cumulative impact tend to influence and sometimes transform political behaviour.

The term social mobilization does not merely imply a collection of changes which can be of different nature and occurring at different levels. It basically implies that these processes tend to go together in certain historical situations and stages of economic development, that these situations are identifiable and recurrent, in their essentials, from one century to another, and that they are relevant for political behaviour. It essentially implies that something is happening to large number of people in areas which undergo modernization, i.e. where advanced, non-traditional practices in culture, technology and economic life are introduced, and accepted on a considerable scale. It is however not identical to the process of modernization as a whole, but it deals with one of its major aspects, or better, with a recurrent cluster among its consequences. These consequences once they occur on a substantial scale, influence in turn the further process of modernization. Thus what can be treated for a short time span as a consequence of the modernization process, appears over a longer period as one of its continuing aspects and as a significant cause, in the well known pattern of feedback or circular causation. Thus viewed over a longer perspective, the concept of social mobilization suggests that several of the changes subsumed under it will tend to go together in terms of recurrent association. For example, any of the firms of social mobilization such as the entry into market relations and a money economy can be expected to be accompanied or followed by a significant rise in the frequency of impersonal contacts, or in exposure to mass media of communication, or in changes of residence or in political or quasi-political participation. The implication of the concept is thus to assert an empirical fact—that of significantly frequent association which can be tested empirically.

In fine, social mobilization refers to a process by which major clusters of old social, economic, and psychological commitments are eroded or broken and people become available for new patterns of socialization and behaviour.[2] Thus the following points may be taken into consideration:

(i) Mobilization is taken to mean a process by which is induced not a mere state or level which can be worked out either from 'hard' objective indices, or simply abstracted from subjective notions like participation, levels of cognition, etc. These latter are treated as second order consequences here. Ideally the most fruitful way of measuring relative states of mobilization through time, or between different societies, would be by use of reference group theory within an action framework. Thus the whole concept of mobilization is related in its comparative or measurable aspects to the notion of substantial changes in defining new referents for identifying different sections of population, as well as to the success of an elite in forcing acceptance of its new reference groups, both normatice and comparative.

(ii) Social mobilization can also be analysed as a function in terms of the social system. In this context, it can be understood in its manifest and latent forms so as to fit the function of political mobilization into the broader political function of goal attainment.

(iii) The concept is neutral with regard to purpose. It is not always necessary to classify different experiences of mobilization at different times in accordance with any latent or declared purpose. One main concern in defining it is more with the instrumental process in relation to the existential goals and values than with any overall assessment of the normative or ethical purposes of mobilization.

(iv) It is necessary, in any case, to define what is involved in the process of mobilization. It is essentially (1) attitudinal a commitment to action, and (2) a means of translating this commitment into action or observed behaviour. This is a composite process involving different stages:

(a) the existence of values and goals requiring mobilization.

(b) action on the part of leaders, elites or institutions seeking to mobilize individuals and groups.

(c) the institutional and collective means of achieving the mobilization.

(d) the symbols and references by which values, goals, and norms are communicated to, and understood and internalized by, the individuals involved in mobilization.

(e) the process by which mobilization takes place in terms of individual interaction, the creation and change of collectivities and structures, the crystallization of roles, the effect on sub-systems and their boundaries.

(f) estimates of the numbers and people (or proportion of a population) mobilized and the degree of such mobilization for different sectors or strata of the population.

Edward Shils has pointed out that images of mobilization and of Manmheims "fundamental democratization" imply two distinct images of the process: (I) the stage of uprooting are breaking away from old settings, habits, and commitments, and (2) the induction of mobilized persons into some relatively stable new patterns of group membership, organization and commitment. In this fashion soldiers are mobilized from their homes and families and integrated into the army which they serve. Similarly, Manmheim suggests an image of large numbers of people moving away from a life of local isolation, traditionalism and political apathy, and moving into a different life or broader and deeper involvement in the vast complexities of modern life, including potential and actual involvement in mass politics.

Social mobilization as defind above, can be related to political theory. For this, it will be necessary to bring it into a form in which it can be verified by evidence, and to develop the problem to a point where the question "how"? can be supplemented usefully by the question "how much". In its intuitive form, the concept of social mobilization already carried with it some images of growing numbers and rising curves. In so far as the constituent process of social mobilization can be measured and described quantitatively in terms of such curves, it may be interesting to learn how fast the curves rise, whether they show any turning points, or whether they cross any thresholds beyond which the process they depict have different side effects from those that went before. Notable among these side effects are any that bear on the performance of political systems and upon the stability and capacities of governments.[3]

The impact of social mobilization can be observed, among other things, on India's hierarchical social and political system. Weiner has observed that social changes accompanying modernization are facilitating the development and not the diminition of community interest in politics. The number of castes, religions, tribal, linguistic and ethnic associations is likely to continue to increase as the rate of social change increases, or even if it stays the same. These community interets may not exist at precisely traditional level of fragmentation or cleavage. Social mobilization in India is not likely to lead to homogeneity, but it already seems to have aggregated some small groups of somewhat greater size. Social mobilization, therefore, does not necessarily freeze the traditional system at the pre-existing level of social cleavage. It may reinvigorate a social cleavage at a high level of interest aggregation.[4]

Jyotindra Das Gupta has observed that the language association of contemporary India have grown as a part of Indian political system. The associations have promoted social mobilization in their own language through literacy and linguistic modernization. Languages have provided for three associations a way of binding people drawn from narrow occupational or local group loyalties into wider regional linguistic frameworks. These associations have also used modern organizational methods of political recruitment and socialization. The politics of language association in India, in short, illustrates the twin aspects of the effects of social mobilization on national integration. On the one hand, groups that shared cultural characteristics and language were able to put aside minor parochial differences and form a larger aggregate. But at this higher, albeit sub-nation state, level of aggregation and cleavage in the traditional system, social mobilization reinforced the divisions with other cultural and linguistic aggregations in India.[5]

We cannot, however, conclude, from the foregoing discussion that social mobilization invariably promotes national disintegration wherever there is differentiation by language or caste, or colour. In a hierarchical system of ethnic or linguistic stratification, with an agglomerative political culture, it is likely that social mobilization will not have disintegrating effects if the political culture of the system prior to the beginning of social mobilization did not legitimate ascriptive group political action. A hierarchical ethnic system includes the acquiscence by the social subordinates to the norm that more honour accrues rightfully to social superiors. An agglomerative political culture, moreover, has institutionalized patterns of social mobility over a long period of time. A long term pattern of individual mobility renders new ethnic group political behaviour by the social subordinates illegitimate and practically impossible. Social mobilization by itself does not automatically create ethnic group organizational capabilities. The social mobilization hypothesis done is insufficient to predict the probable political outcome. It is also necessary to specify the prior context and experiences of ethnic group political behaviour.

Morner and Pitt-Rivers have emphasized in their study of the historical development of Latin America, a hierarchical ethnic system, an agglomerative political culture, and individual mobility. When social mobilization came, social sub-ordinates did not organize politically as groups. Social mobilization opened new channels for individual change and thus reinforced, rather than changed, the preexisting pattern. This can be examined in the following figure that illustrates Latin Americas position in comparative perspective.

| *Ascriptive Culture* | *Political Culture* | *Mobility Pattern* |
|---|---|---|
| Parallel (Belgium, Lebonan, Canada, Nigeria) | | |
| Hierarchical | Assimilative (United States Liberia, South Africa) | Group (India) |
| | Agglomerative | Individual (Latin America) |

*Source*: Samuel A. Huntington and Jorge I. Domingnez, Political Development in Macro-political theory by Fred I. Greenstein and N.W. Polsby, *op. cit.* p. 70.

It has been also found that individual mobility and social mobilization do not disrupt the traditional system. They reinforce it. The normative justification for the persistence of inequality has not been shaken, while new avenues for personal mobility have been opened. It does not follow, therefore, that the mere existence of social difference indicates the existence of drastically different cultures within a country or that social inequality leads automatically to violence. Brazil had a single shared culture for blacks and whites, which includes the recognition that blacks and whites are unequal and that individual upward mobility—permissible and desirable—requires cultural 'whitening', while downward mobility leads to cultural blackening. This common inegalotarian and normatively justified culture has been reinforced by social mobilization.[6]

It has been further empirically demonstrated that social mobilization, though closely associated with political variables, does not automatically lead to long-range implications for politics. A more automatic relationship appears in parallel ethnic systems or in those hierarchical ethnic systems with political culture that legitimize ethnic, caste, or religious group behaviour. But however these traditional legitimizing features have been lacking, the political effects of social mobilization on ethnicity are minor. And where the coercive power of the state is put at service of radical assimilation/exclusion policies, the dominant groups continue to rule. For example, in Latin America, dominant ascriptive social strata rule with little apparent cost but also in the presence of considerable individual mobility; in South Africa they rule at considerable political, social, economic, and personal costs in order to freeze an ethnically immobile system with an uncertain long-term future.[7]

In fact, there are only three processes of systematic long-term social mobilization en masse; military, religious, and political. Since all three fulfil broadly similar functions in creating community they have much in common. For one thing, they all relate people tightly together in a distinct and often novel form, by evolving particular structures and by giving people common goals and references groups. In doing so, mobilization process either substitutes new priorities for previous ones, or creates conscious priorities on a general scale for the first time, where it did not exist previously.

Question arises as to how political mobilization differs from other form of mobilization and from the notion of social mobilization generally. One possibility is to analyse the problem in terms of sub-systems; politics is one normative integration, economic activity and kinship relations are others. We can measure their interaction in terms of changing range and density; thus we may often find in system predominant at any one time (dominant religion during the reformation, kinship in primitive societies, economic in communist societies)—the phase model. A second possibility is to introduce politics at an upper stage of the progression of value—addition in forms of collective behaviour. But norms and value-oriented movements have largely political reference, though they do not necessarily exhaust themselves exclusively in political action at the level they become past of societies goal—attainment function. The movement we are dealing with norms and beyond, we are also dealing with norm or decisionmaking machinery and are therefore in politics. A third version—which can be treated as a logical extension of the latter alternative, is simply to define political context narrowly or broadly (change of policy, change of policy—making personnel or structures, change of value components of structure) and to take that part of any given social action, or any social situation for that matter. This really implies a completely different definition of politics—in term of authority roles or actions concerned with the exercise of power. Such a defrnition approximates most closely to Lasswell/Kaplan and Dahlls definition of politics or Dahrendorf's model of society. The political process now becomes a component of social action all the way through the hierarchy from values down to individual roles. In one sense, it is probably the most satisfactory method since it avoids arbitrary and brittle classifications of process and action. However, it suffers from the grave disadvantage that it makes the political component of action or situations almost impossible to isolate. Comparison becomes very difficult and comparison in terms of change is the prerequisite of the analysis of political and mobilization.

The second method of analysing political mobilization in accordance with the scale and level of its societal impact is most easily related to constitutional or elitist political cultures. In a strongly constitutional polity, norm oriented attack on, as well as defense of, the existing rules of the game will quickly reach the limits of the normatively possible if it carries sufficient impetus escalation to value - orientation will be manifest and dramatic. This is because constitutional societies tend to incorporate their formal structures into their perspective ideology, and into the general definition of this given situation. Malfunctioning is therefore rapidly and closely identified with constitutions; any part is held to be functionally dependent on the whole and both antipathetic political action as well as sympathetic assertion escalate easily to value orientation. We see this clearly in countries like France, Germany, and Italy, in new democracies like Nigeria and Turkey and in United States. In Apter's definition, all these are consummatory cultures as far as the dimension of their major political institutions is concerned. In elitist societies, by contrast, conflict over norms encompasses a much larger but more self contained area. Escalation is more difficult, because the institutional structure of the polity is porous, flexible and in the last resort expendible we have this situation primarily in Britain and the Soviet Union, to a lesser extent in post war Germany and Japan; among the newer countries in Pakistan and Indonesia. On the constitutional dimension these are thus relatively instrumental political cultures. Perhaps it should be emphasized that the issue here is the social possibility for antipathetic normative movements to escalate into value oriented ones, not the functional instrumentality or structural conduciveness for mobilization offered by elitist or constitutional politics.[8]

India, Switzerland, and Sweden, with composite cultures, represent a relatively difficult case. In India, it can hardly be indicated that this or that kind of cultural orientation will prevail in the polity. In the structure independent of, or indifferent to, those presently managing it. Is congress a stable party or an unsufficiently differentiated womb for the Indian political universe? Can antipathetic political mobilization be contained in a struggle for norms, however acute (which might include the transformation of the political and institutional structure of, or will it escalate to engulf the very existence of the Indian Union. A substantial amount of the evidence regarding norm oriented mobilization and counter mobilization in India has accumulated as a result of the issue of linguistic states. Between the decision of Bombay state into new linguistic states in 1956, and the similar decision of the Punjab in 1966, there has been regular and highly organized rioting of the traditional collective behaviour type. At times, it has escaped the control of the authorities, who in the whole have maintained that each new linguistic state must be the last. Yet these severe challenges have so far been contained at a norm - oriented level, often even at a collectivity level; partly by concessions, partly by the ready collapse or deflation of the movements after a short while. The gloomier predictions for India have yet come to pass—though the resistence and authority of Mrs Gandhi's government seemed severely shaken by the end of 1966.[9]

It follows, from the foregoing discussion, that it would be useful to consider the nature of mobilization in the context of the four basic components of the social hierarchy - roles, collectivities, norms, values. To some extent, this is a simple progression, as we have observed herein-before. Mobilizing people makes then either into a mode (if non-institutional but based on some general belief) or a collectivity by coercion (if institutional but not based on a general beliei, press-gangs, enforced savings, etc.) Mobilizing people plus norms equals the minimum of political action. Mobilizing people plus values might be called a revolution or, if institutionally induced, a mobilized nation-at-arms. But in real life things are not often as simple as this. No doubt social and political action increases in scope and intensity as issues more from the lowest level of roles to antipathy or support for norms or even values emerge. But the effect we have already described as compression or short-circuiting prevents these components from being simple alternatives or even additives. The mobilization of collectivities (or conversely theirs identification as social and political obstacles to mobilization) need not end with escalation to the next highest category on our scale of norm-oriented action. In elitist societies, antipathy to individuals is often a sign and means of escalation from normative preoccupations to value-oriented ones; individuals may become the symbol of norm-oriented change.

**References**

1. Karl W. Deutch, *"Social Mobilization and Political Development"* in Jason L. Finkle and Richard W. Gable, Political Development and social change, (New York: John Wiley & sons Inc., 1966) p. 2-5-26.
2. Karl Deutch observes "Other things assumed equal, the stage of rapid social mobilization may be expected, therefore to promote the consolidation of states whose people already show the same language, culture, and major social institutions: whose population is already divided into several groups with different languages or cultures or basic ways of life," Nationalism and National Development: An Interdisciplinary Bibliography Cambridge, Mass: MIT Press, 1970; also see his social Mobilization and political Development in American Political Science, Review, 55: 453-514.
3. Karl Deutch, *op. cit.*
4. Myron Weiner, Politics of Scarcity: Public Pressure and Political Response in India Chicago: (Chicago Univ. Press. 1962)
5. Jyotindra Das Gupta, Language Conflict and National Development, Group Politic and National Language Policy in India (Berkly: Univ. of California Press; 1970)
6. Samual P. Huntington & Dominguez, *op. cit.* p. 70.
7. Ibid. p. 73.
8. J.P. Nettls Political Mobilization: A sociological Analysis of Methods and concepts (London: Faber and Faber Ltd. 1967)
9. Selig H. Marrison, India: The Most Dangerous Decades, (Princeton, 1960)

# Bibliography


Aaenger, G.H.-"Social Status & Political Behaviour", *American Journal of Social Forces,* Sept. 1945, pp. 103-13.

Agger, R.E. and Goldrich, D.-"Community Power Structure and Partnership", American Sociological Review, 1938, 23, pp. 383-92.

Agger, R.E. and Swasm, B.E.-*Rulers & Ruled: Political Power and Importance in American Communities* (Newyork) John Viley, 1964.

Akinchan, S.-"Sociological Theory and Social Determinism Towards a Dialecticised Perspective of Research", *Journal of Social and Economic Studies,* 1976.

Akinchan, S.-*Urban Growth and Political Socialization* in India, Janaki Prakashan, New Delhi, 1981.

Akinchan, S.-*Urban Growth & Political Socialization,* Delhi-Janaki Prakashan, 1982.

Alkers, H.R.-"Casual Inference & Political Analysis" in J.L. Bernal (ed.) Mathematical Applications in Political Science, Southern Methodist, University Press, Dallar, 1966.

Almond & Colman (ed.)-The Politics of the Developing Areas, (Princeton: Princeton Univ. Press; 1960) p. 59.

Anthony, M.-"A Reappraisal of Social & Political Participation of Negros", *American Jr. of Sociology* Vol. 72, 1966, pp. 32-46.

Ashby, W.R.-*Design for a Brain,* Widley, Newyork, 1960, p. 82.

Arendt, H.-*The Origins of Totalitarianism,* Newyork, Harcourt, 1954.

Arneson, B.A. & Wills, W.N.-"Voting Behaviour in 1948 as compared with 1924 in a typical Ohio Community", *American Political Science,* Junem 1950, pp. 432-34.

Aron, R.-"Power and Status Relations", *European Journal of Sociology,* Vol. I (2) 1960, p. 260-61.

Axelrod, M.-"Urban Structure and Social Participation". *American Sociological Roview,* 1965, 21, pp. 13 18.

Banfield, E.C.-*Politics, Planning.*

Bay, Christian, -A critic of behavioural politics, designates it as 'Pseudo-Politics' or Counterpart Politics'. A Critical Evaluation of Behavioural Literature, "*American Political Science Review* (March, 1965, pp 39-51).

Beale, C-"Economics Affects Vote", *Science,* Vol. 58, 1950.

Benedix, R. & Lipset-*The Field of Political Sociology* p. 26.

Bently, A.F.-*The Process of Government.*

Bentor, V.J.-"Leadership: A Study of Social Interaction", quoted in Bernard M. Bass, *Leadership, Psychology, & Organizational Behaviour,* (New York: Harpar & Row).

Berelson, P.F. & Mephea, W.N.-*Voting,* Chicago, Univ, of Chicago Press, 1954.

Bertrand, R.-Power: *A New Social* Royal Press, Newyork, 1953.

Bhamberi, C.P.-"Functionalism on Politics", in Indian *Journal of Political Science,* Delhi, Vol. XXXIV, No. 4, Oct-Dec., 1973, p. 455.

Bhatta, A.-*Caste, Class, and Politics, in aprial Profile of Social Stratification in Modern India,* New Delhi: Manohar Book Service, 1975.

Biesanz, M. & Biesanz, J.-*Modern Society.* (New Jersey : Parentice Hall, 1968).

Biswas, D.K.-Political Sociology, Calcutta: Firms KLM Pvt. Ltd. 1978 pp. 49-50.

Biswas, D.K.-Political Sociology, Calcutta-Frims KLM Pvt. Ltd. p. 131.

Blondel, J.-*An Introduction to Comparative Government.* (London: Weiderfold and Wiebolgon, 1969). p. 223.

Bluhn, W.-*The Theories of Political System.*

Bogardus, E.S.-"Leadership & Social Situation, *Sociological Research,* 16, pp. 164-170.

Bower, D.R.-*Political Behaviour of the American Public* (Columbia, Ohio: C.E. Merril Pub. 1968) p. 4.

Brotz, H.I.-"Social Stratification and Political Order". *American Journal of Sociology,* May, 1957-64 (6), pp. 571-78.

Brown, H.R.-"Interpretation of voting in the Allocation of Economic Resources", *Quarterly Journal of Economics,* No. 1943, Vol. 58. pp. 27-48.

Brown, A.R.-*Structure and Function in the Primitive Society,* (London-Cohen and West Ltd.) 1959.

Brown, R.R.-*Explanation in Social Science.* (Chicago : Aldine 1963). pp. 109-32.

Bulparompil, J.K.-Models of Nation-building : A Critical Appraisal (New Delhi : New Publications, 1975) pp. 77-78.

Carl, H.-Leaders, Factions, and Parties—The Structure of Philipine Politics, New Haven: Yale University South East Asian Studies Monograph, No. 6, 1965.

Campbell, A. and Khan, R.C.-*The People Elect a President,* Ann Arbor, University of Michigan, Sinves Research Centre Publication-9, 1952.

Campbell, A. & Miller, W.E.-*The Voter decides Evanson,* Illinois, Row Peterson.

Cantril, H.-"Why we Vote the Way" We do, *New York Time Magazine,* September 24, 1944, p. 12.

Catlin, G.E.G.- *Systematic Politics,* (Toronto Univ. of Toronto Press, 1962) p. 299.

Cornetius, W.-"Principal Research Findings Relating to Political Participation Among low-income Rural migrants to Mexico City". Harvard Univ. Centre of International Affairs, Cambridge, Mass 1972.

Charles, A.-*Sociology*: An Introduction (New Lersey: Parentice Head, 1972).

Chodak, S.-*Societal Development: Five Approaches with Conelasions from Comparative Analysis* (New York: Oxford University Press, 1937) pp. 233.

Chodak, S.-*Societal Development* (New York : Oxford University Press 1973).

Clawde, E.W.-*Political Modernization,* (Blemnt, California, Wadsworth Publishing Co., 1971).

Cohham, S.A.-"Ethics and the Decline of Political Theory", Political Science Quarterly (Sept., 1953) p. 335.

Cole, G.D.H.-*Studies in Class Structure,* (London: Routledge and Kegan Paul 1955, pp. 102-103.

Crick, B.-*The Pererican Sance of Politics,* Routhdge and Kegan Paul, London, 1959.

Cornel, R.W.-*The Childs Construction of Politics,* Melbourne, Australia: Melbourne Univ. Press, 1971.

Dahal, R.A.-*"The Behavioural Approach in Political Science: Epitaph for a monument to a Successful Protest",* in *American Political* Science Review (Dec. 1961) pp. 763-72.

Dahl-*Modern Political Analysis.*

Dahl, R.-*Who Gorerns,* (New Haves: Yale Univ. Press 1961).

Daminguer, J. & Samuel, Huntington-"Political Development in Science" in Handbook of Political Science, Vol. 3, *op. cit,* p. 2.

Dances, Bell-"Towards the year 2000: Work in Progress", *Daecllas special Number,* 96, (Sammn 1967) p. 642.

Daniel, Lorner-*The Passing of Traditional Society,* (New York: Free Press: 1953).

David, E.-*A Frame work for Political Analysis.* (Englewood Cliffs, Parentice Hall, 1965). pp. 125-32.

David, A.- The Politics of Modernisation (Chicago: Chicago Univ. Press), 1965.

David, E.- Theoretical Relevance of Political Socialization", *Canadian Journal of Political Science,* 1, 1968.

Davis, I.- *Social Mobility and Political Change* (London Pall Mall; 1970) p. 97.

David, M.-"Political Socialization: The inflict Assumptions Questioned", *British Journal of Political Science,* 1971, 453-65.

David, -"Review of the R. Hess and J. Torney, The Development of Political Attitudes in Children", Harvard Educational Review, 1968, 38: 571-78.

Dawson, R.E.-*Political Socialization,* Little Brown, 1969.

Dawson, R.E. & Kenneth- *Premitt and Political Socialization* Boston: Little Brown, 1969.

Dennis, J. & David, E.- "The Child's Image of Govt." Annals of the American Academy of Political and Social Sciences 1965, 361: 40-57.

Dennis, J. -*Children in Political System,* McGraw Hill, Newyork, 1969.

Dennis, J. & David, E.-Children in the Political System: *Origins of Political Legitimacy,* Newyork, McGraw Hill, 1969.

Deutch, K.W.- 'The Growth of Nations : Some Recurrent Patterns of Political and Social Integration, *World Politics,* Vol. V., January, 1953.

Deutch, K.W.- *The Nerves of the Government : Models of Political Communication and Control,* The Free Press, 1966.

Deutch, K.W.-*Political Development and Social Change,* (Newyork: John Wiley & Sons Inc., 1966) p. 2-5-26.

Deutch, K.W. -Social Mobilization & Political Development in *American Political Science Review,* 55.

Deutch, K.W.- "Nation-Building and National Development: Some focus for Political Research", in Karl W. Deutch & W.J. Foltz (eds.) *Nation Building* (New York: Aldine Atherton: 1971) pp. 11-12.

Duncan, P.J. -"Peasant Society and Clientalist Politics in *American Political Science Review,* 64: 411-25, 1970.

Dunningham, N.E. Sydner, G.S.- "Voting in Early America", *America Heritage,* No. 4, Sept. 1952, p. 6-8.

Dwight, W.- "The recent period: Political Science World War II, Handbook of Political Science, *op. cit,* p. 58.

Dye, T.R. -*Politics, Economics and Public,* Rand one mally Chicago, 1966.

Easton, D.- The Political Systems *An Enquianynto the State of Political Science,* Alfred Aknopt, Chicago, 1953, pp. 96-97.

Edenger, L.J. -*Political Leadership in Industrial Societies : Studies on comparative Analysis (Newyork* : Robert E. Kriger Publishing Co. 1976.)

Edward, S.- Political Socialization, Newyork, Acherton, 1970.

Edward, S. - Old Societies & New States : *The Question modernity in Asia and Africa,* Newyork : Free Press of Glencoe, 1963, p. 22.

Edward, S. - "On the Comparative Study of the New States", in Clifford Greertn (ed) *Old Societies and New State,* (New Delhi: Amerind 1971) pp. 1-2.

Eispentdt, S.N. -*Modernization : Protest and Change,* (New Delhi, Prentice Hall of India : 1969) p. 1.

Edersveld, S.J.- "Theory and method in voting Behaviour Research, in H. Eulaw, S.J. Eldersveld and M. Janritz (eds.) *Political Behaviour*: A reader in theory and Research, Glencoe III. Free Press 1956. pp. 276-77.

Emerson, Robert - *From Empire to Nation : The Rise to Sect Assertion of Asia & African Peoples,* Calcutta : Scientific Book Agency, 1960.

Ernest, R. -"The meaning of Nationality", in Hans Kohan, *Nationalism: Its meaning and History,* Princeton, N.J. : Van Nortrand (1955) p. 136.

Etzioni, A.- *Modern Organizations,* New Delhi : Prentice Hall of India: 1965.

Eulan, Heizz - "The Ecological Basis of Party System, The case of Ohio", Mo *Journal of Political Science*, Vol. I, 1957, pp. 225-35.

Faridi, J.- "Job Reservation : How much, For whom and How long?" *The Hindustan Times Magazine*, Nov. 23, 1980, p. 1.

Fleishman, E.A. - Leader Behaviour : Its Description and Measurement (Ohio : Ohio State University, 1957).

Frugelman, E. and Flaginan, W. - "Functional Analysis in James C. Chanesworth (ed) *Contemporary Political* Analysis (New York: Free Press, 1967, p. 72.

Frugelman, E. & Flagnan, W. - "Functional Analysis in James C. (ed) *Contemporary Political Analysis* (New York: Free Press 1967), p. 72.

Friedrich, C.J. -*An Introduction to Political Party*, (New York : Harper & Raw, 1967) p. 175.

Gabriel, A. & James Colman - *The Politics of Developing Areas*, Princeton University Press, Princeton, 1960.

Gallup G. "How 55 million Vote", U.S. News, May 23, 1955, pp. 5-7.

Gaugrade, K.D.- Emerging Pattern of Leadership : Comparative Study of Leadership & Social Structure (Delhi : Ralhna, 1974) pp. 5-7.

Gerlh, H.H. & Mills, C.W. -*From Max Weber, Essays in Sociology* (London : Routledge & Kegan Paul, 1967).

Geertz, C.- "The Integrative Revolution : Primordial Sentiments and Civic Politics in the New States", in Clifferd Gertz (ed) *Old Societies & New States* (New Delhi: 1971).

Gillin & Gillin- *Cultural Anthropology.*

Gladden, E.N.-*Approach to Public Administration* (London : Stapless Press, 1966).

Glaser, W.A. - "Fluctuations in Turn-out", in W.N. Mcphel & W.A. Glaser (eds.), *Public Opinion and Congressional Elections*, New-york, The Free Press of Glencoe, 1962, pp. 19-51.

Greenstein, F.I. -*Children and Politics*, New Haven, Yale University Press, 1985.

Greenstein, F.I.- *Personality and Politics*, Chicago : Markban 1969.

Greenstein & Nelson -*Handbook of Political Science, Vol.* 2 Micro Political Theory, Addison Wesley Publishing Company, California, 1975, pp. 93-153.

Greenstein, F.I. - *Macro Political Theory, A Handbook of Political Science*, Vol. 3, Addison Wesley, London 1975, p. 42.

Gupta, J.D. - *Language Conflict and National Development, Group Politic and National Language Policy in India* (Berkly : University of California Press; 1970).

Hanser, N.R. - *Patterns of Discovery* (Cambridge : Cambridge University Press, 1961).

Harris, L. -*Is there a Republican Majority,* Newyork, Harper, 1954.

Hastings, P.K. - "The Voter & the Non-Voter", *American Journal of Sociology* 1956, 62, pp. 302-307.

Hawley, Amo H. -*Human Ecology,* Newyork Ronald Press, 1950, p. 204.

Hayman, H.R. and Wright, C.R. - "Voluntary Association Memberships of American Adults : Evidence from *National Sample Survey.*

Hayman, H.R. & Wright, C.R. - "Voluntary Association Membership of American Adults : Evidence from National Sample Surveys", *American Sociological* Review, 1958, 33, pp. 284-94.

Heinz, Eulou - *The Behavioural Persuation in Politics,* 1963.

Hempel, C.G. -"The Logic of Functional Analysis" -Llewellyu Grocs (ed) *Symposium on Sociological Theory,* p. 278.

Hensehel, A. - "Relationship between Values and Behaviour : A Development 'Hypothesis' "*Child Development,* 1971, 42 pp. 1977-2007.

Herbert, T.-*Political Behaviour : Studies in Election Statistics,* Bedminster Press, Totowa, N.J. 1963.

Howard, A.S. - "Voter turn cut in Canada", *Midaert Jr. of Political Sciences* 5 Nov. 1961, pp. 351-364.

Haghes J. and Robert Edowse - Political Sociology, (John Wiles and Sons, London 1972) pp. 2-3.

Hontington, S.P. -*Modern Political Theory,* (Delhi Vikas, 1965, p. 303).

Huntington, S.P. - *Political Order in Changing Society*. Yale University, New Hever, 1968.

Hyman, H.H. -*Political Socialization : A Study in the Psychology of Political Behaviour,* Glencoe III, Free Press, 1954.

Hyman, H. -*Political Socialization,* Glencoe, III, Free Press, 1959.

Inkless, A.- "Participation Citizenship in Six Developing Countries", *American Political Science Review* 63, pp. 1120-41.

Ithiel de Sola Pool - "Political Communication", in *International Encyclopaedia of the Social Sciences,* Op. let pp. 91-95.

Iuoyd, R. & Radolph, E.H. -*The Modernity of Tradition,* Chicago, University of Chicago Press, 1967.

Jansen, B.M. -*Changing Japanese Attitudes, Towards, Modernisation* (Princeton : Princeton Univ, Press 1965) pp. 23-24.

Johnson, H.M.- *Sociology : A Systematic Introduction* (Allied Publication 1960).

Johnson, H.M. -*A Systematic Introduction* (Bombay : Allied 1970).

Johari, J.C. -*Contemporary Political Theory,* Sterling Publishing House, New-Delhi, 1972.

Jonocisitz, M. -*The Community Press in an Urban Setting,* Glencoe III, Free Press, 1952.

Katz, E. & Lazarsfeld, P.F.-*Personal Influence,* Glencoe, III, Free Press, 1955.

Kay, V.O. Jr. -*Public Opinion and American Democracy,* New York Knopft, 1960, pp. 110-18.

Key, O. (Jr.) - Southern Politics in State & National New York, Knopf 1949, p. 5, 11-13.

Key, V. Jr. - *Politics, Parties, and Pressure Groups,* New York, T.Y. Growell, 1952.

Kenneth, P. and Powell, C.B. - "Social Structure and Political Participation : Developmental Relationships", *American Political Science Review,* 63, pp. 361-78.

Khan, H. -"Why Reservations", *Hindustan Times.*

Khare, B.B. -*India : Political Attributes & Social Change,* New Delhi.

Kini, N. G.N. -*Urban Voter in India* : A Study of *1967 General Election in Nagpur.* (New Delhi : Abhinav : 1974).

Kirkpatrick, S.A. and Morgan, D.R. -*Urban Political Analysis : A System Approach,* (London : The Free Press, 1972), pp. 67.

Kornabauser, W. *The Politics of Mass Society,* (London : Routledge Kagen Paul, 1965) p. 51.

Lal, S.K. -*The Urban Elite* (Delhi : Thompson Press 1974).

Landuyt & Harduick, C.T. -*Administrative Strategy,* (New York : Simons Broadman Publishing Corporation, 1961) p. 33-34.

Lane, R. -*Political Life*; Glencoe III, Free Press 1959.

Lasswell, H.D. -*The Future of Political Science,* Alberton Press, New York, 1963.

Lasswell, H. -*Who gets what, when and why?*

Lazassfeld, P.F. & Hazel, Claudet -*The Peoples Choice,* New York, Dwell Sloan & Peace, 1944.

Lerner, D. & Laswell, H.D. -*The Comparative Studies of Elites* (Standford : Heaver Institute Studies, 1952) p. 6.

Levy, M. -*The Structure of Society* (Princenton Univ. Press, New Jersey, 1952) pp. 36-38.

Levy, M.J.- *Modernisation & Structure of Societies* (New Jersey: Princeton Univ. Press) 1966.

Lewis & Davis -*Models of Political Systems* (Delhi-Vikas, 1971).

Lipset, S.M.- *Agrarian Socialism*, Berkeley, University of California Press, 1950.

Lipset, S.M. & Coliman, J. -*Union Democracy*, Glunce, III. Free Press, 1956.

Lipset, S.M.- *Political Man*, Mercurey Book, London, 1960, p. 21.

Lipset, S.M. & Benedix, R. -*Social Mobility in Industrial Society*, Berkeley, Univ. of California Press, 1960.

Lipset, I.M. & Stein, R. (ed) -*Party System, & Voter Glignments : Cross National Perspective*, Free Press, Newyork, 1967.

Lonald, D. & Joel, J. - The Structuring Principle. Political Socialization & belief system" *American Political Science Review*, 1973, 67, 415-32.

Lowie, R. - *Social Organization*, (London : Routledge and Kegan Paul, 1956).

Maccoby, E.E. & Merton, R.K. - "Youth and Political Change? *Public Opinion Quarterly*, 1954, 15, pp. 23-29.

Malinowrki, B. -*A Scientific Theory of Culture & Other Essays*. (Farolina : The Univ. of North Carolina Press) 1944.

Maclver, R.M. -*Politics and Society*.

Mann, R.S. -*Social Structures, Social Change and Future Trends*, Jaipur: Rawat Publications, 1979.

Marrison, S.H. -India, *The Most Dangerous Decades*, (Princeton, 1960).

Marropm, J. *International Encyclopaedia of the Social Sciences*, Mac Millan & Free Press, Newyork, 1968, pp. 21-25.

Martin, S., Lazorfel, P.F. & Berton, A.H.- "The Psychology of Voting": Analysis of Political Behaviour in Gardener Lindzey (ed) *A Handbook of Social Psychology*, Vol. 2, Reading, Mass Addison - Wesley.

Massarik, F. & Weschler, I.R. -*Leadership & Organisation, A Behavioural Science Approach* (New York : Mc Graw Hill Book Co.).

Mechan -*The Theory and Method of Political Analysis* (Homei Wood III : Dorsey Press, 1965).

**Merkel, P. -*Political Continuity & Change*** (New York: Harper and Row: 1967) p. 430.

Merton, R.K., Broom, K. and Coratell, L.S. (ed) - *Sociology Today, Problems and Prospects*, Happer Torch Books, New York, 1953 p. 83.

Merton, R.K. -*Social Theory & Social Structure* (Rev. Ent. Ed.) Glencoe, III, Free Press, 1957.

Merrion, C.E. and Goshell, H.F. -*Non-Voting Causes and Methods of Control*, Chicago, University of Chicago Press, 1974.

Merrian, C.E. -*The Making of Citizens*, Chicago : University of Chicago Press 1931.

Merriman, C.E. -*New Aspects of Politics.*

Merrian, C.E. -*Systematic & Politics*, University of Chicago Press (Chicago : 1945).

Milbrath, C.W.-*Political Participation*, Rand Mcorally, Chicago, 1965.

Milhu, J.B.D. -*The nature of politics.*

Mills, C.W. - *The Power Elite*, (Newyork : Oxford Univ. Press, 1959) p. 13.

Milton, R. -*The nature of Human Values*, Free Press, New York, 1968.

Mitchell, W.C. -*The American Polity*, New York : Free Press, 1962.

Mitchell, W.-'System Analysis' in *International Encyclopaedia of the Social Science.* Vol. 15, The Macmillan Co. & the Free Press, 1968, p. 473.

Mosca -The Ruling Class (New York: The Gran Hill, (1939), p. 50.

Mukhopadhyaya, A.K. -*Political Sociology.*

Mulkay, M.J. -*Functionalise Exchange and theoretical strategy.* (London: Lishthedge Hegan Paul, 1971) p. 56.

Mulkay, M.J. -*Functionalise Exchange and Theoretical Strategy*, (London: Lishthedge Hegan Paul, 1971) p. 56.

Nadel, S.F. -The Concept of Social Elites: *International Social Science Bulletin*, VIII (3) 1956, p. 415.

Nadel, S.F. -The Foundation of Social Anthropology, (London : Cohen and West Ltd.) 1958.

Nelson, J.M. and Samuel P. Huntington -*Socio-Economic* Change and Political Participation, Cambridge Mass : Harvard University Press, 1976.

Vettls, J.P. -*Political Mobilization : A Sociological Analysis of Methods and Concepts* (London : Faber Ltd. 1967).

Norbert, W.- *The Human Uses of Human Beings*, Doublday, Garden City, 1956.

Northrop, P.S.C. -*Logic of the Science and Humanities*, (New York: Meridian Books, 1959) pp. 40-49.

Organiski, A.F.K.- *The Stagis of Political Development*, Alfred and Knopt, New York, 1965.

Parry, G.- *Political Elites* (London : George Allen & Unavin Ltd. 1969) pp. 30-31.

Parsons, T. -*Politics and Social Structure,* (New York: The Free Press 1969) pp. 15-16.

Parsons, T.- *The Social System,* New Delhi, Amerind : 1977, p. 456.

Parsons, K. -The Grammar of Science.

Pigors, P.-*Leadership of Domination,* (Boston : Houghton, Mifflin, 1935) p. 10.

Piaget, J.-*Structuralism,* Basic Books, New York, 1970

Prathro and Irish -*Politics of American Democracy,* pp. 15-17.

Presthas, W.R. & Piffner, J.M. - *Public Administration,* New York.

Prewilt, K. "Political Socialization and Leadership Selection", *Annals of the American Academy of* Political and Social Science, 1965, 361, pp. 86. III.

Pye, L.- *Aspects of Political Development* (Borton Little Brown, 1966) p. 33.

Raymond, T.- "*Toward a Theory of Political Development*" Midwes *Jr. of Political Science,* II, 1967, pp. 145-172.

Rapport, A.- "System Analysis : General Systems theory", *International Encyclopaedia of Social Science,* op. cit.

Rene, L. and Keith Legg -"Political Clientatism and Development: A Preliminary Analysis ", *Comparative Politics,* 4: 149-75, 1972.

Rice, S.F. - *Quantitative Methods* in Politics, Knspt, New York, 1978.

Rocker, W.H. -*Political Coalition* (New Haven : Fole Univ. Press 1962).

Rinehart, H. & Winston - *Contemporary Political Thought : Issues in Scope,* Values & Direction, (New York 1969) pp. 118-36.

Robinson, J.A. & William S. -"The case of Indians" *Journal of Politics,* Vol. 22, Feb. 1949, pp. 96-111.

Richard, G.N. & Kent, M.- "The transmission of Political Values from Parent to Child", *American Political Science Review,* 1968, 62: 169-84.

Robert, M.- *Political Parties : A Sociological Study of the oligarchical undeneies of Modern Democracy* (New York : Callier 1962).

Rogers, E.M. -Modernization Among Peasants : *The impact of Communication,* Newyork : Halt Rainhard & Winston, 1969).

Rogo, N. -*Recent Trends in Occupational Mobility,* Glencoe, III, Free Press, 1953.

Rokkam, S. - "Models and Methods in the Comparative Study of Nation-Building" in A.R. Desai (ed) *Essay on World Modernization of Underdeveloped Societies,* Vol. I (Bombay Thack & Co. Ltd. 1971), P. 226-27.

Rossim, P.M.- "From Land marks in voting Research" in E. Burdick & A.S. Broadhack (eds.) *"American Voting Behaviour"*, Free Press Glencoe, 1959.

Roster, W.W. -*Stages of Economic Growth*, (London : Cambridge University Press : 1960) p. 39.

Rassel, B.-*Power : A New Social Analysis*, (London : Unuin Books, 1962) p. 25.

Runciman, W.G.- "*Social Science & Political Theory*" Cambridge University Press, 1975, p. 34.

Sahay, B.N. -*Dynamics of Leadership* (New Delhi : Bookhive, 1969) pp. 1-2.

Satishk, A.- *The Political Communication. The Public Language of Political Elites in India and the United States*, Holt Ringhort and Wintson, Inc., New York, 1969.

Schnidhauser, J. & David Gold -"Urbanization and Party Competitiveness", Midwest Journal of Political Science, Vol. 4, 1960, pp. 62-75.

Scott, L.C.- "Corruption, machine politics and political Change", *American Political Science Review*, 63 : 1142-58, 1969.

Siegal, R. -"Assumptions about learning of Political Values " *Annals of the American Academy of Political and Social Sciences* Philadelphia, 361, 265, Sept. 1965, pp. 1-9.

Sitaram, A.-*Urban Growth and Political Socialization : A Study of Rural Urban Differentials in Value Preferences and Leadership Behaviour in Bihar*, Janaki Prakasha 1982.

Smelser, N.J. and Davis, A.J. (Eds.) -*Sociology*, Prentice Hall, New Jersey, 1969, pp. 85-86.

Stephen, W.-"The Concept of Political Development", *The Annal of the American Academy of Political and Social Science* 358 (March 1965) p. 1-13.

Stephen, L. & Waxby -*Political Science : The Discipline and its Dimensions. An Introduction*, Scientific Book Agency, Calcutta, 1970, p. 170.

Suri, S.-"New Perspective", *Seminar*, May 1974, p. 34.

Tanehauss, J. & Soniet, A.-"Trends in American Political Science", *American Political Science Review*, 62: 933-947.

Tarrow, S.G.-*Peasant Communism in Southern Italy*, New Haven : Yale University Press, 1967.

Tead, O.- *The Art of Leadership*, (New York : Mc Graw Hill Book, 1935) p. 20.

Tingsten, H.-"Political Behaviour" in Studies in Election *Statistics "Stockhom Economic Studies*, No. 7, London, P.S. King, 1937.

Tingsten, H.-"Political Behaviour: Studies in Election Statistics", P.S. King, London, 1937.

Trucman, D.B.- *The Governmental Process.*

Tummin, M.- *Social Stratification : The Forms and Function of Equality,* Englewood Cliffs, Prentice Hall, 1967, pp. 17-18.

Turner, J.E. and Holt R.T.- *The Political Basis of Economic* Development. (Bombay : Vakils, Fuller and Linambm 1966) p. 8.

Ullan, A.B. & Samuel, H. -*Patterns of Government* (New York : Random House, 1968) 8th Printing, p. 22.

Vallian, C. & Pauttina, M.- *The Political Socialization of Young People: A Panel Survey of Youngster in a San Fransico Bag Areas,* Berkley: University of California Ama., 1972.

Verba, S. & Almond, G.- *The Civic Culture,* Little Brown Boston, 1965.

Verba, S. & Norman, H.N. -*The Modes of Democratic Participation: Across National Comparison. Comparative Politics Series,* Vol. -013, Vol. 2, Sage, Bevarly Hills, California, 1977.

Verma, S.P. -*Modern Political Theory,* (Delhi-Vikas 1975) p. 168-69.

Verma, V.P. -"The behavioural Research & Political Philosophy : Some Aspects", *Indian Journal of Political Studies,* Jodhpur, Vol. 1976, p. 72.

Victor, C.F. -*Technological Man. The Myth and the Realities* (Calcutta: Scientific Agency, 1971) p. 27.

Walin, S. -*Politics and Vision,* Little Brown Baston, 1960, pp. 434-552.

Warner, W.L. & Abbegller, J.C. -*Big Business Leaders in America,* Newyork, Harper, 1955.

Warner, W.L. and Pauls, C.-The Social Life of a Modern Community, (New Haven : Yale Univ. Press) 1965.

Wasley, L. -*Political Science The Discipline and its Dimensions,* Calcutta : Scientific Book, 1972, pp. 48-9.

Weber, Max- *Protestant Ethique* & Rise of Capitalism.

Weinbeny & Shabat - *Society and Man.* Parentice Hall Inc., 1976, p.7 pp. 1.

Weiner, M.- Politics of Scarcity : *Public Pressure and Political Response in India,* Chicago Univ. Press, 1962.

Weingrad, A.-"Patterns, Patronage, and Political Parties", *Comparative Studies in Society and History,* 10: 337-400, 1968.

Weissberg, R.- "Adolescents Perceptions of Political Authorities" Another look at Political Virtue & Power, *Mialwest Journal of Political Science,* 1972, 16, 147-68.

Weiner, & John O.F. (eds.) -*Electoral Politics in the Indian Status*, Monmohan Books, 1975.

Wiley, M.- 'Unemployment and the Vote'. Michigrone State Univ. (Unpublished Master Thesis), 1959.

Wilson, H.E. -*Education for Citizenship*, Newyork: Mc Graw Hill 1938.

William, E.-"Social Involvement and Political Activity: A Replication & Elaboration", *American Sociological Review*, 29, 1964, pp. 29: 198-215.

Young, O.R.- *System or Political Science*, Englewood Cliffs, New Jersey, Parentice Hall, 1968) p. 29.

Zdeny, D.-"Characteristics of Group Leaders", *Sociology & Social Research*, 24, pp. 140-49.

# Index